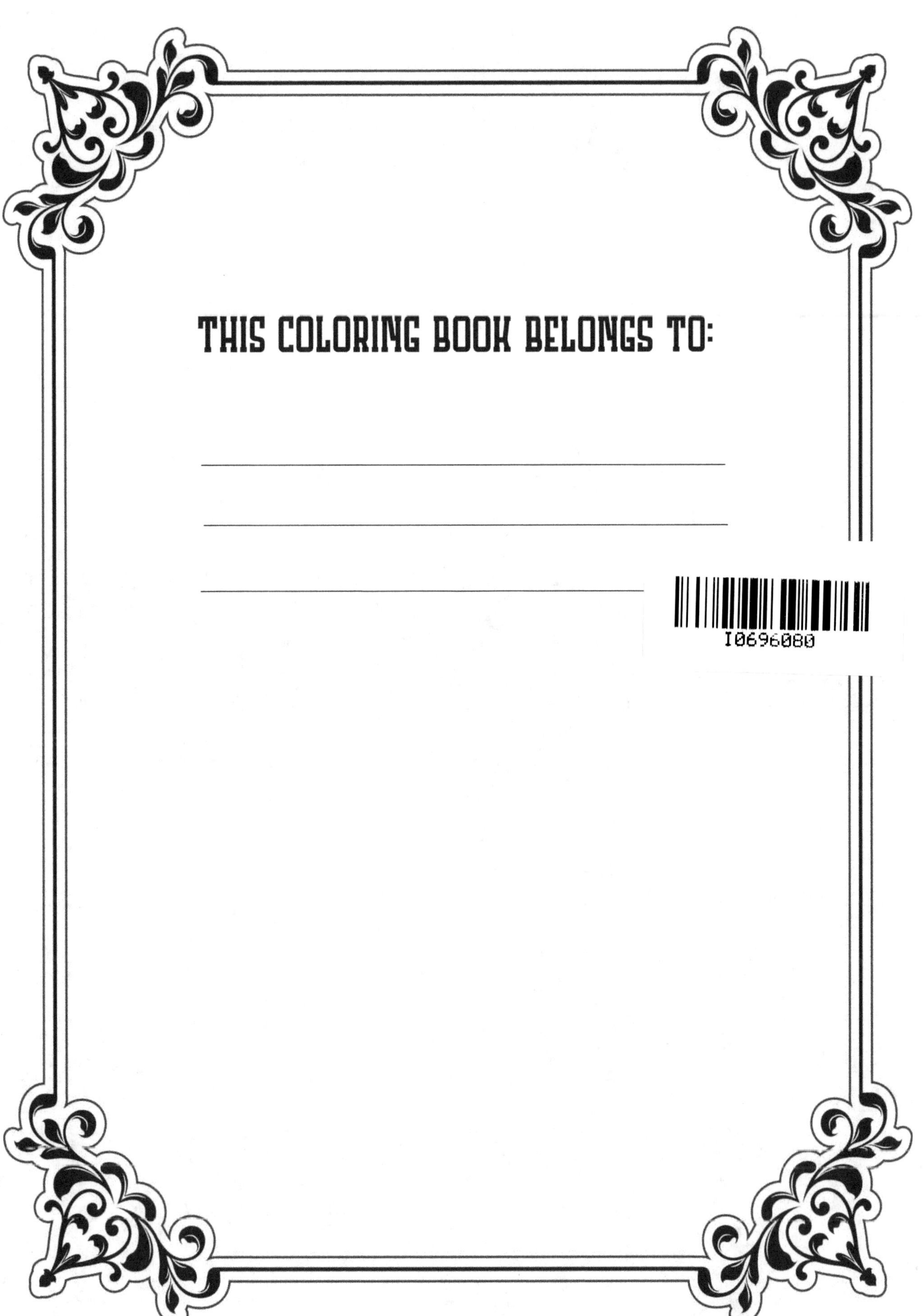
THIS COLORING BOOK BELONGS TO:

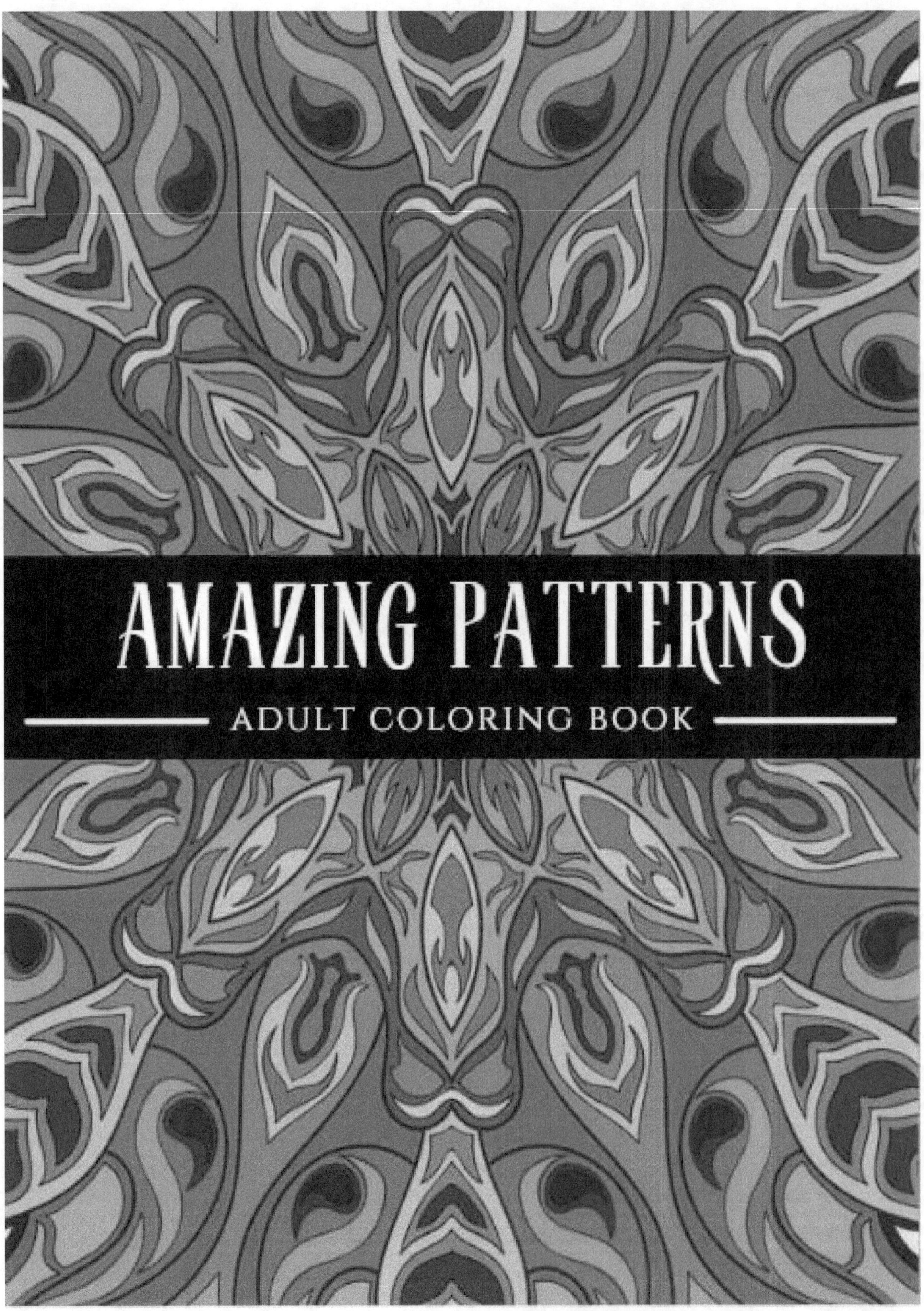

AMAZING PATTERNS
ADULT COLORING BOOK

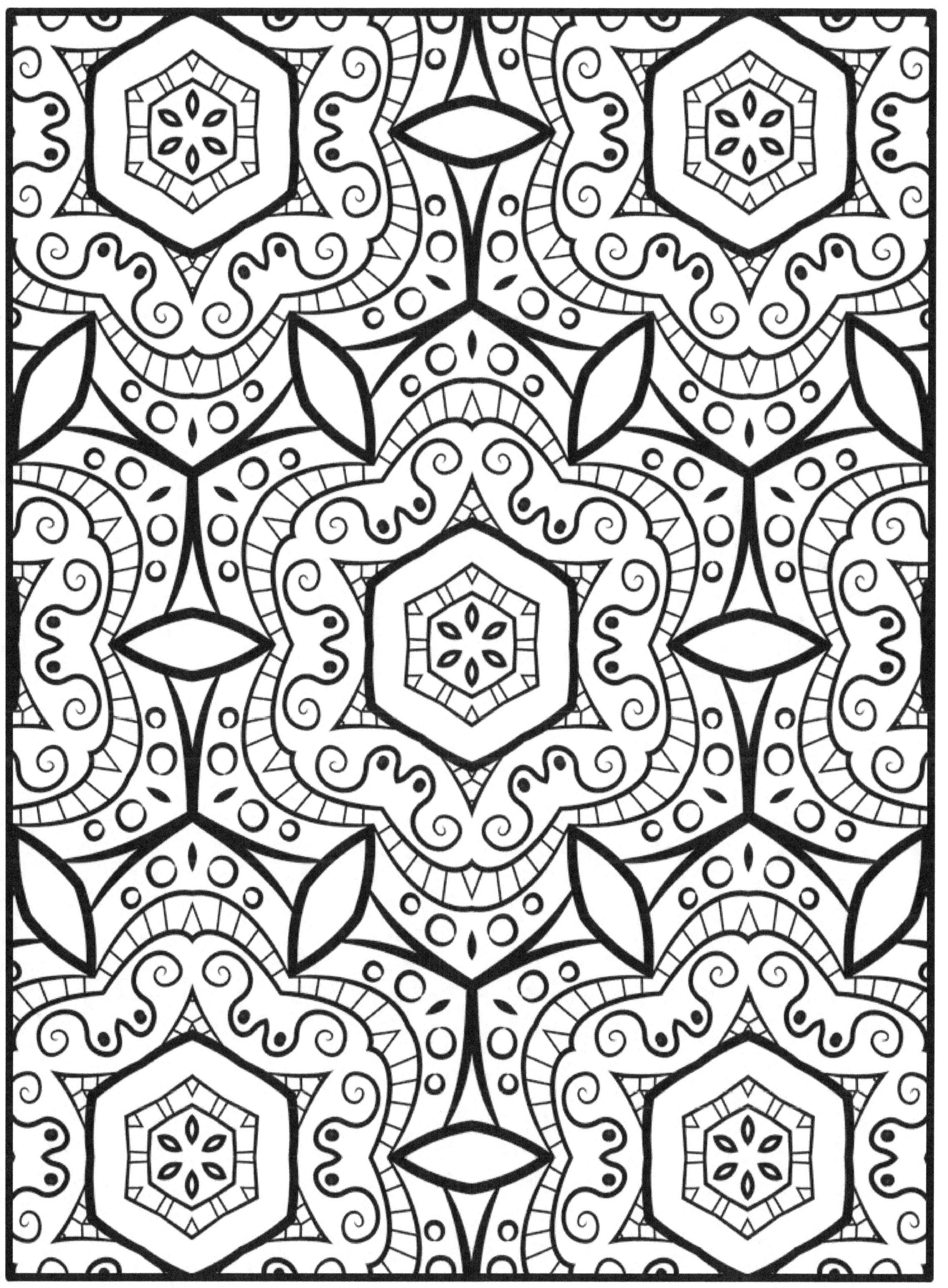

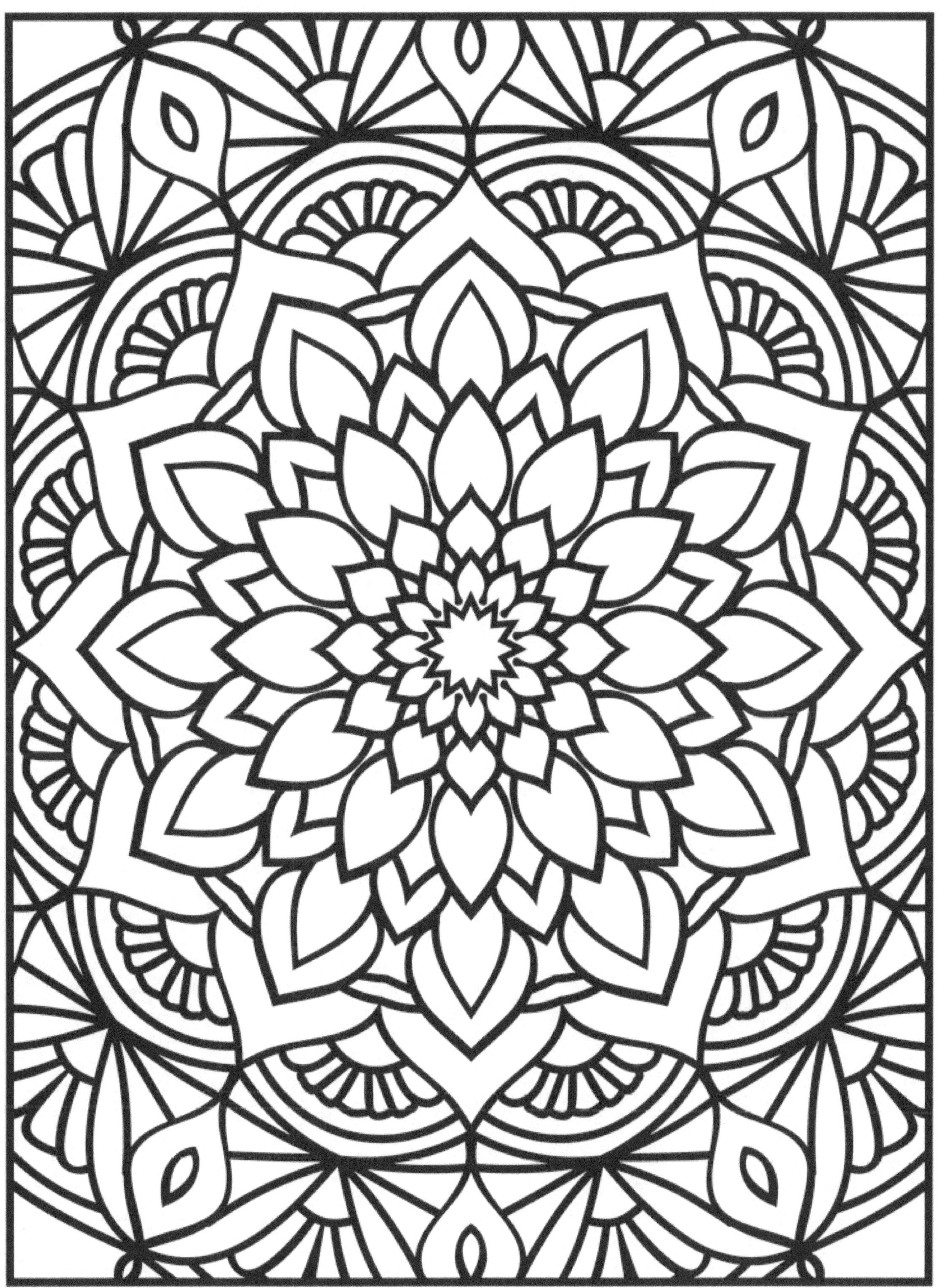

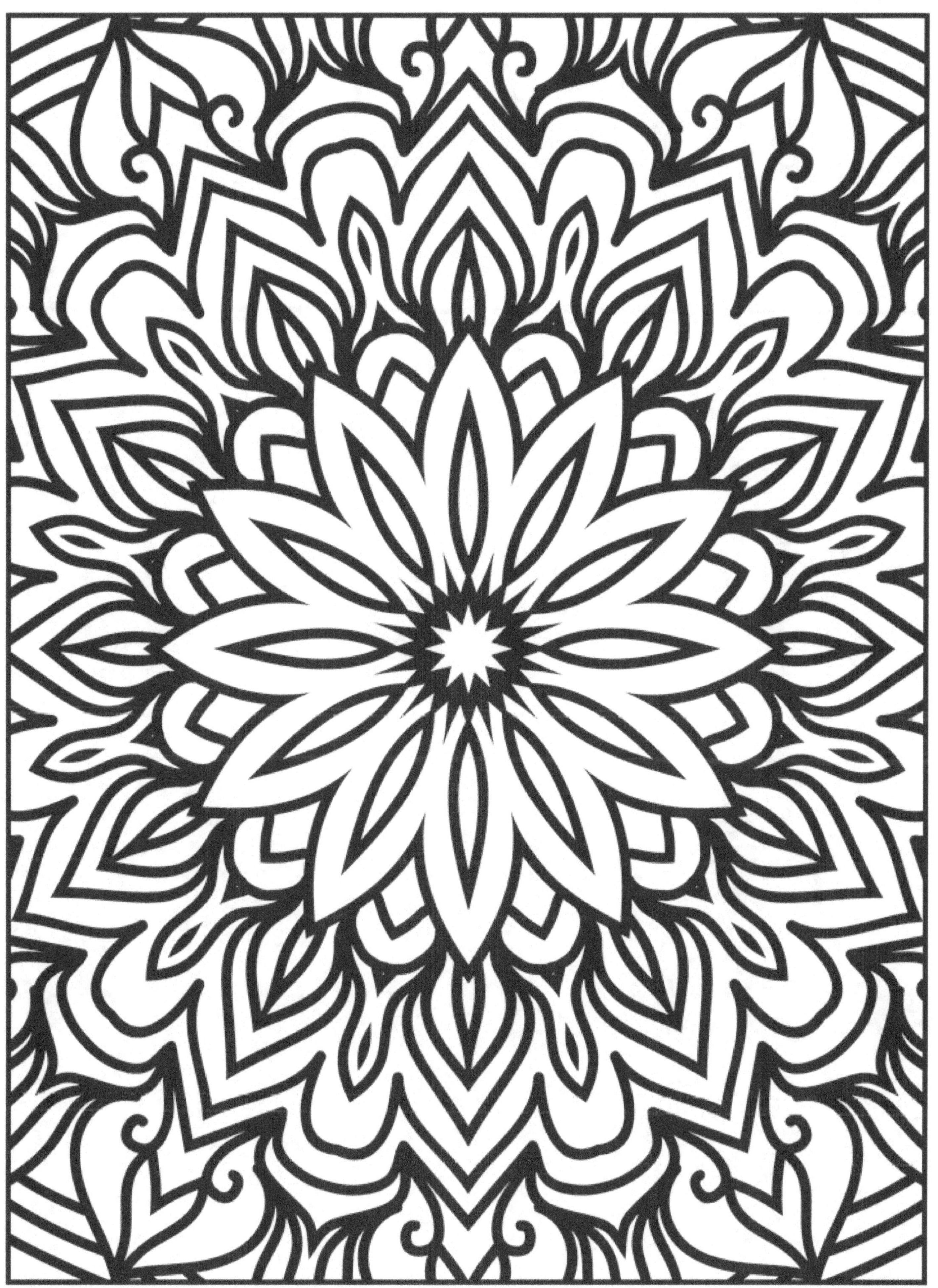

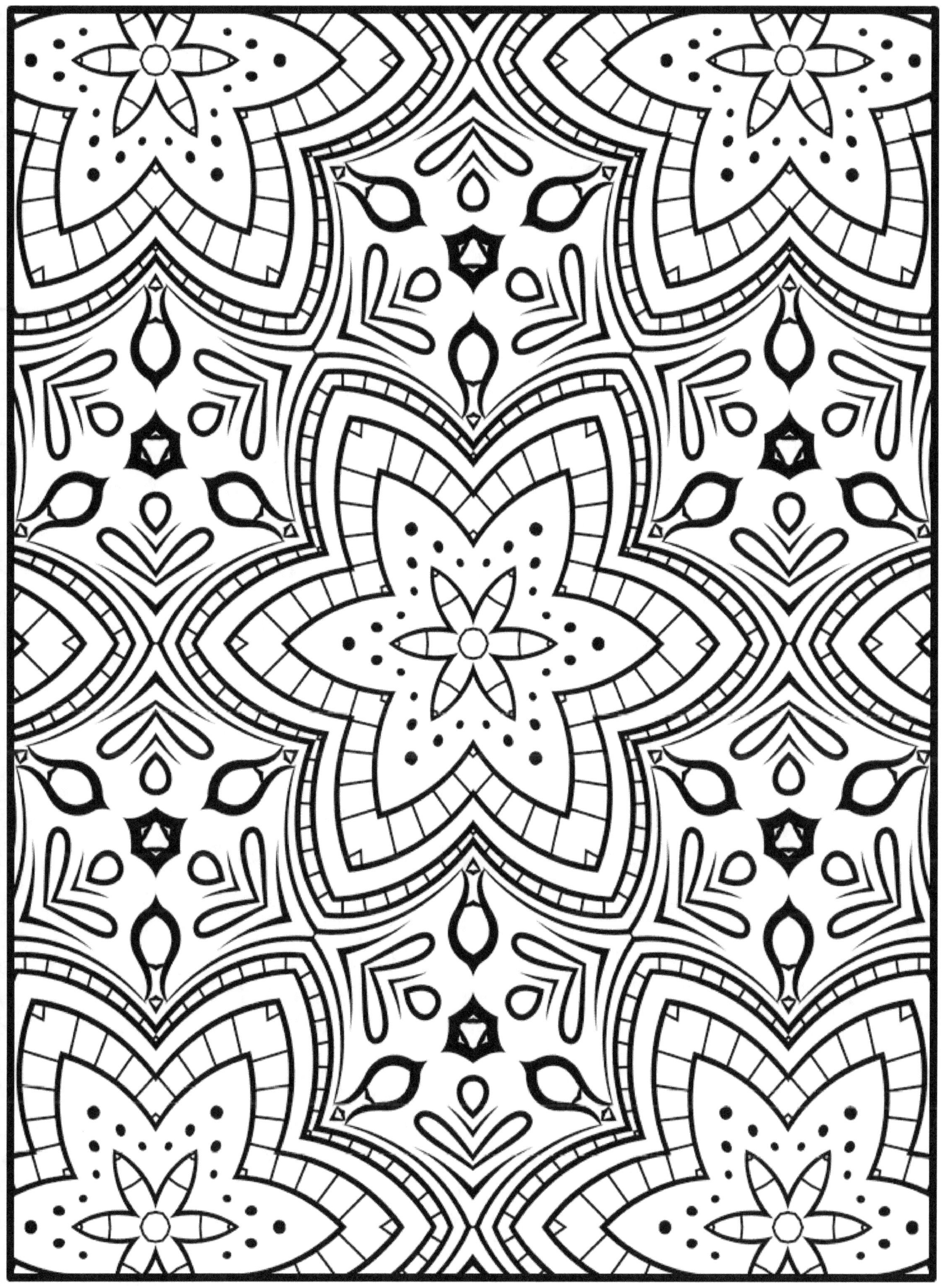

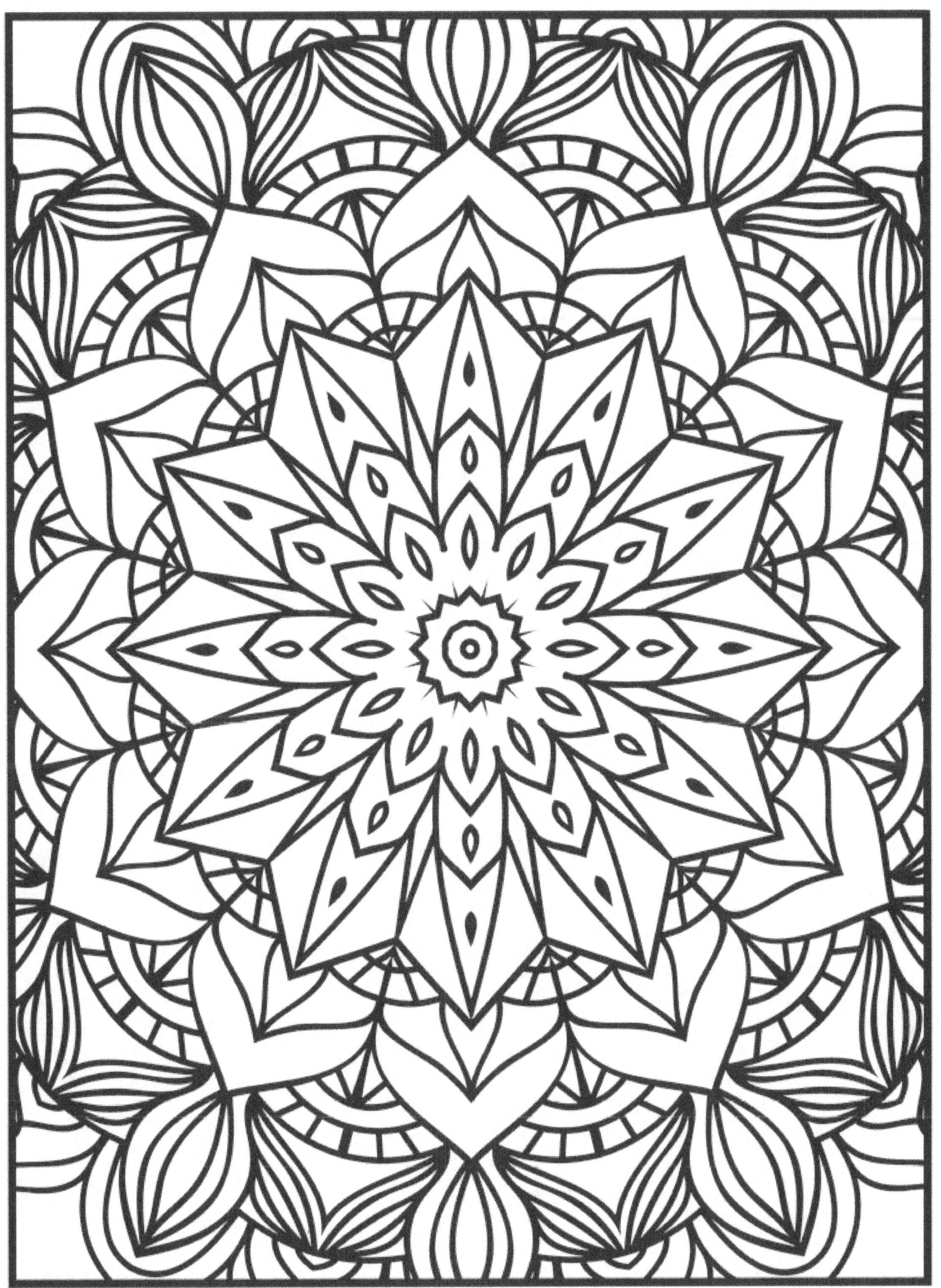

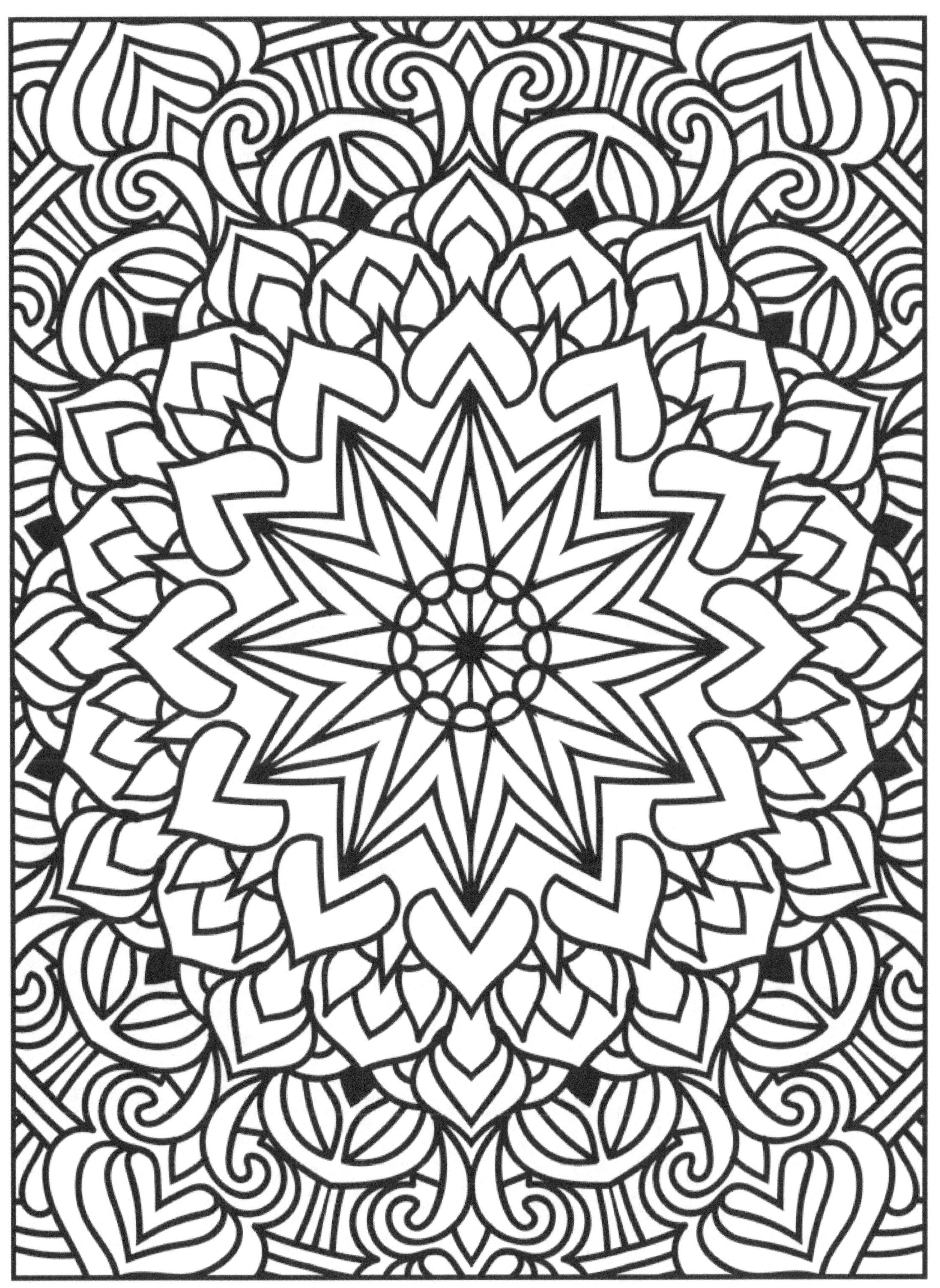

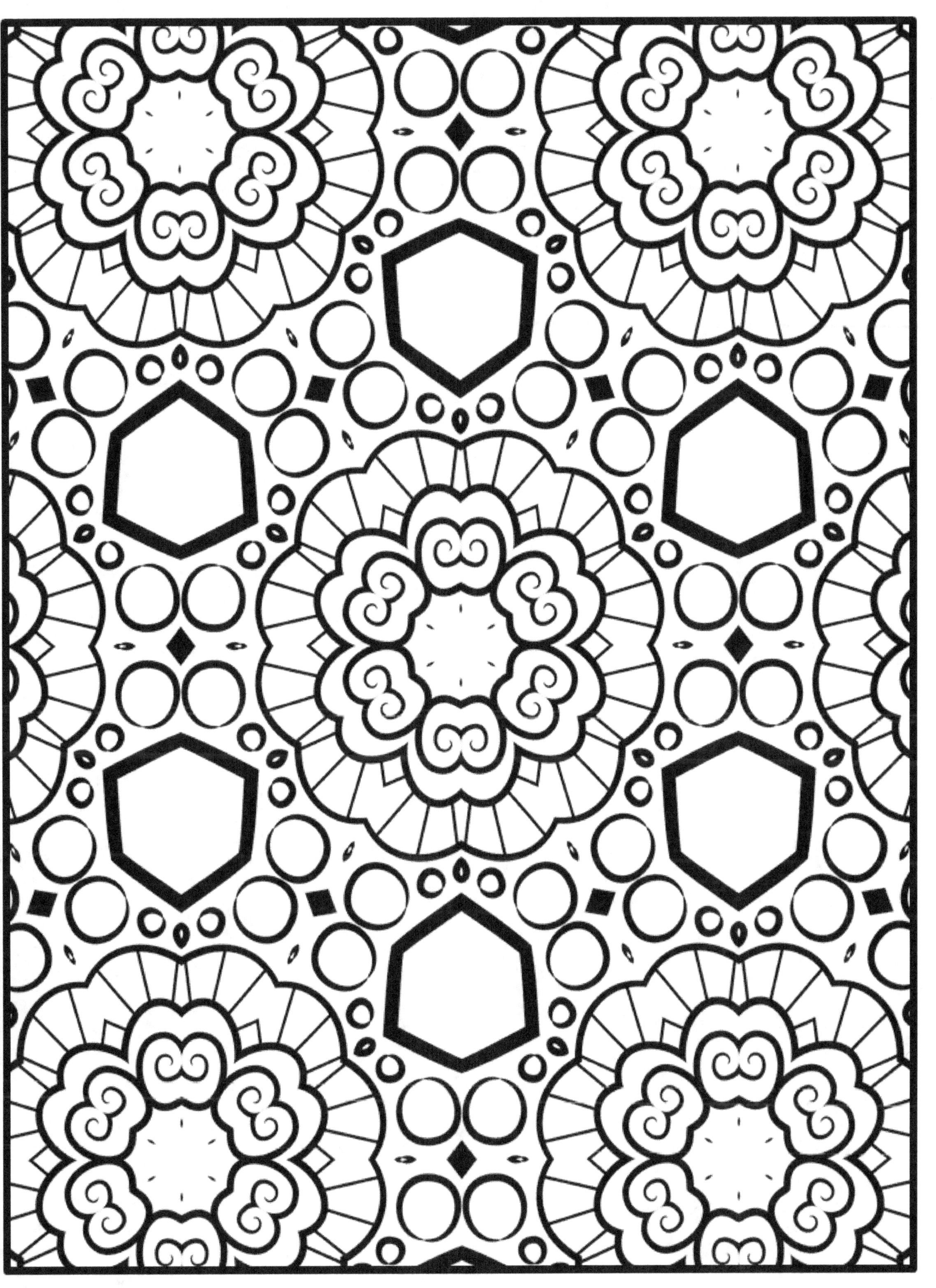

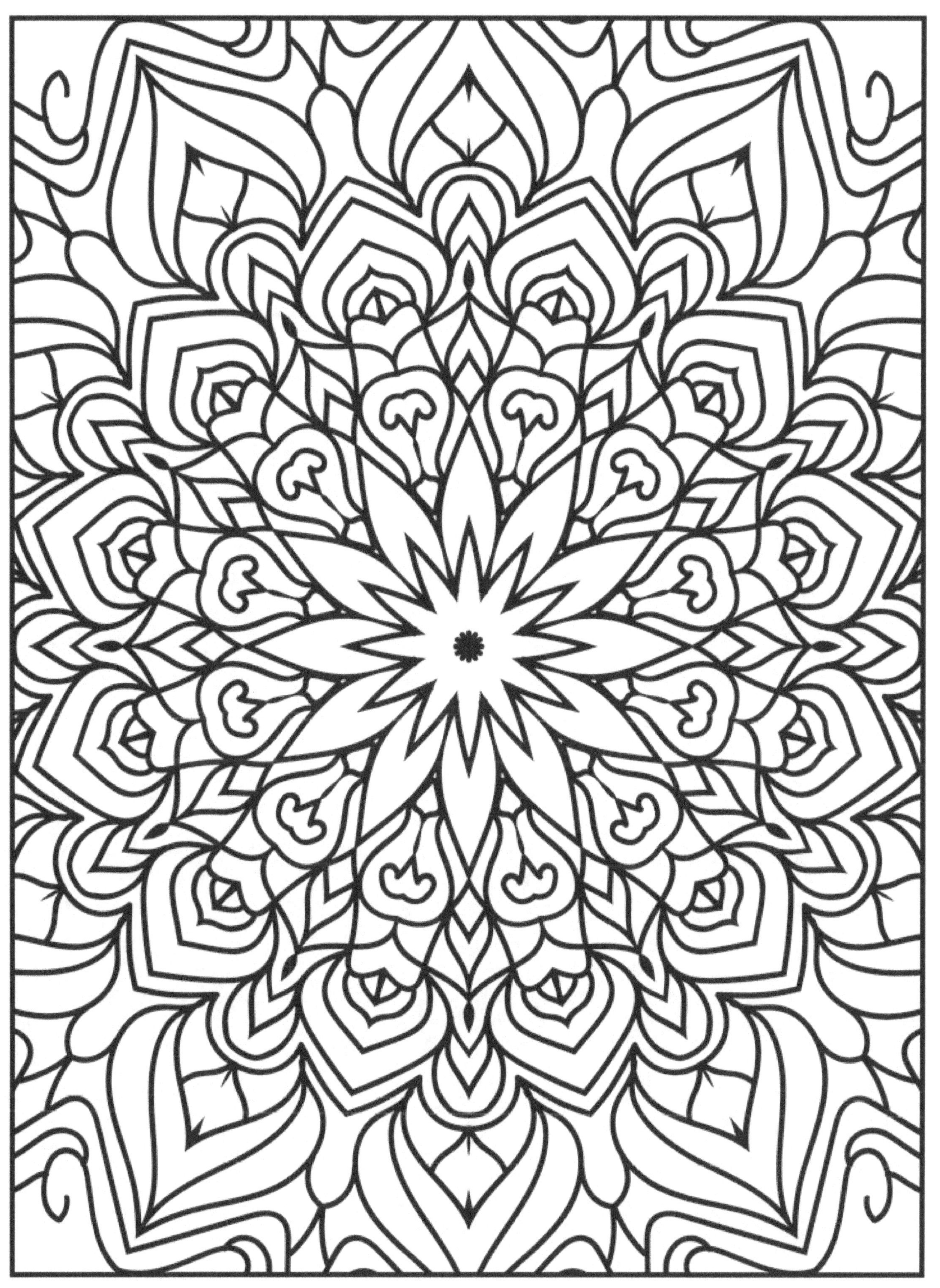

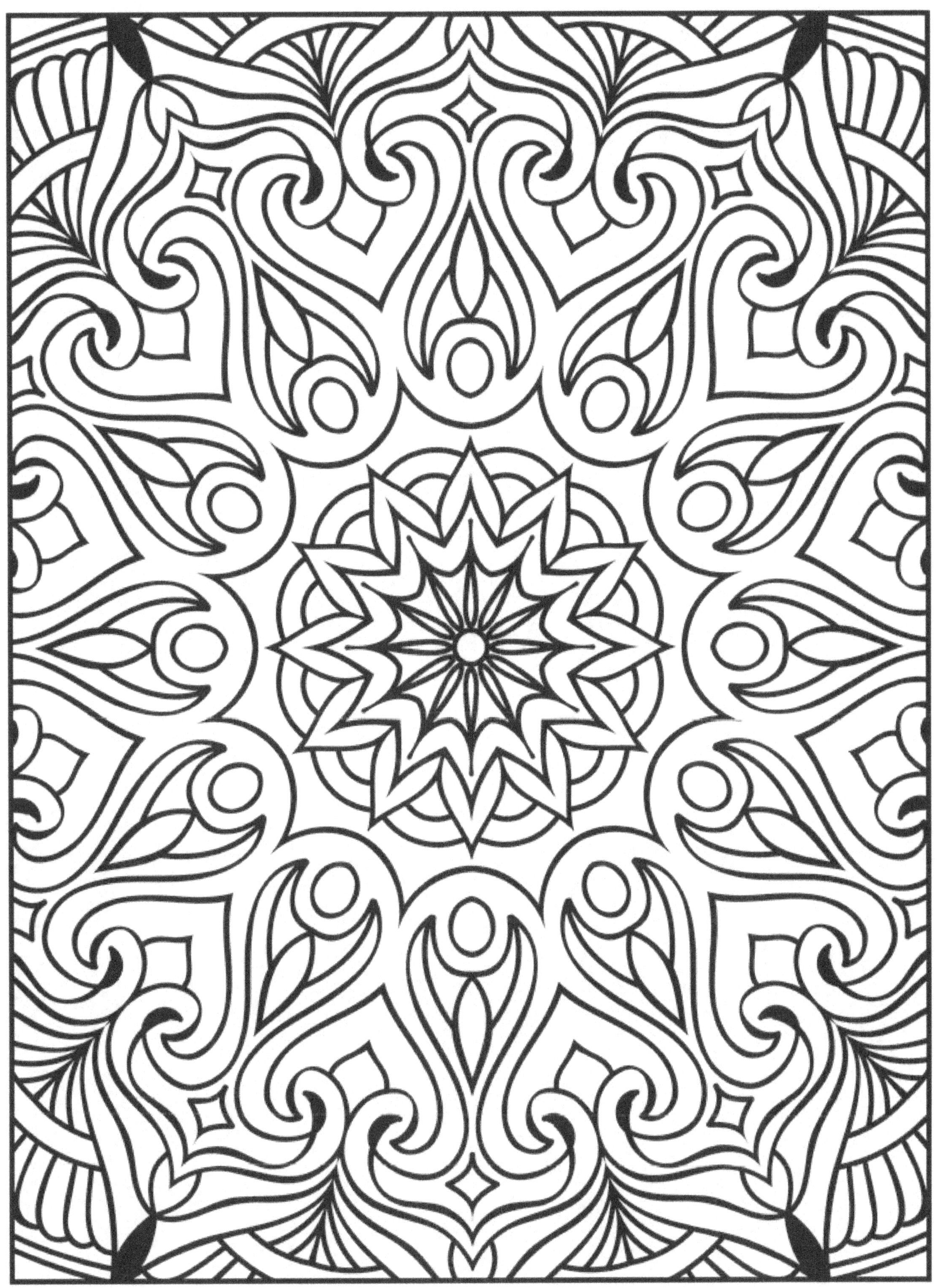

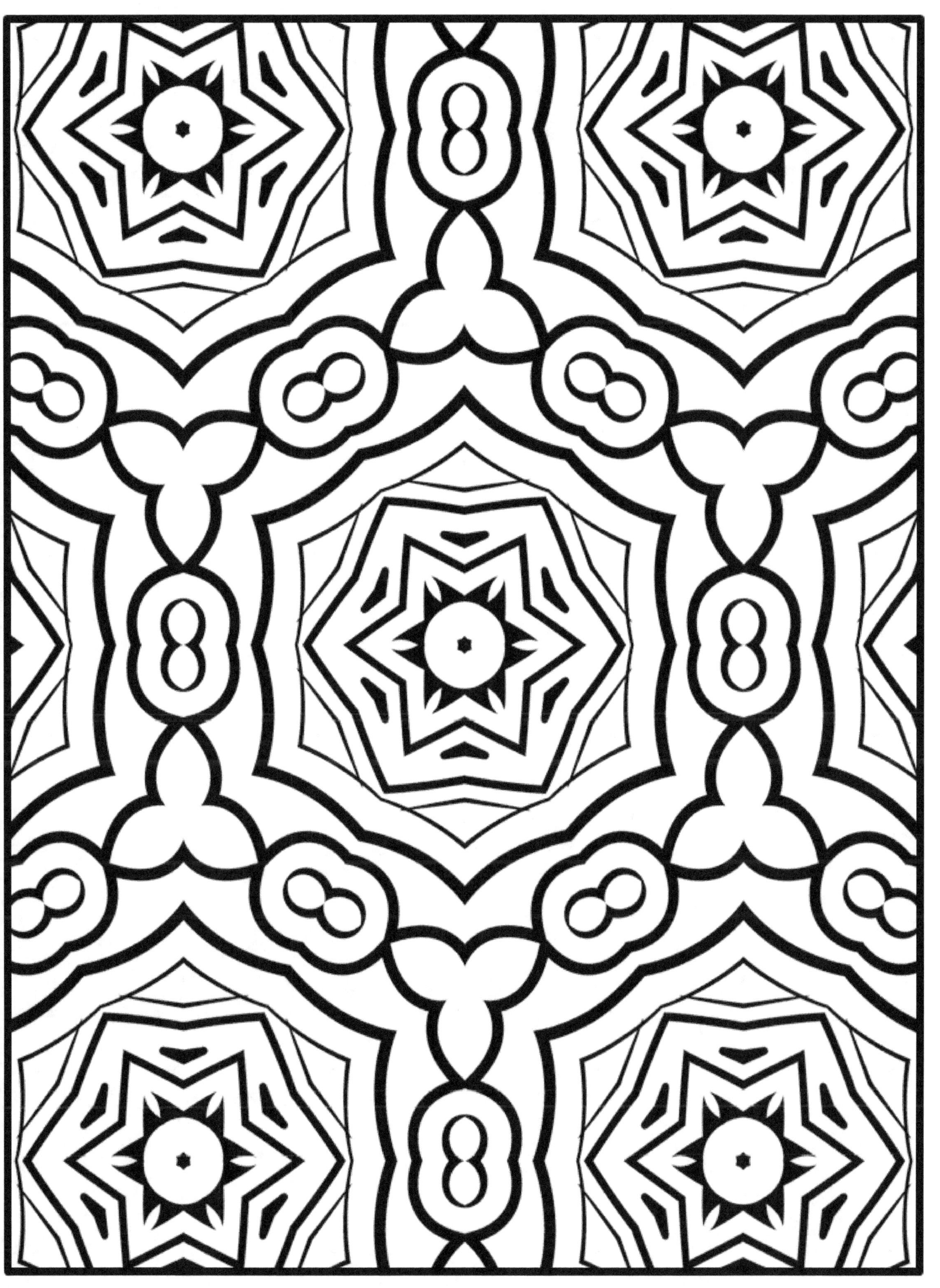

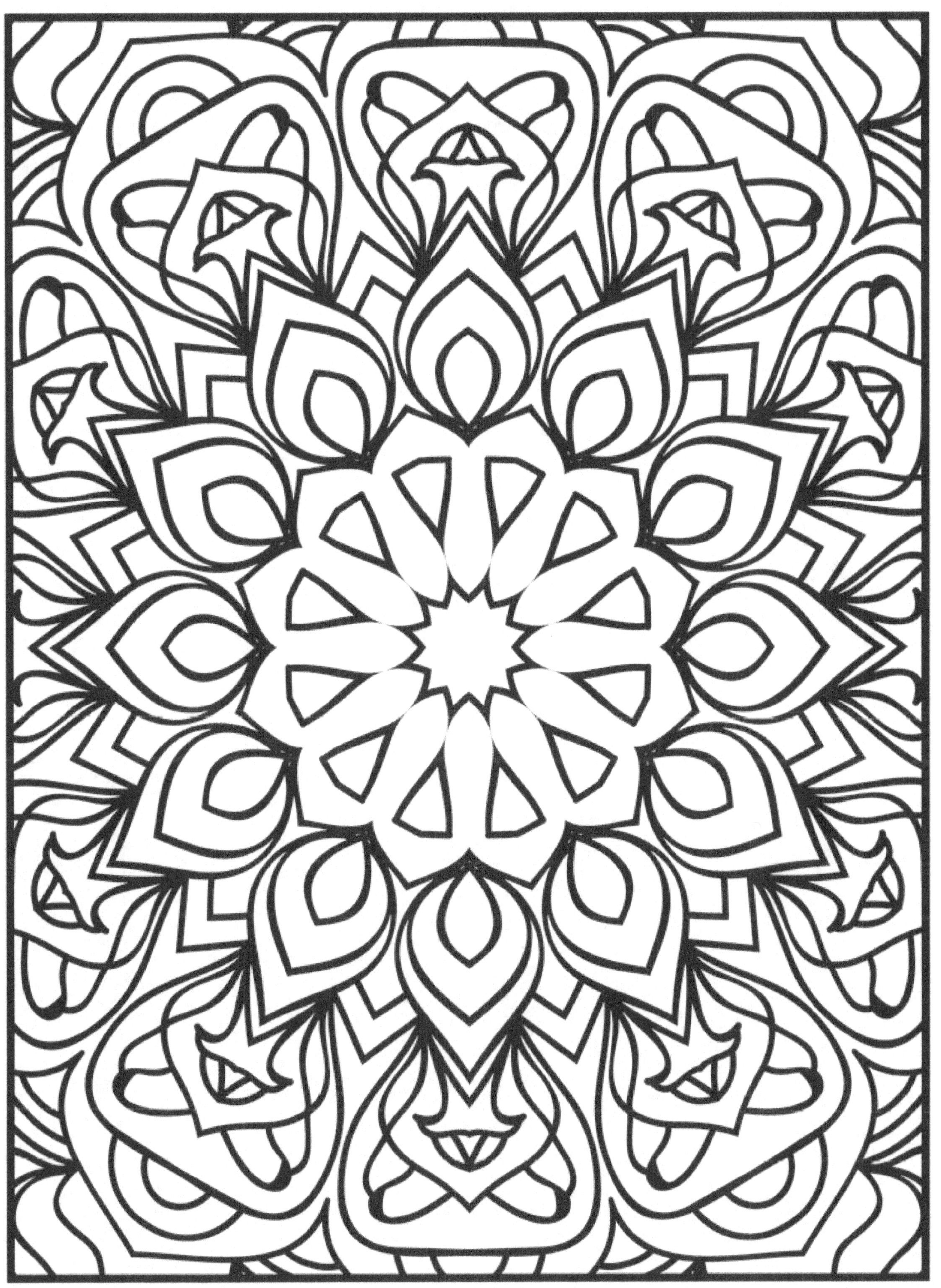

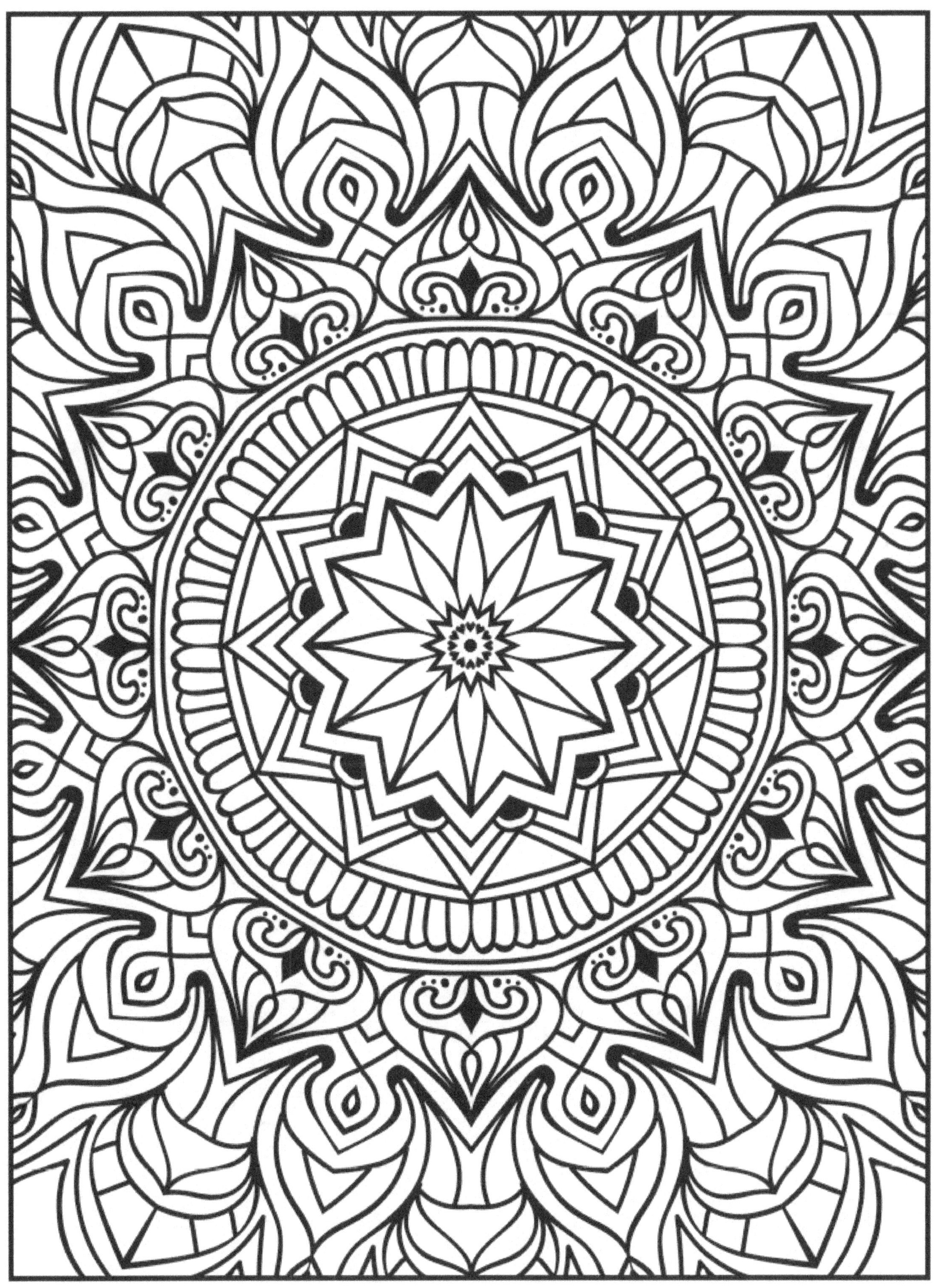

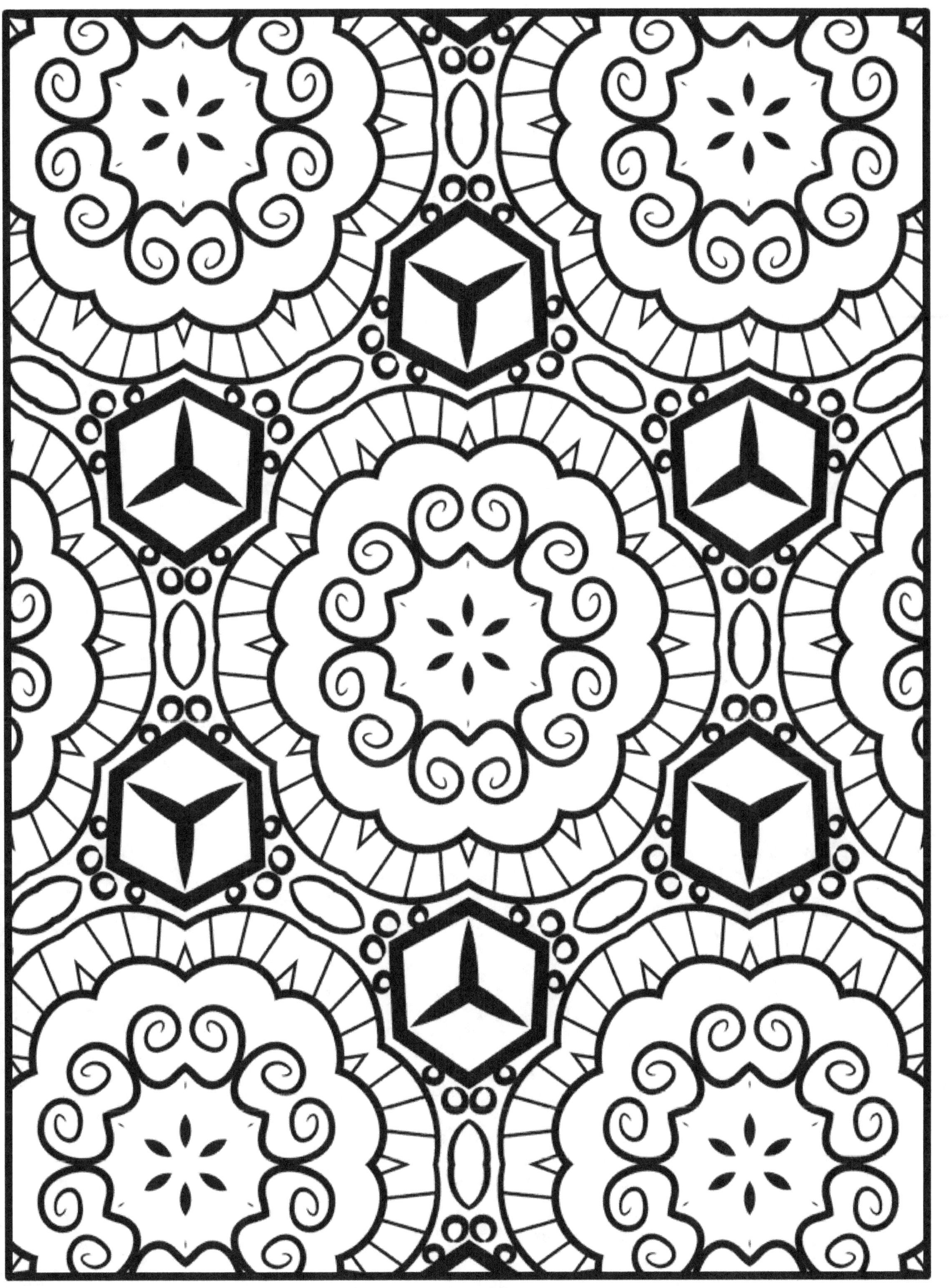

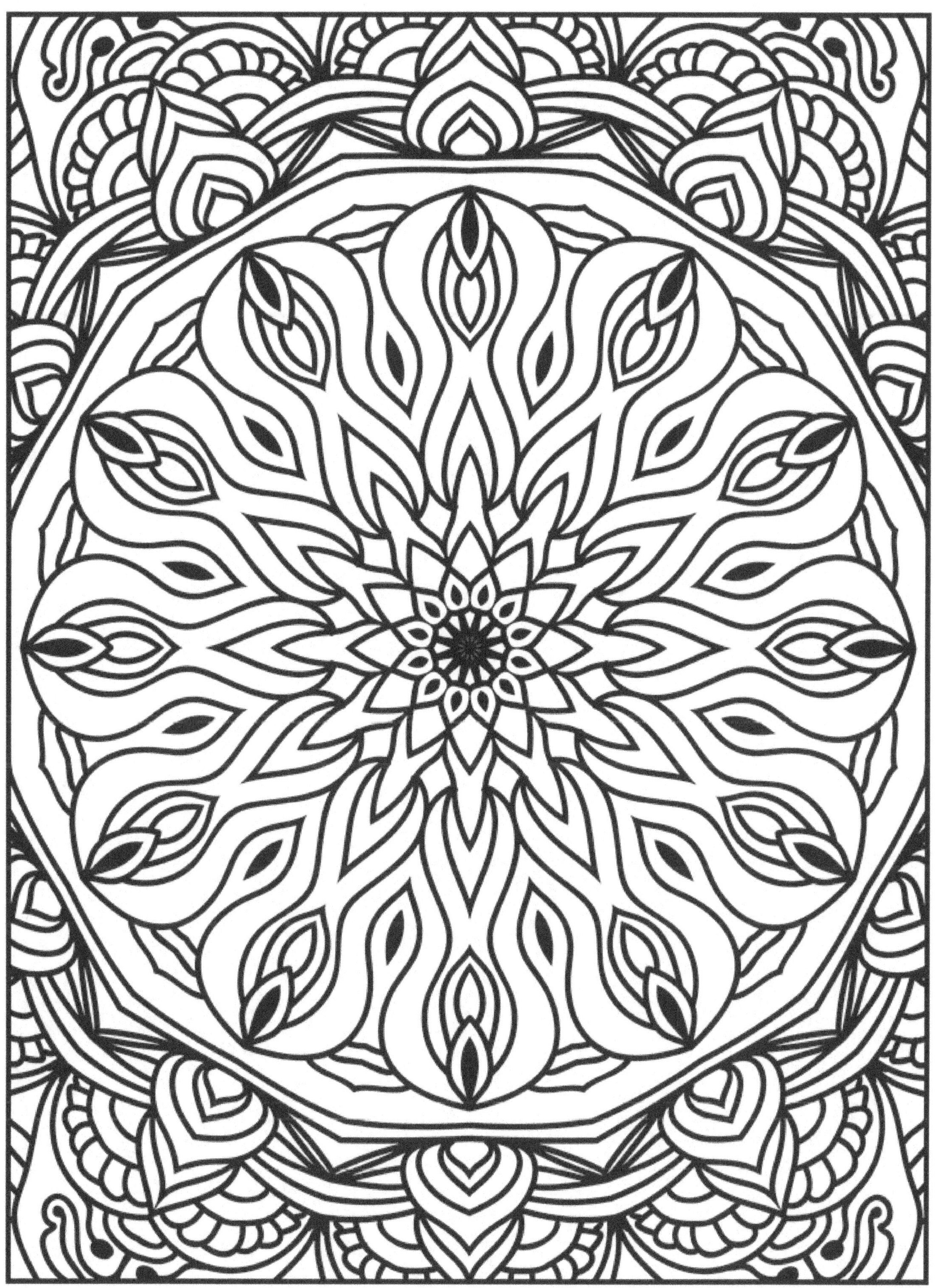

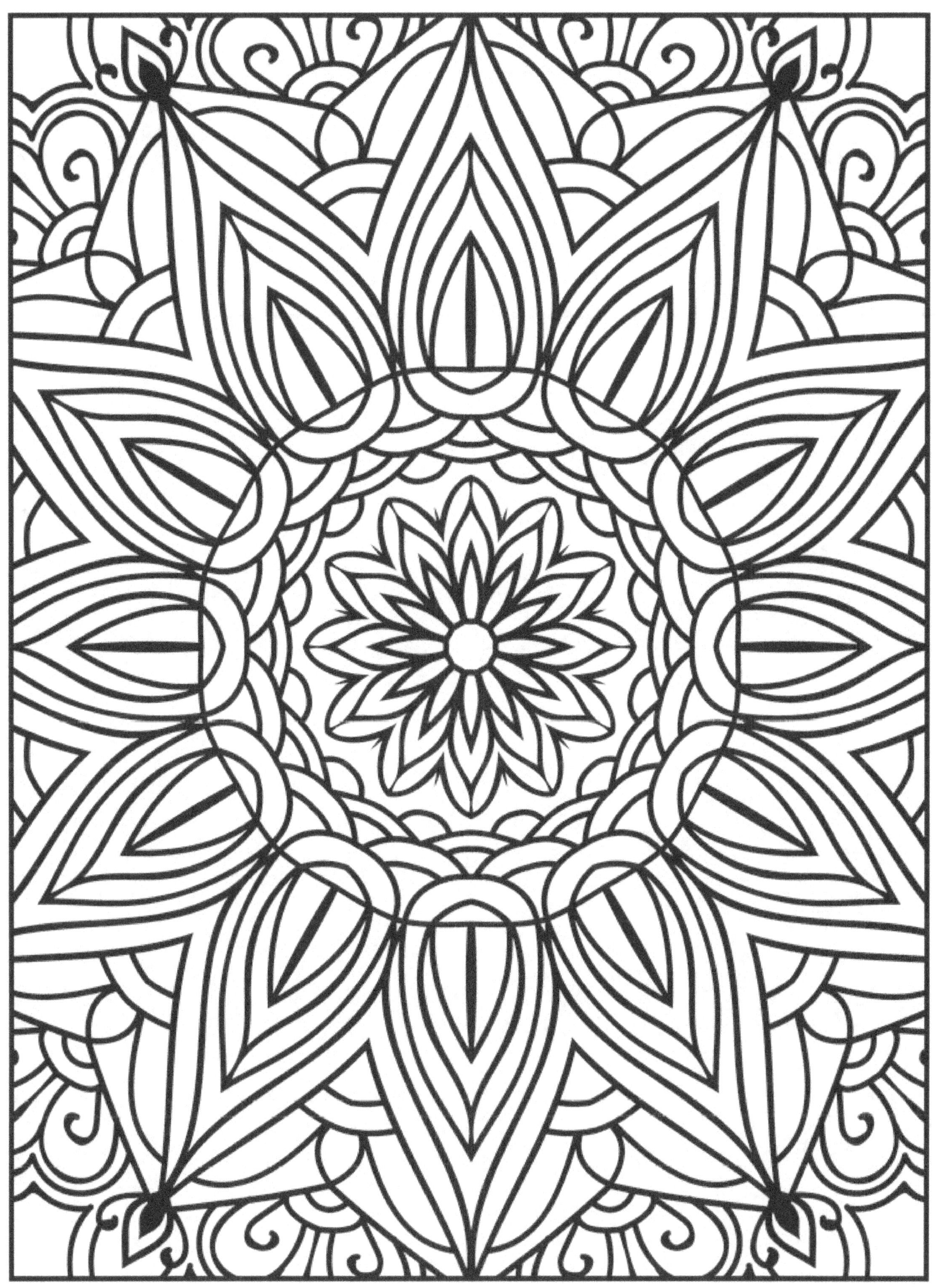

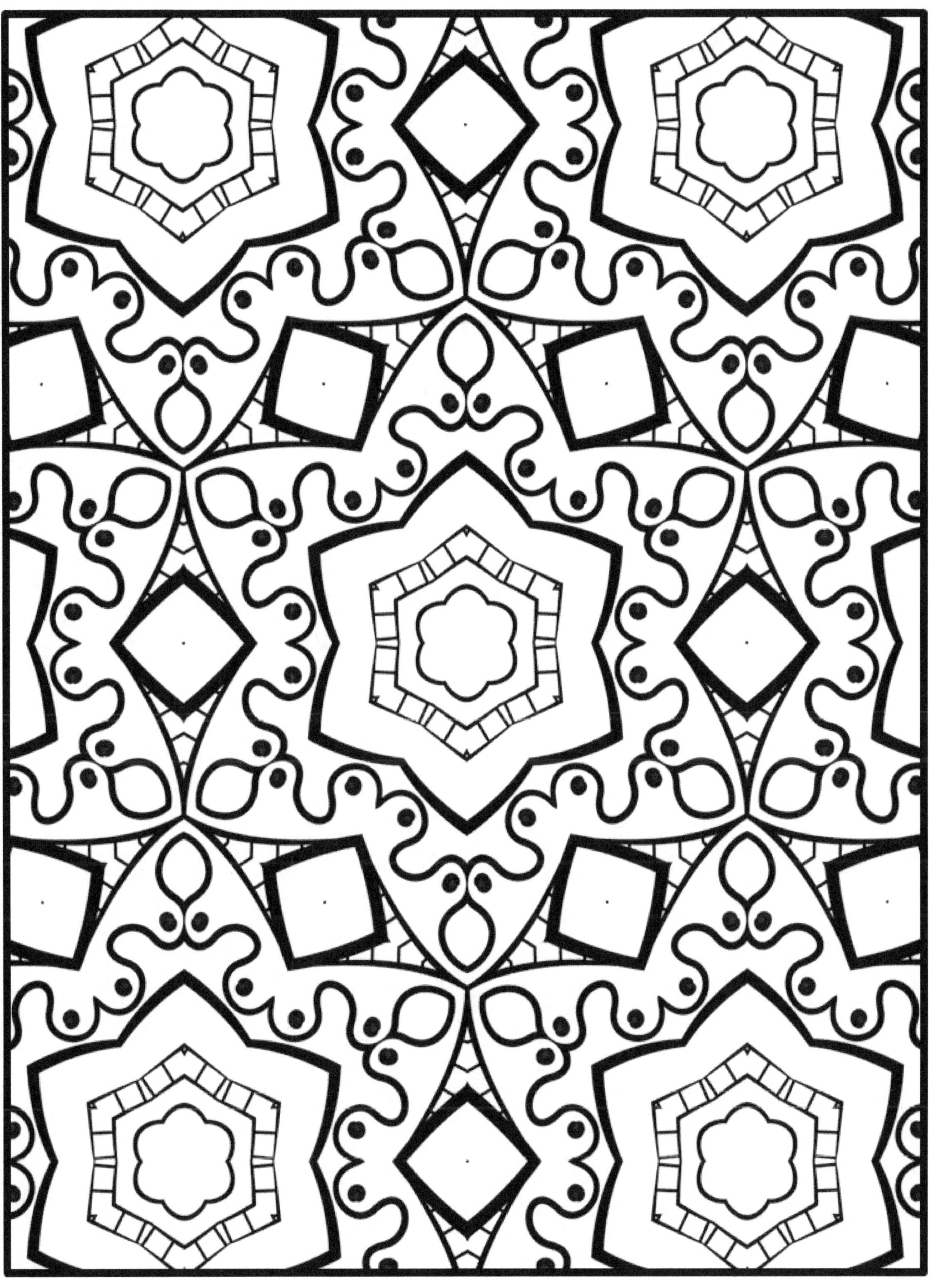

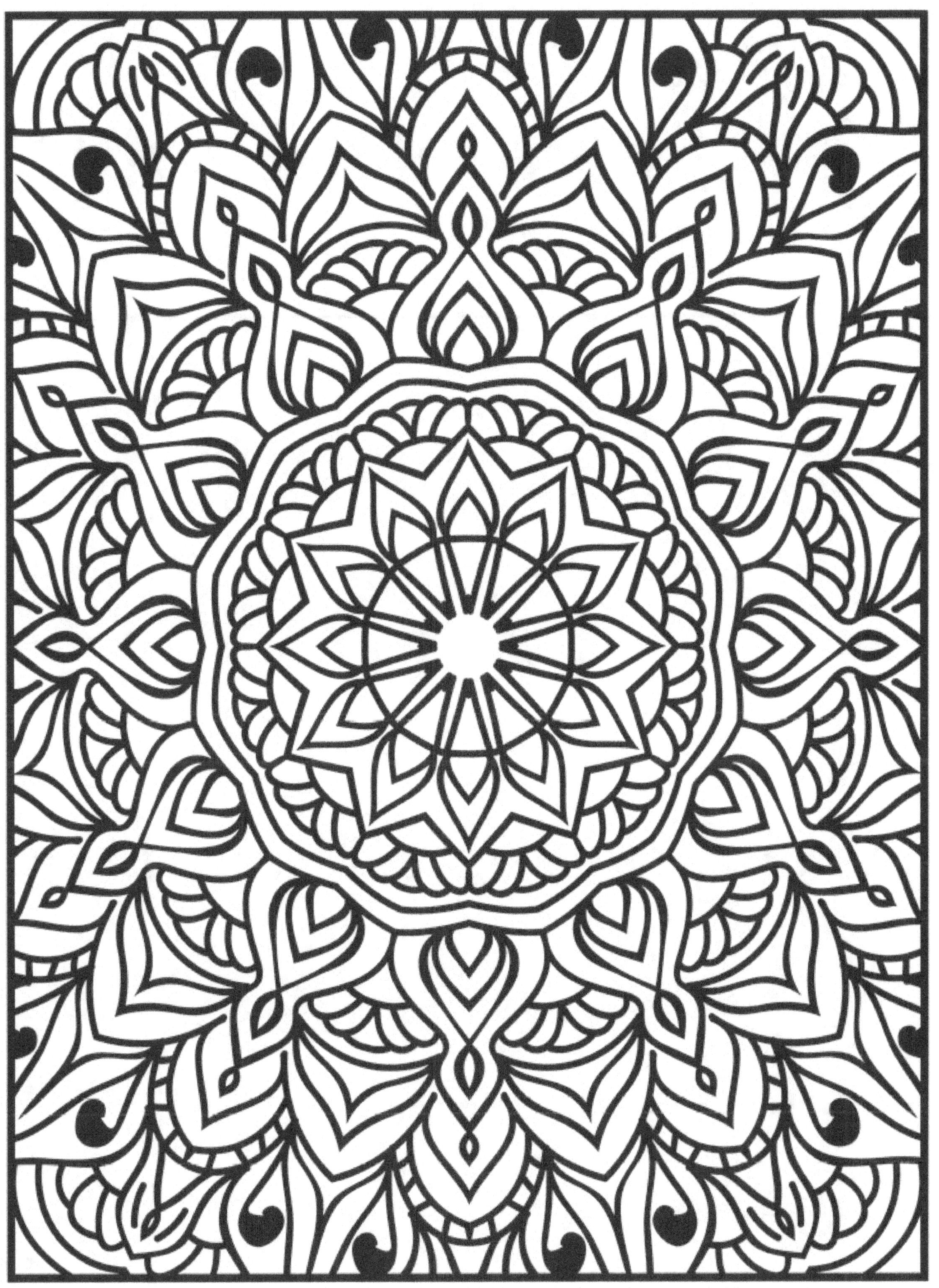

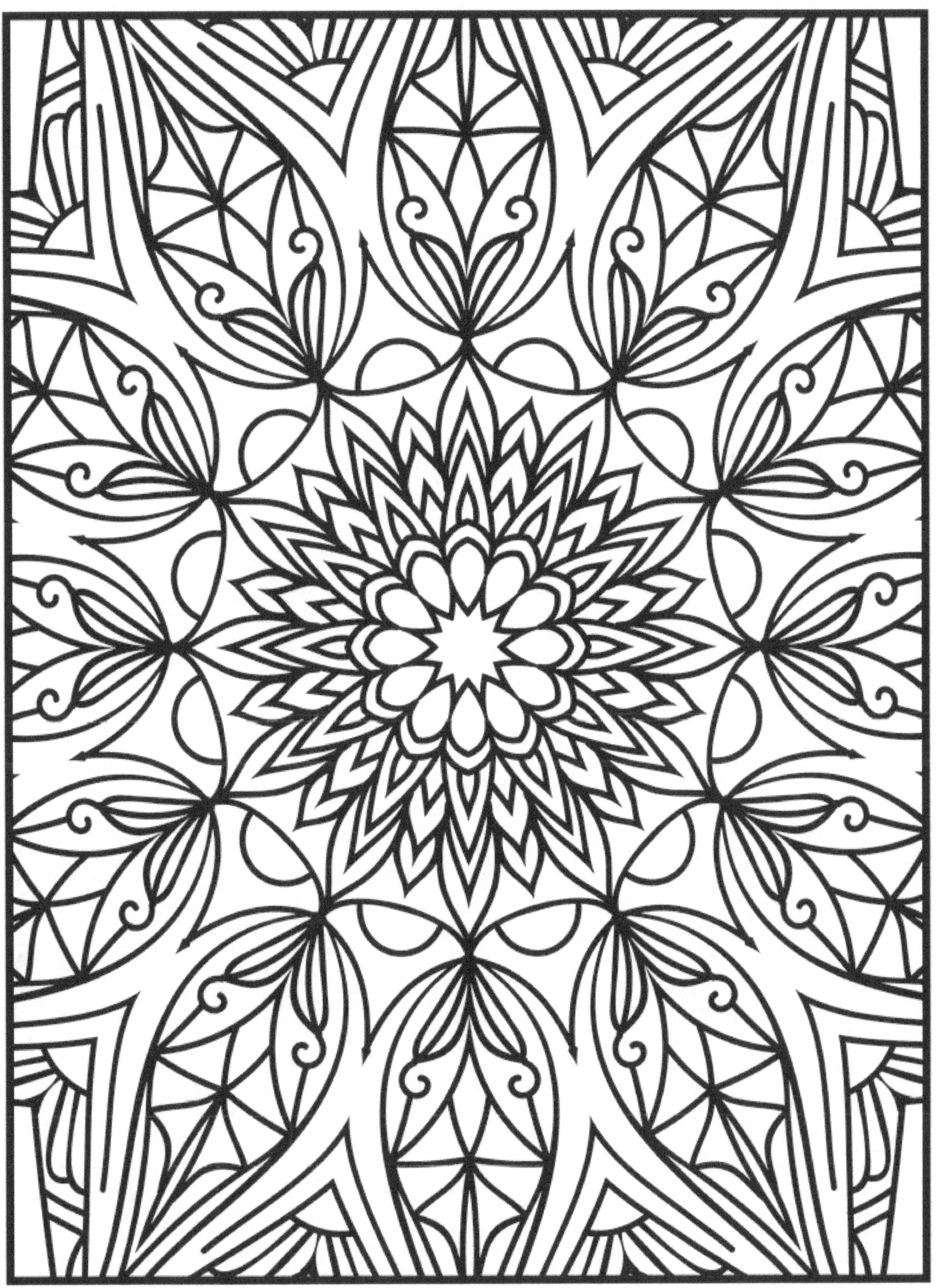

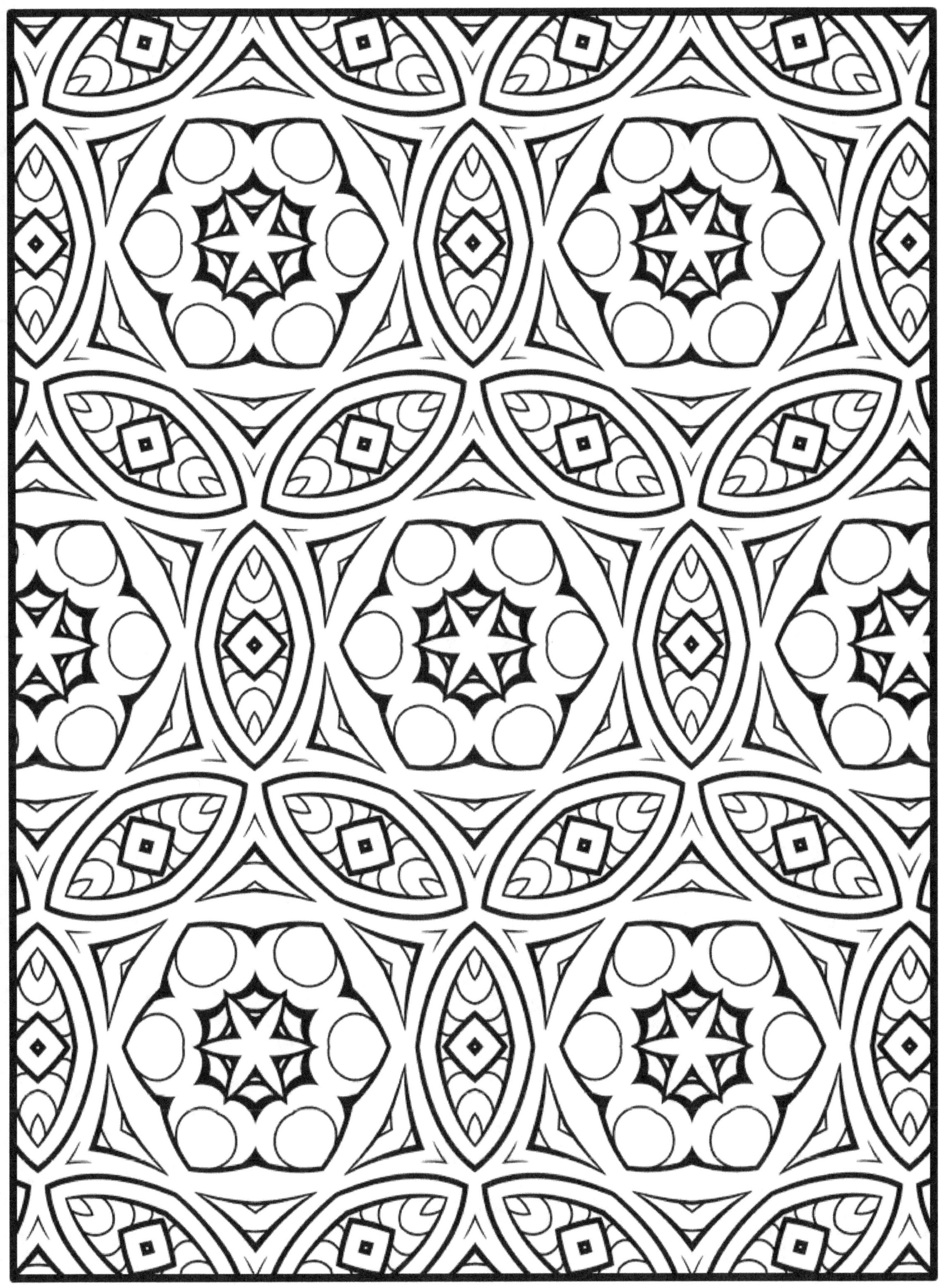

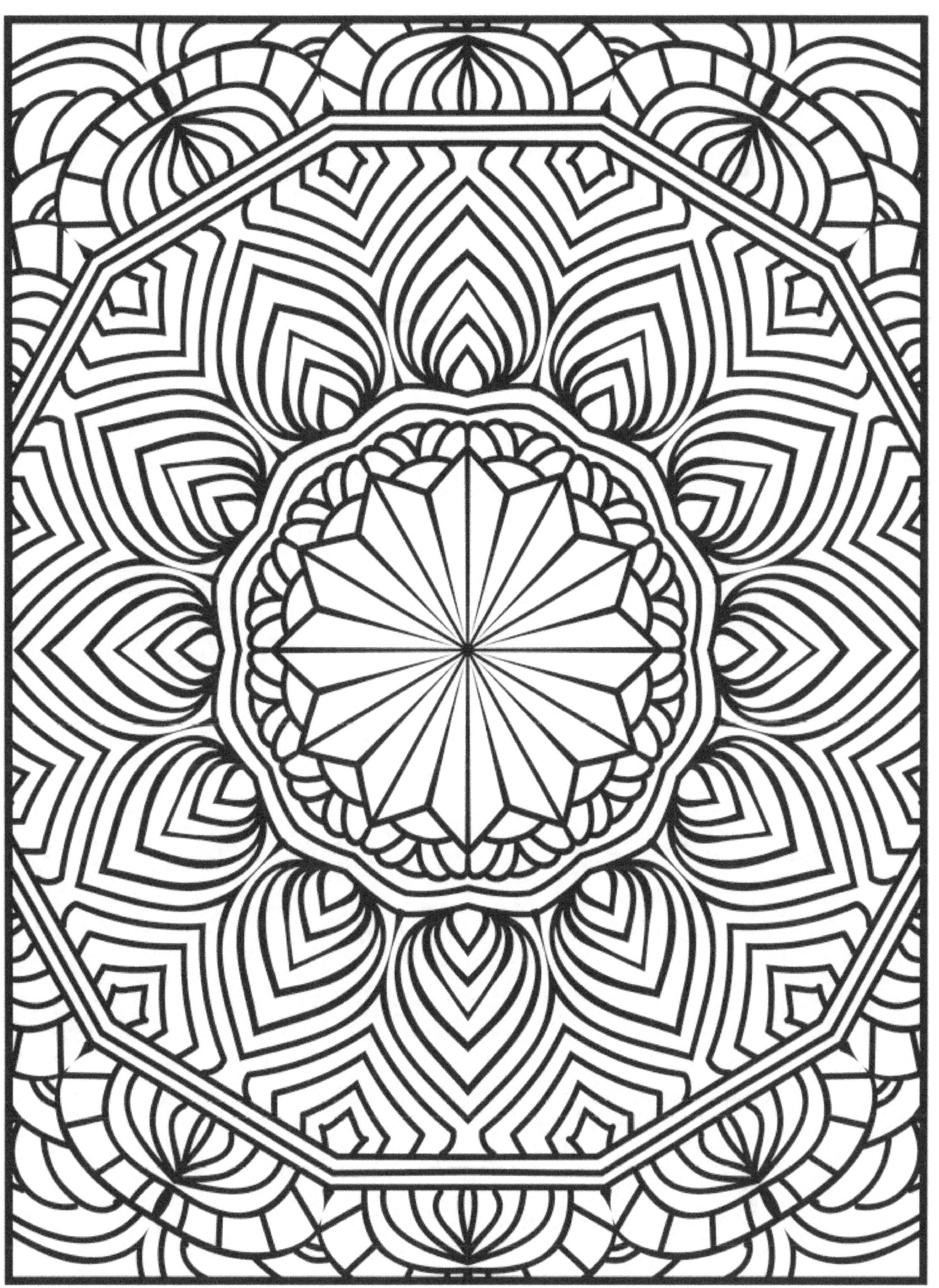

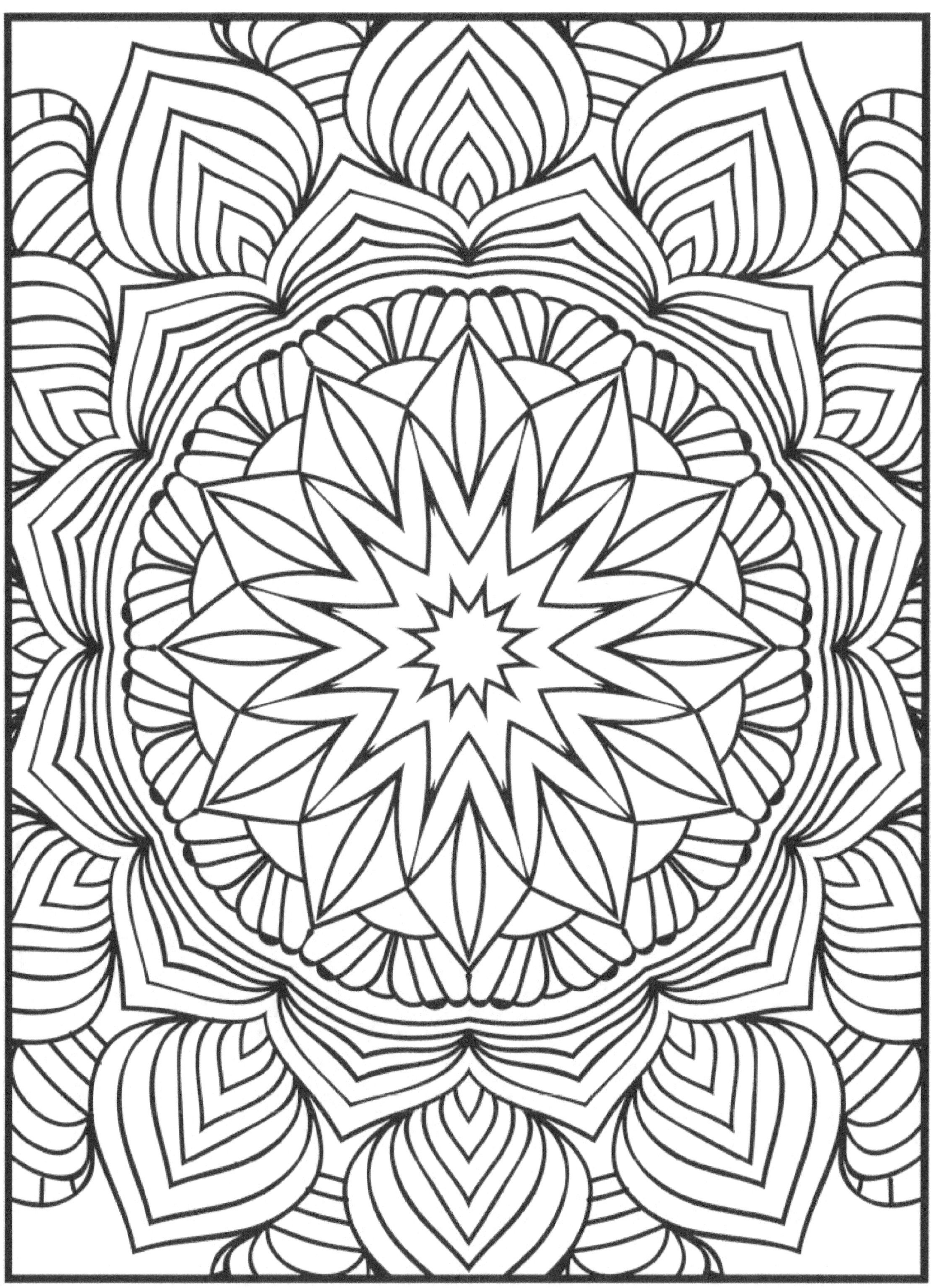

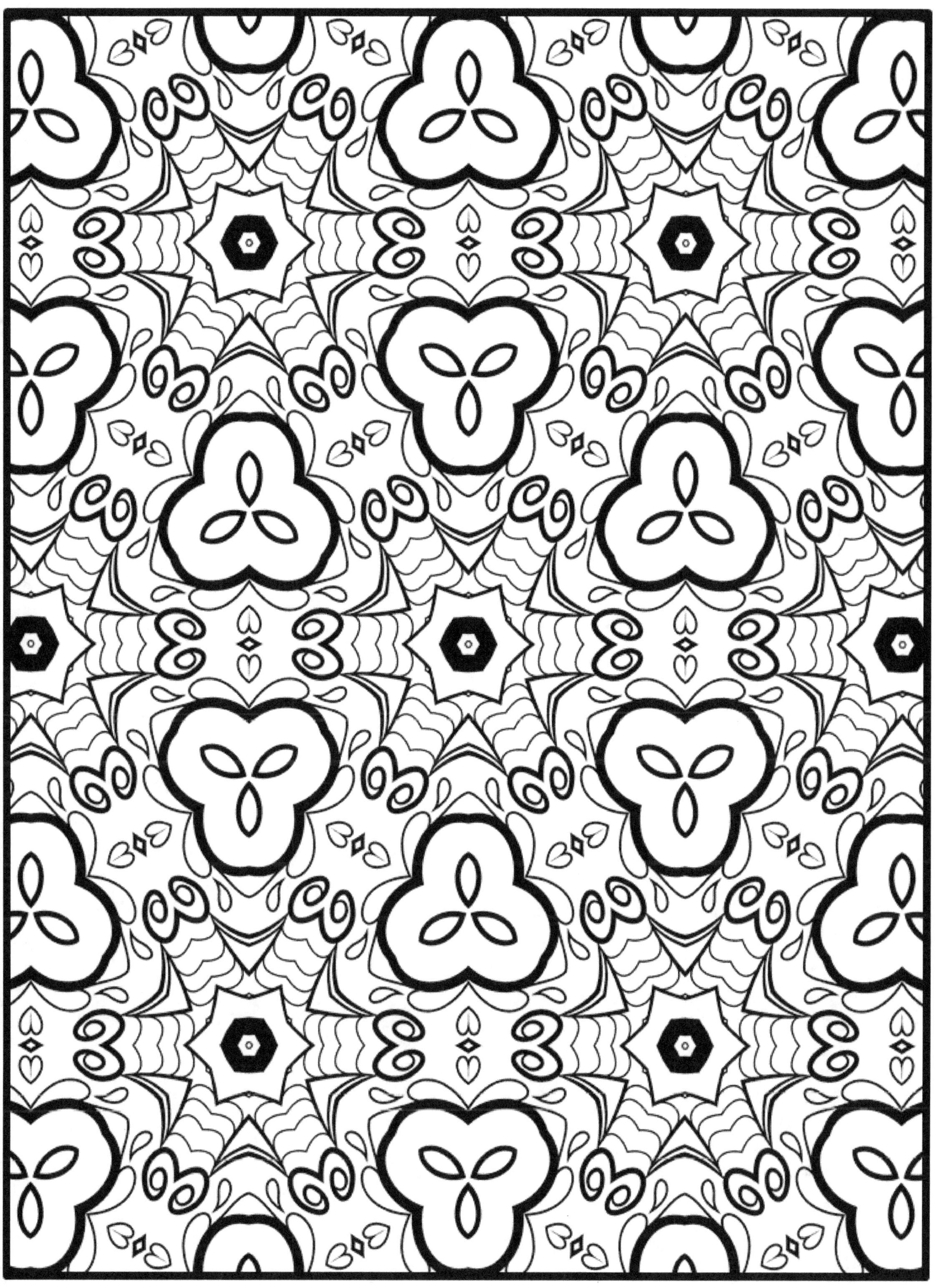

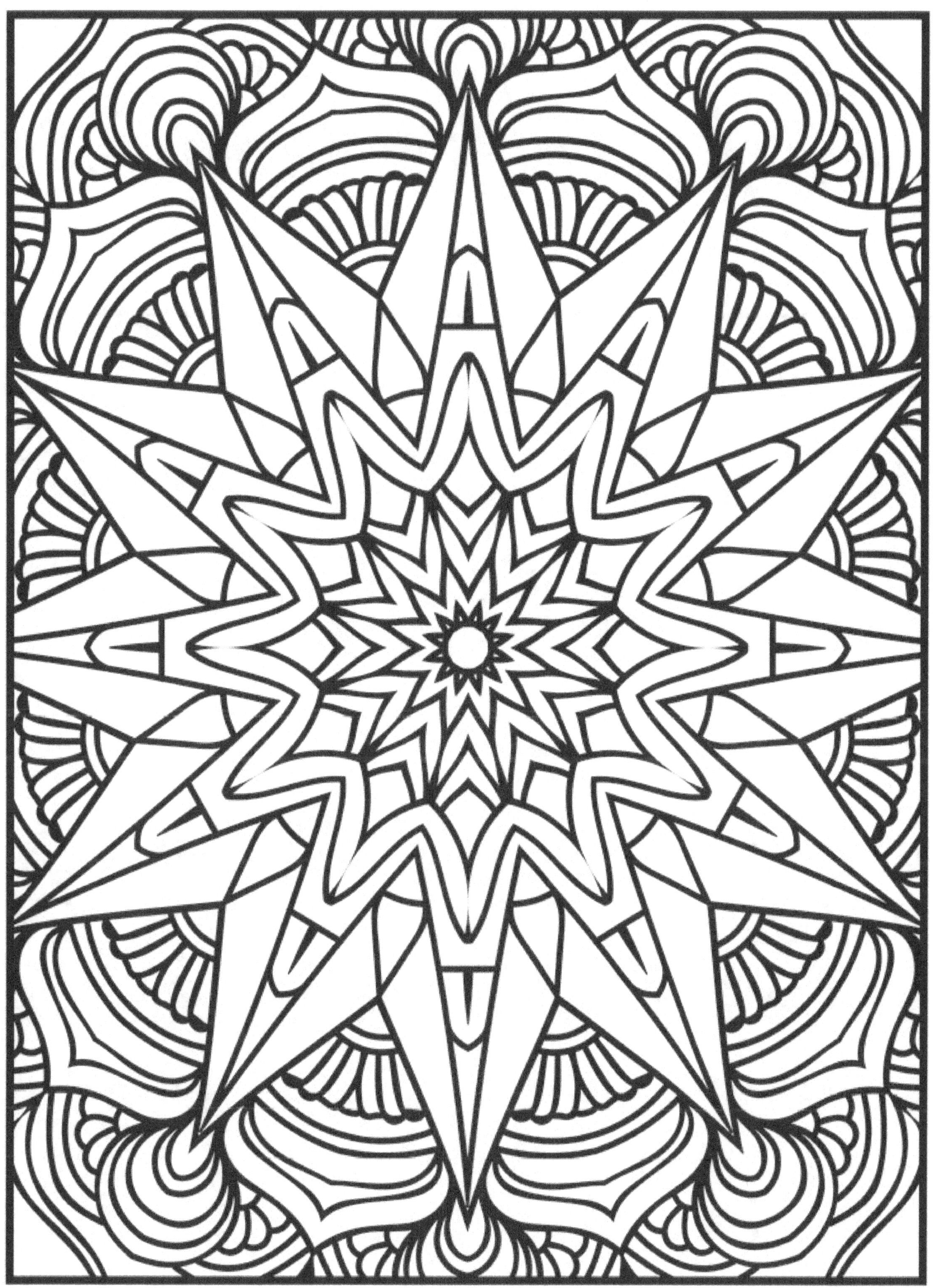

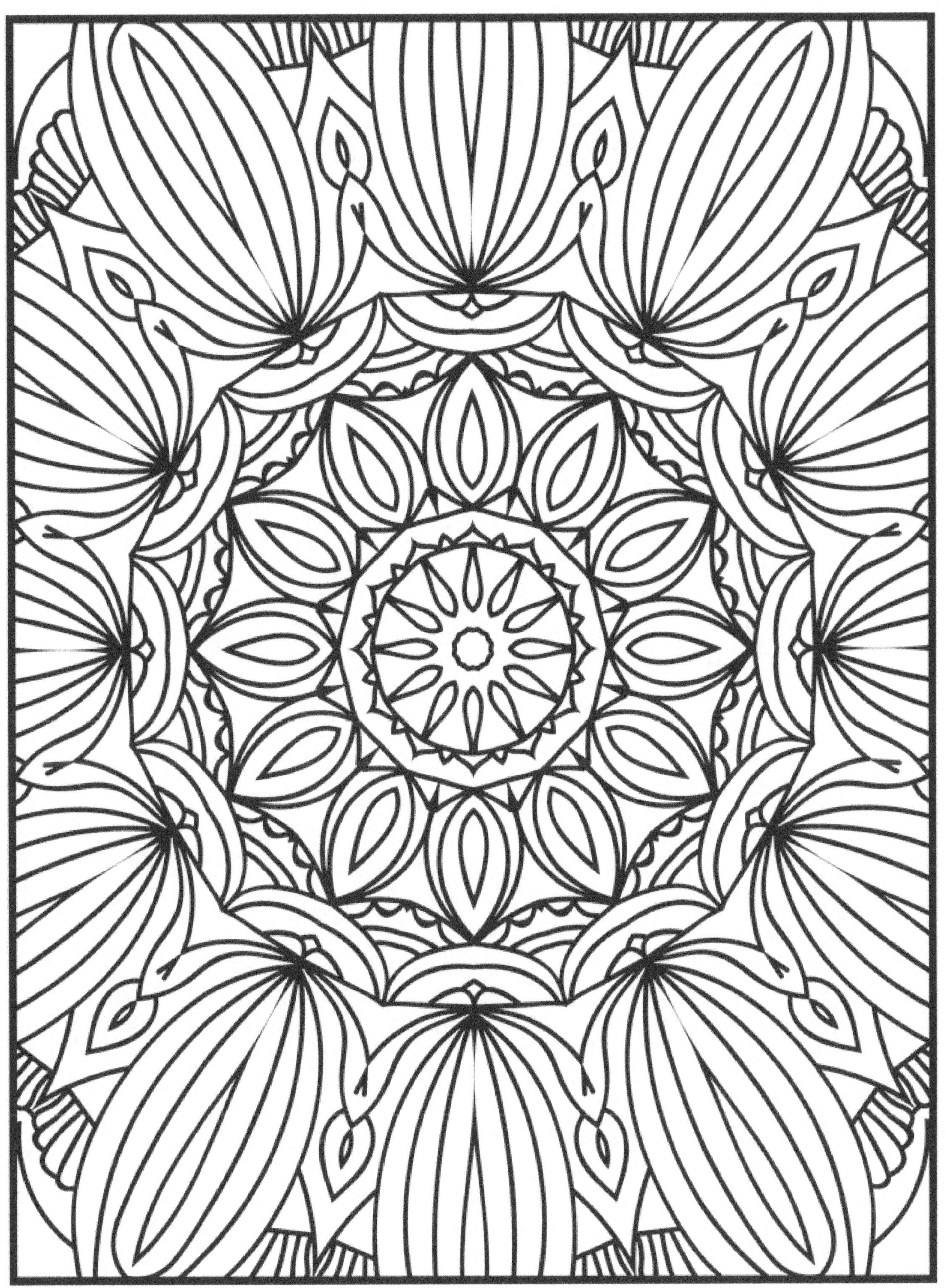

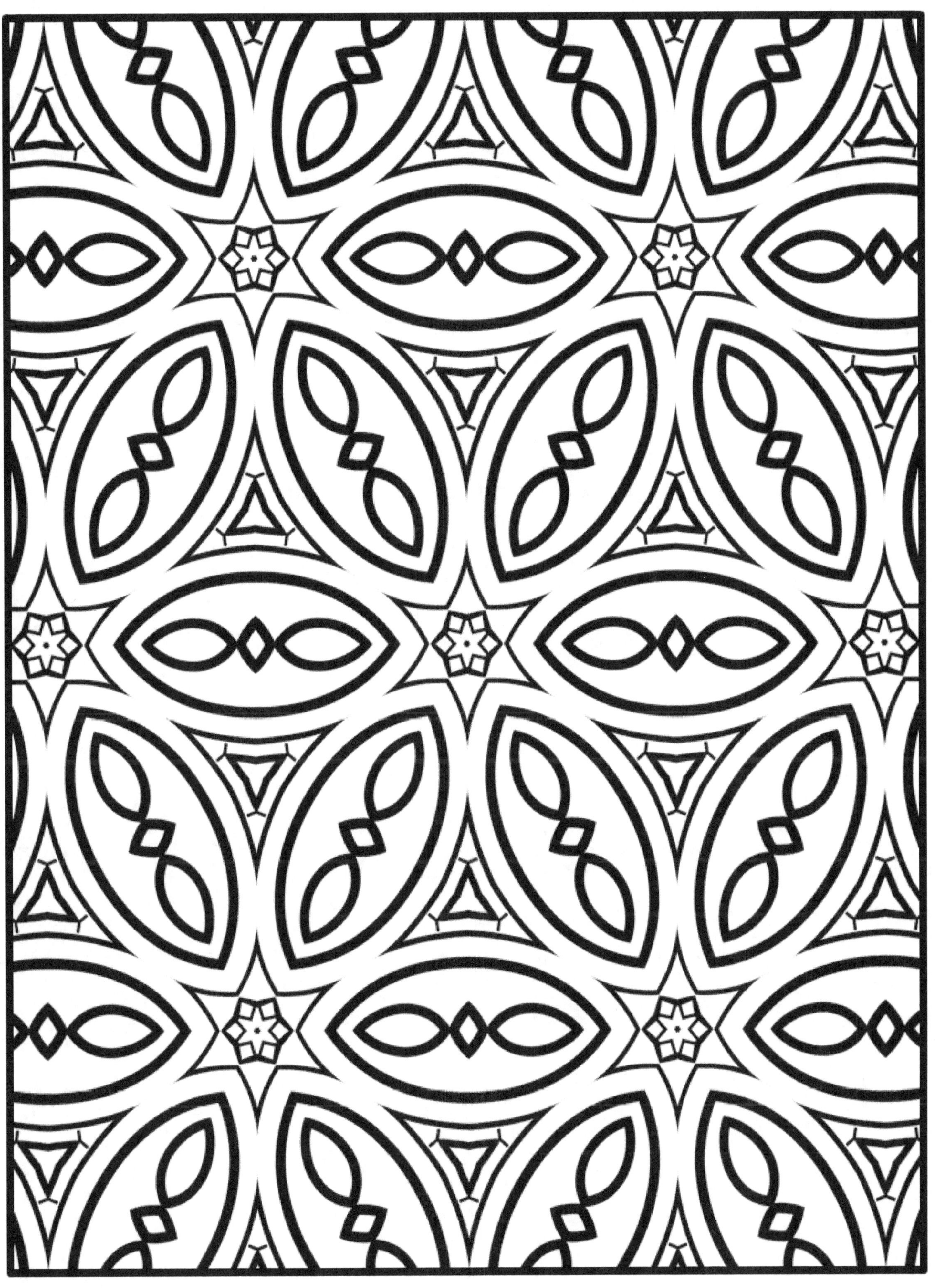

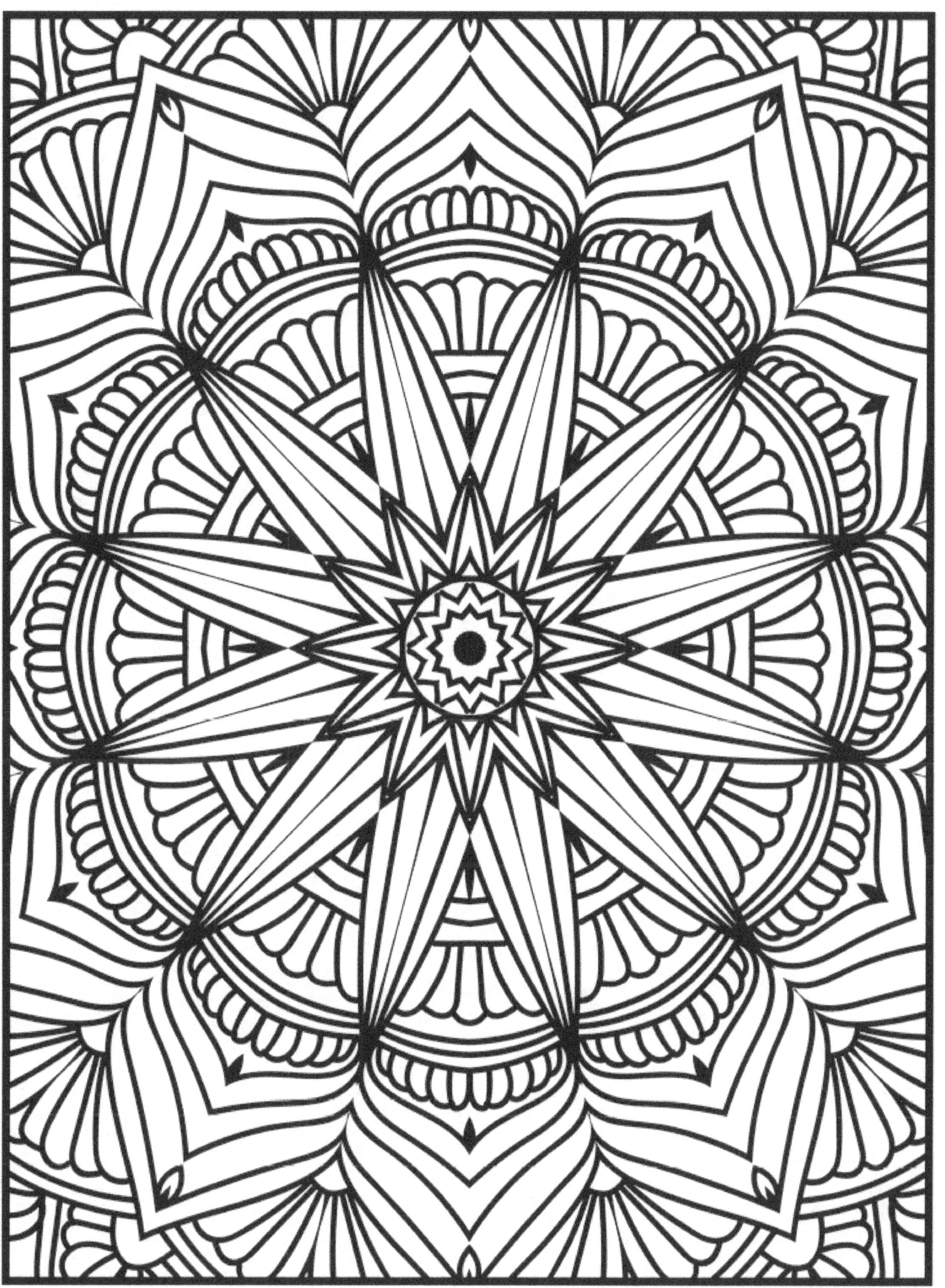

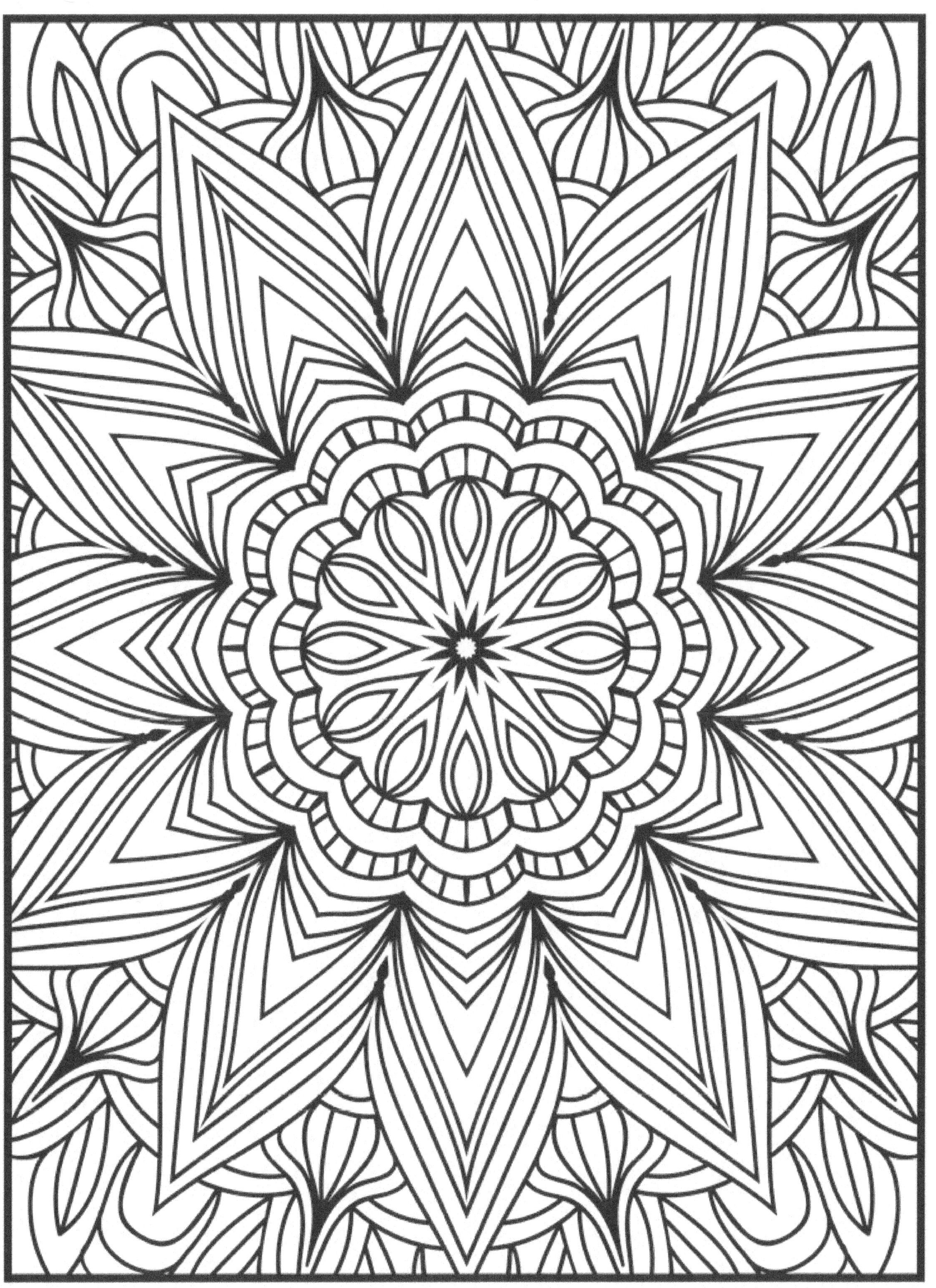

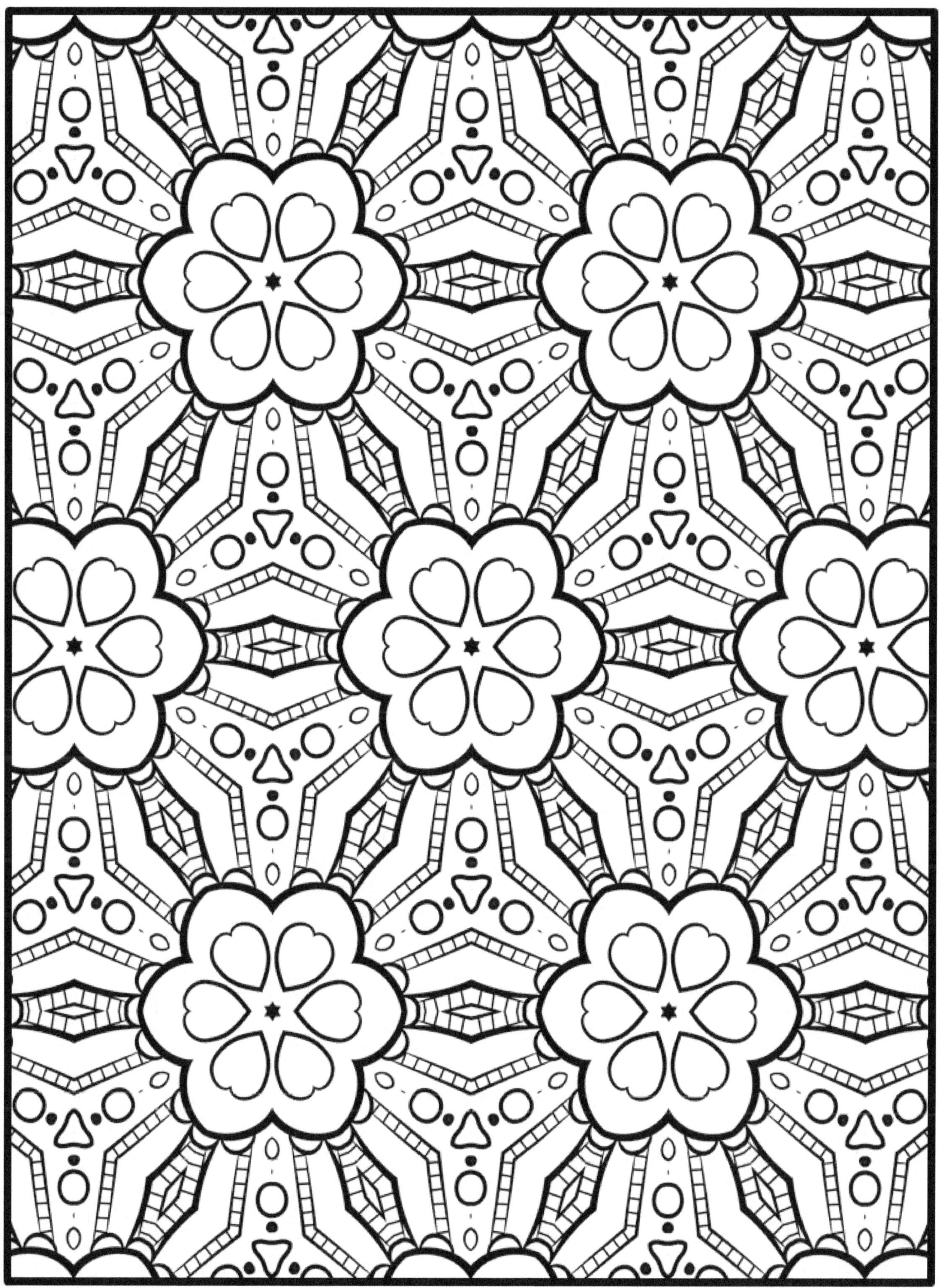

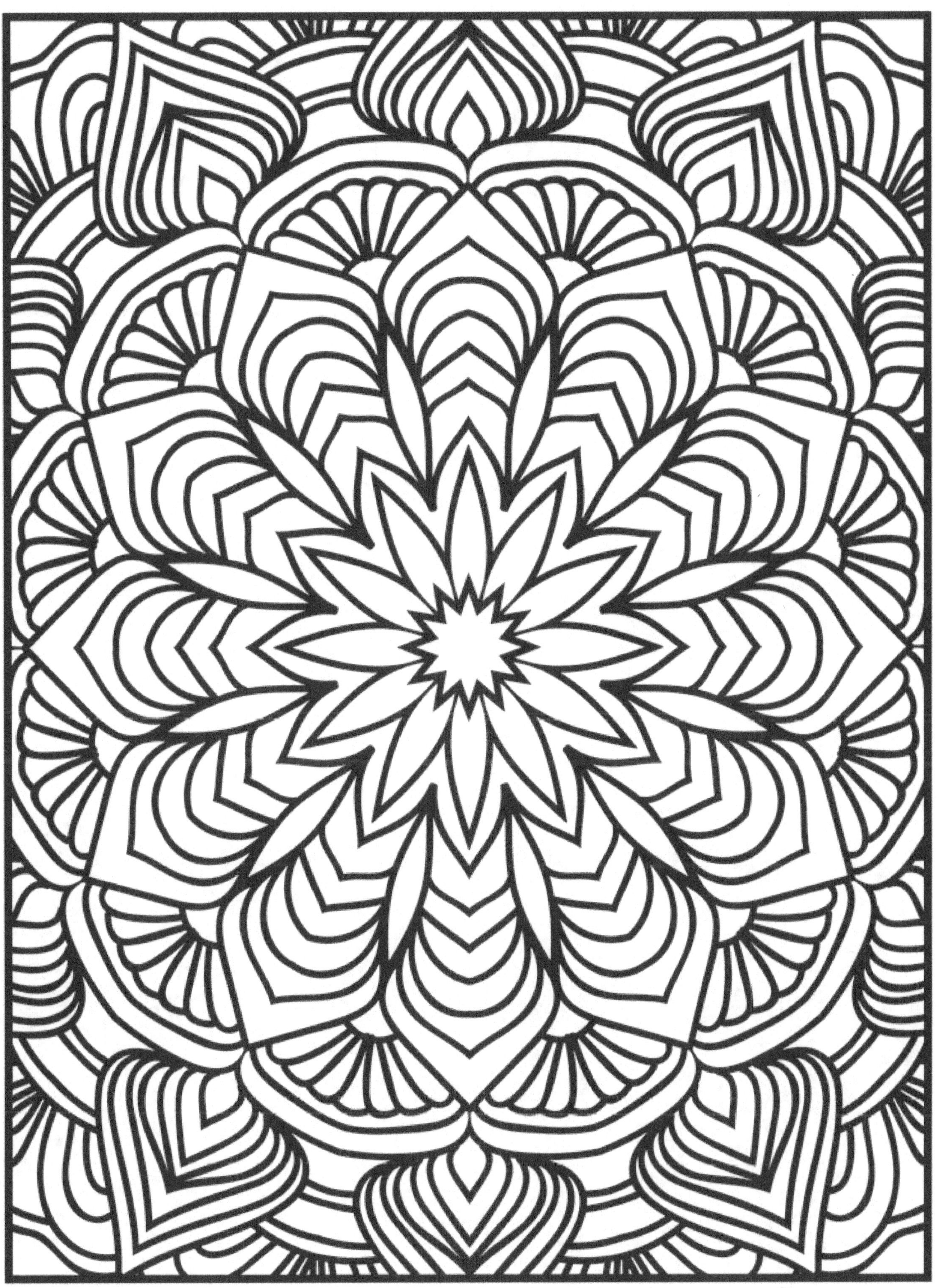

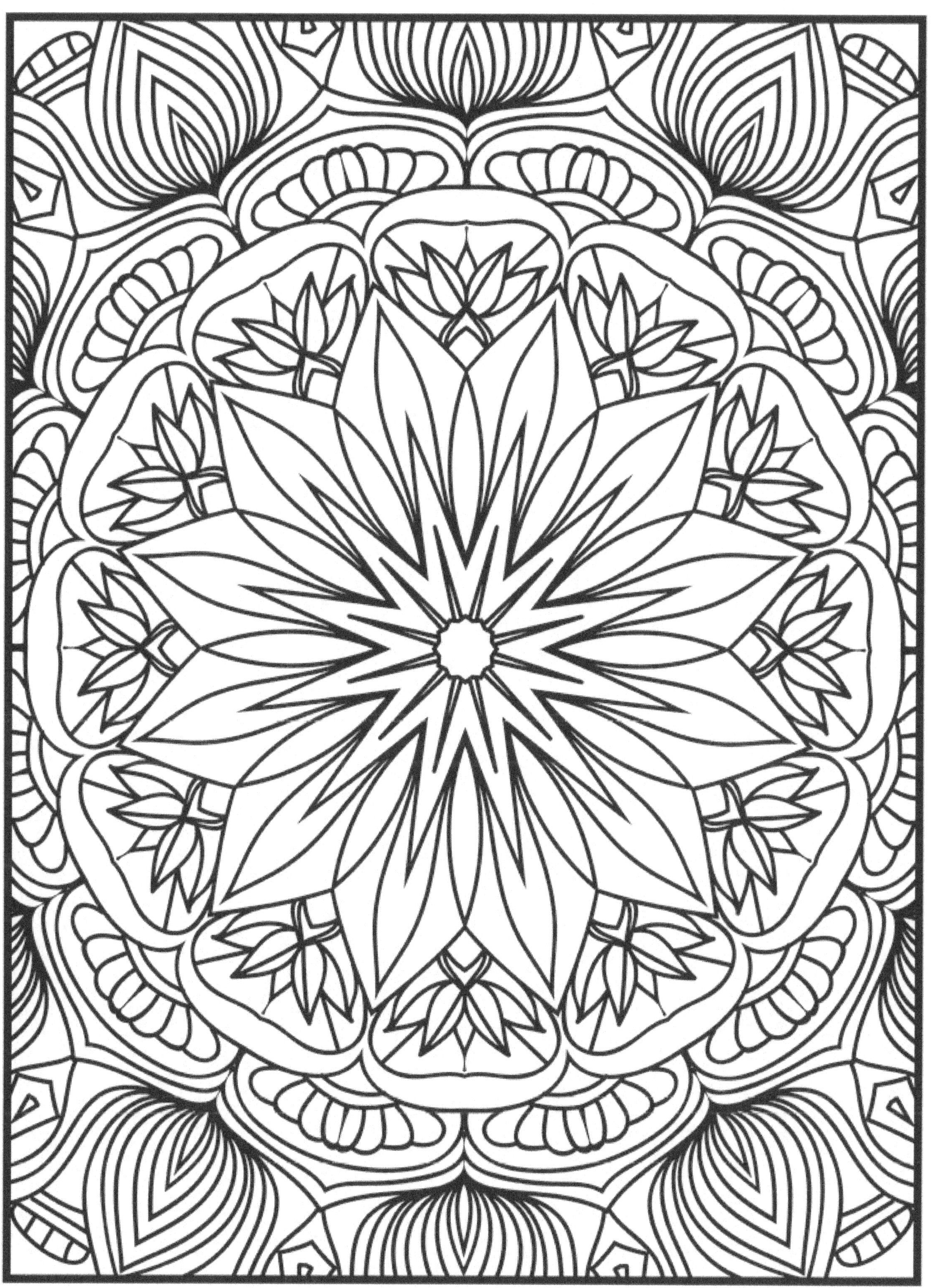

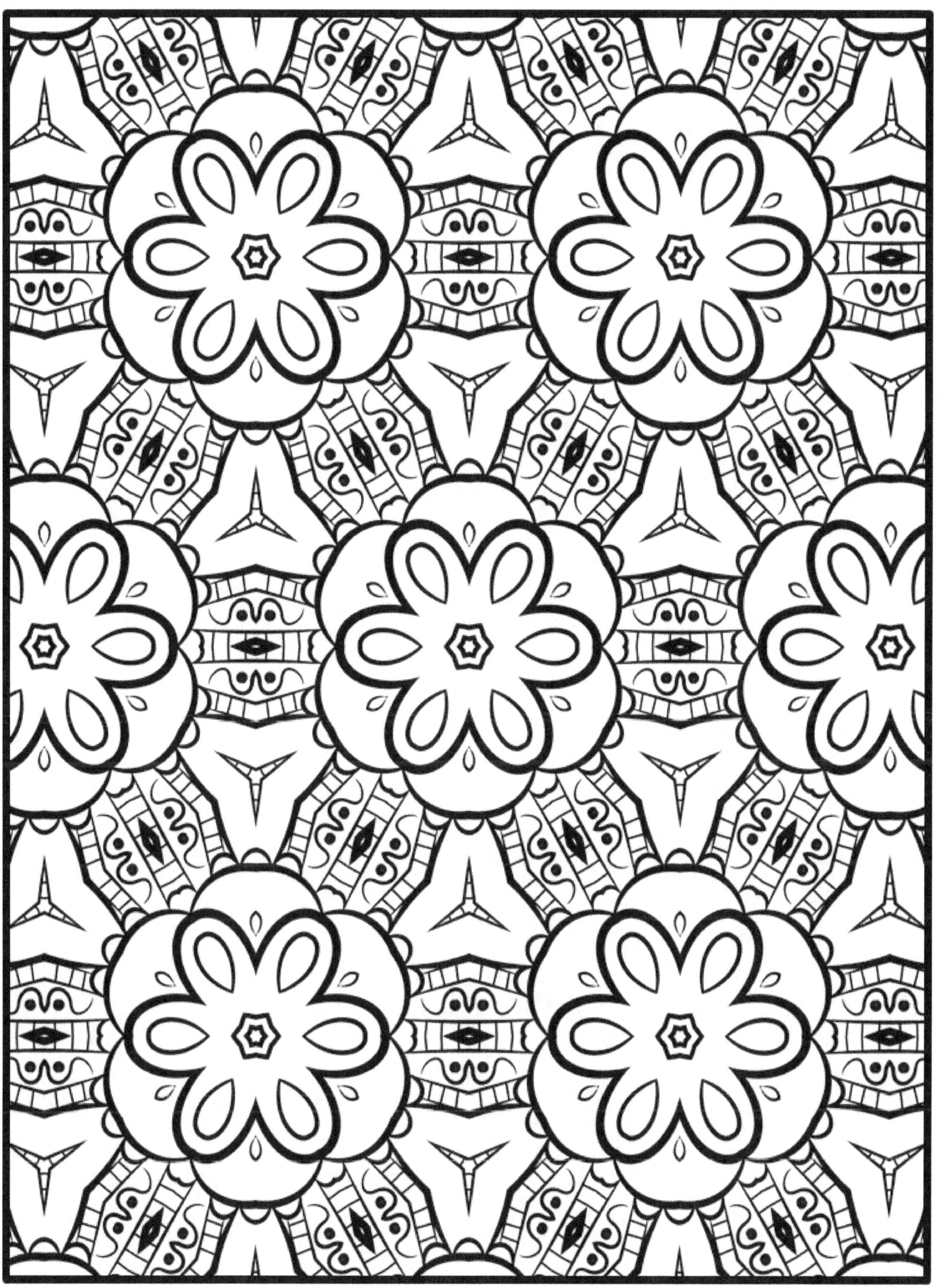

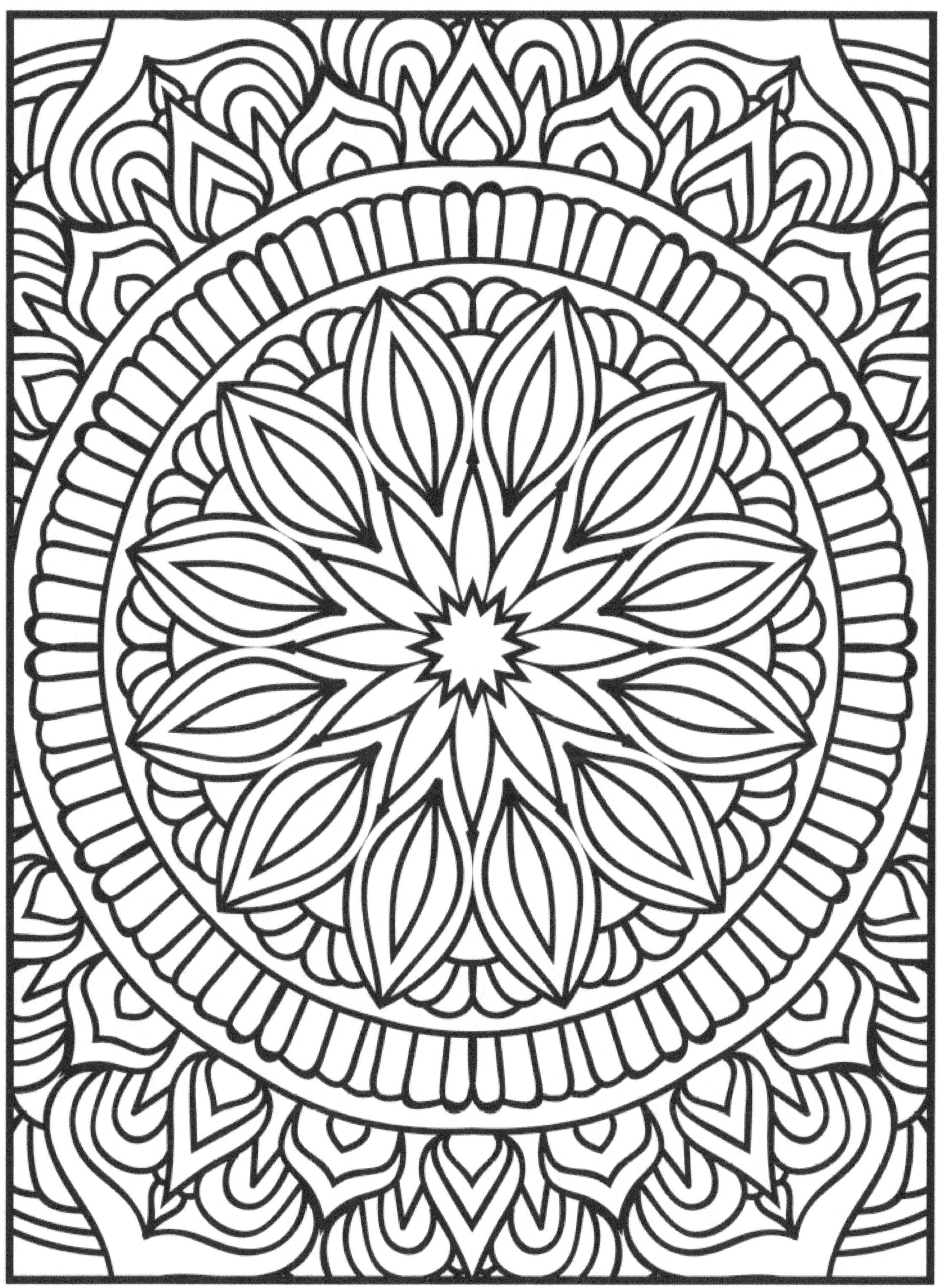

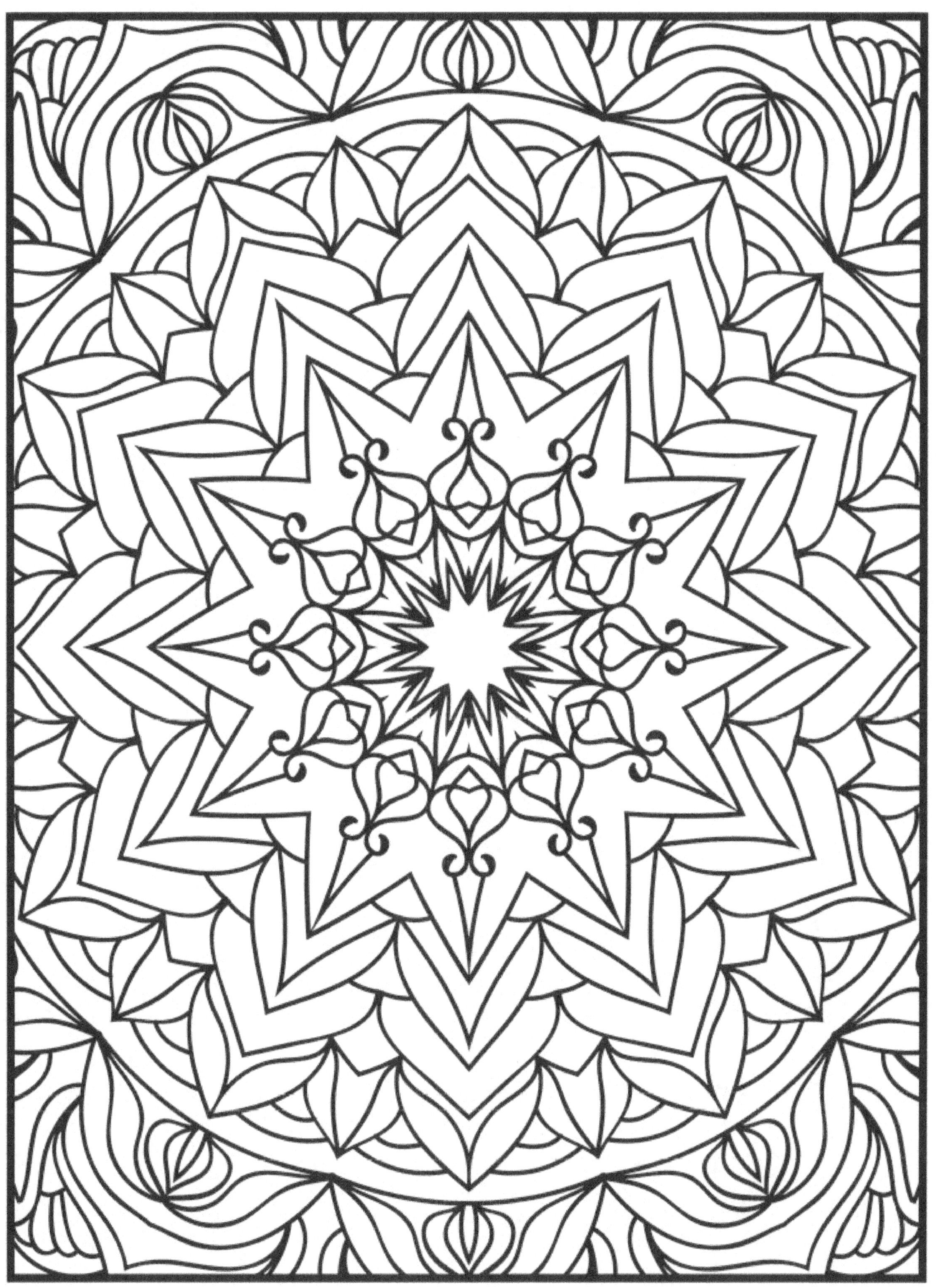

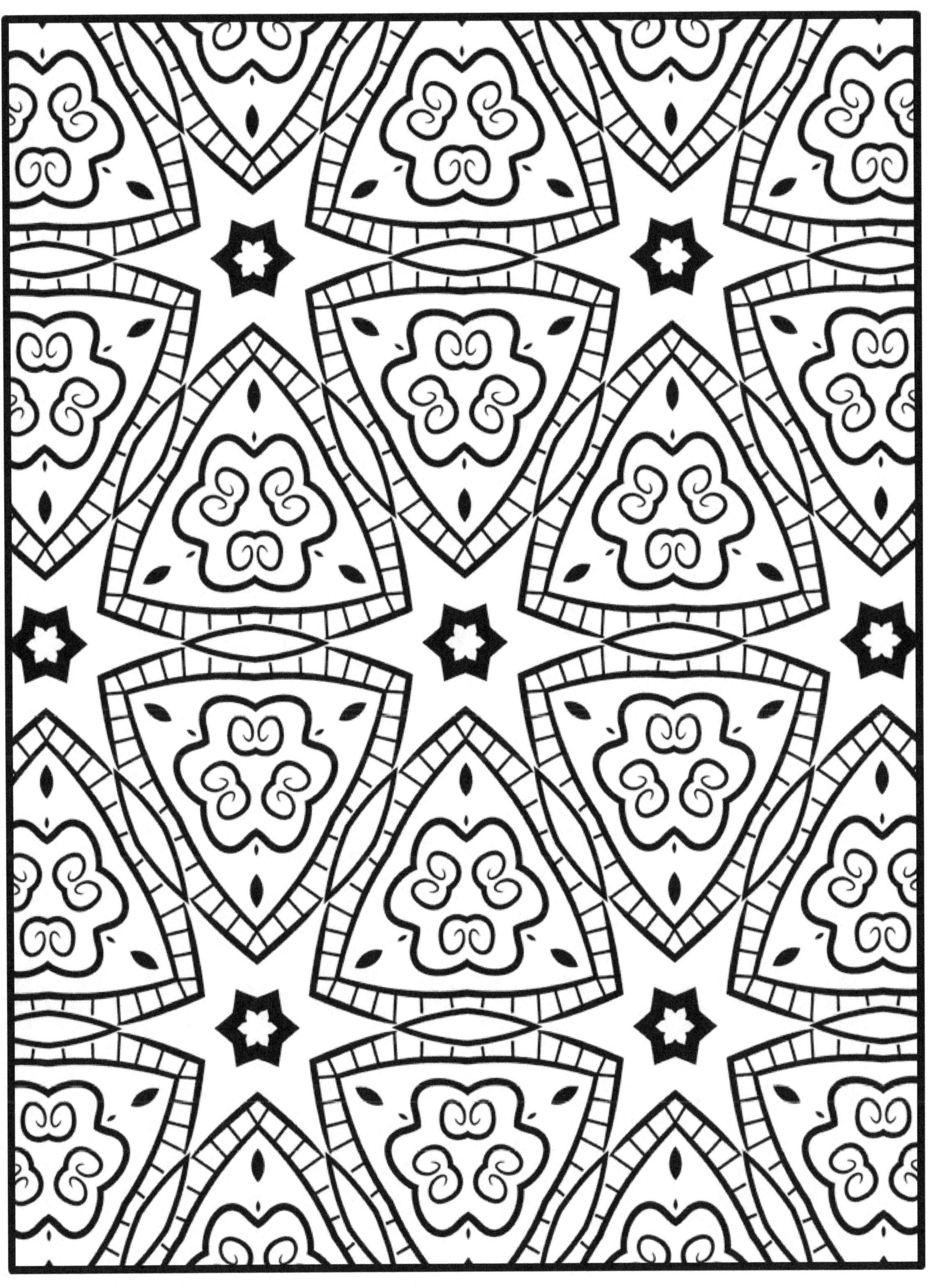

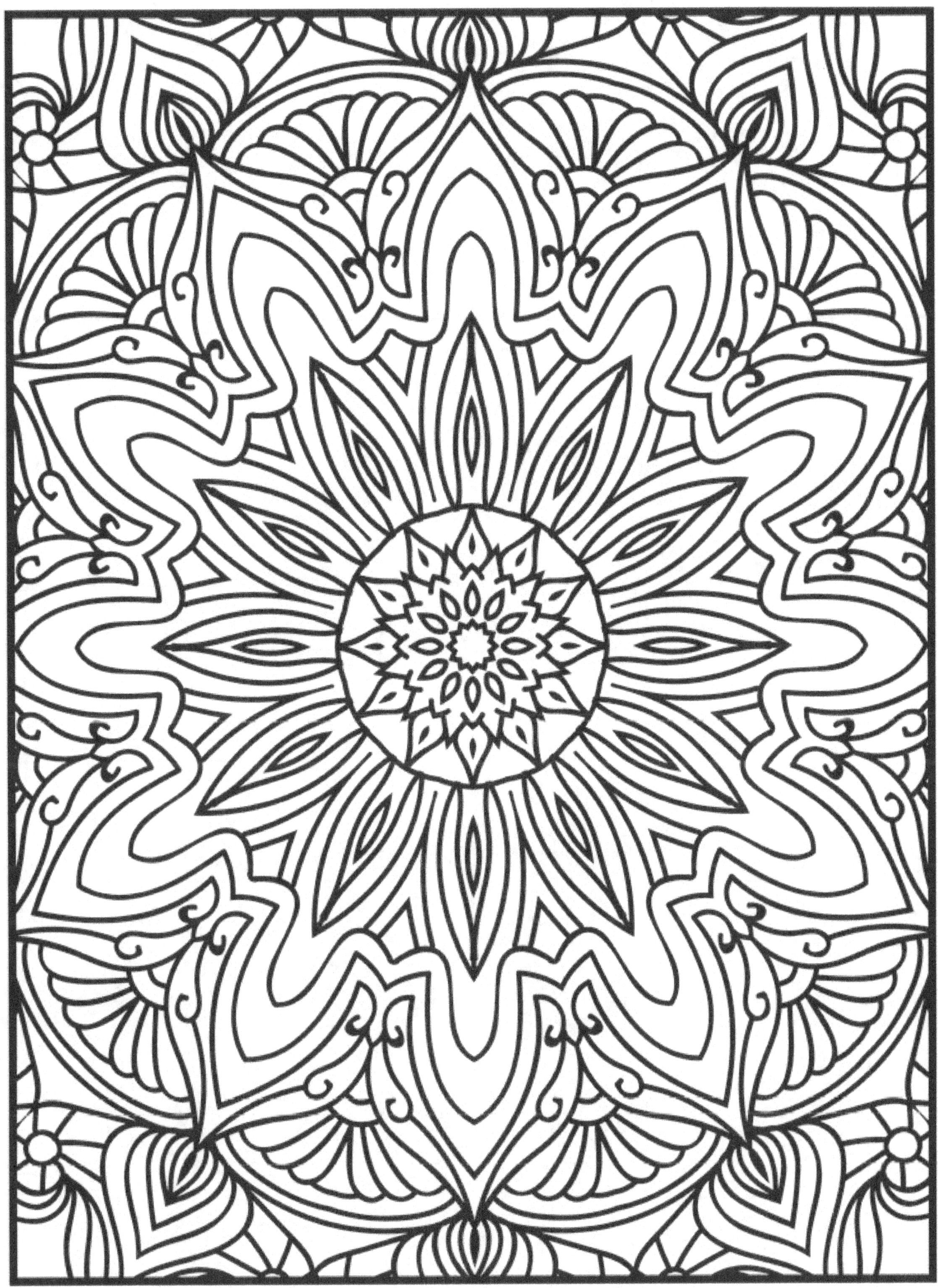

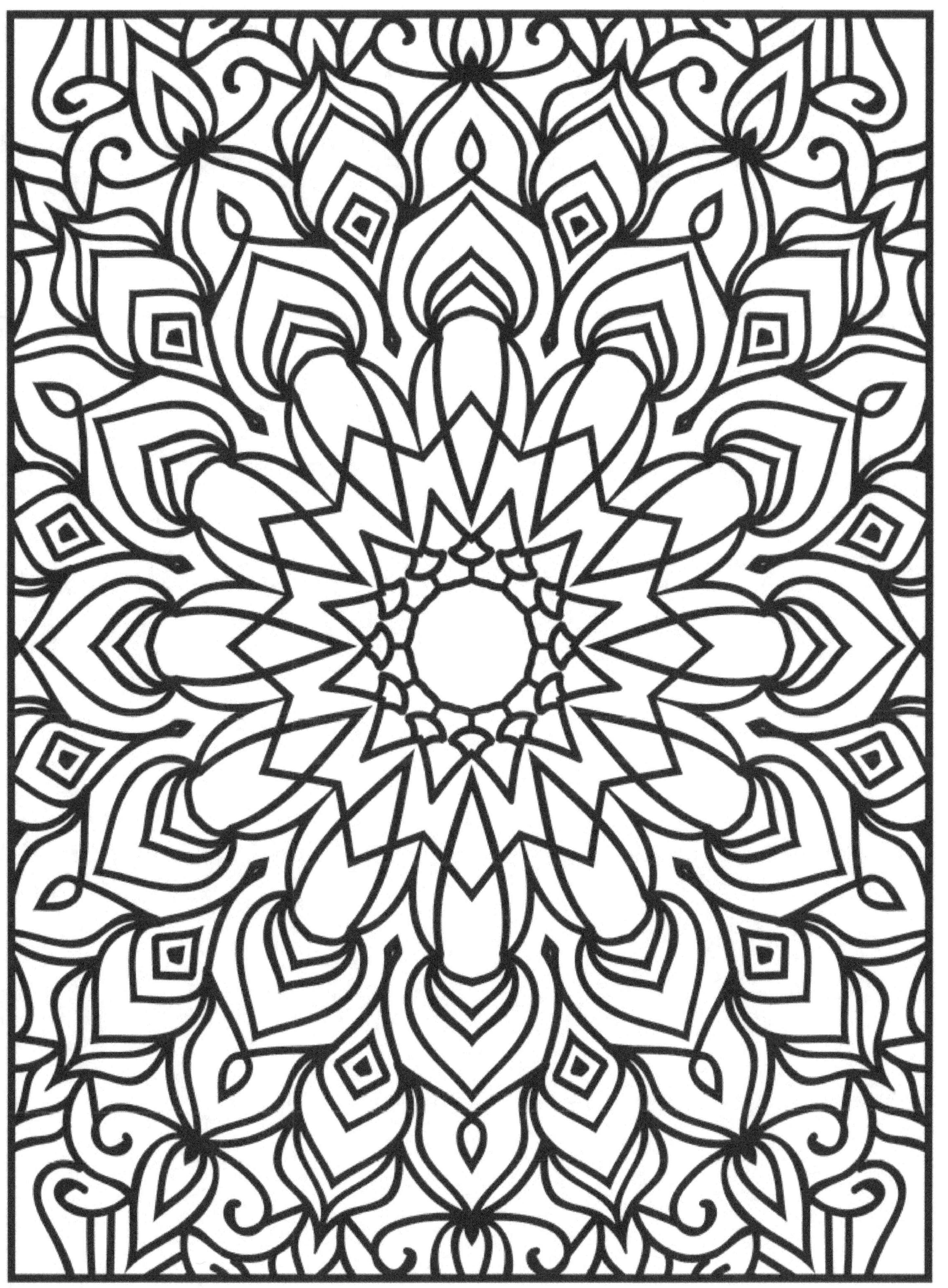

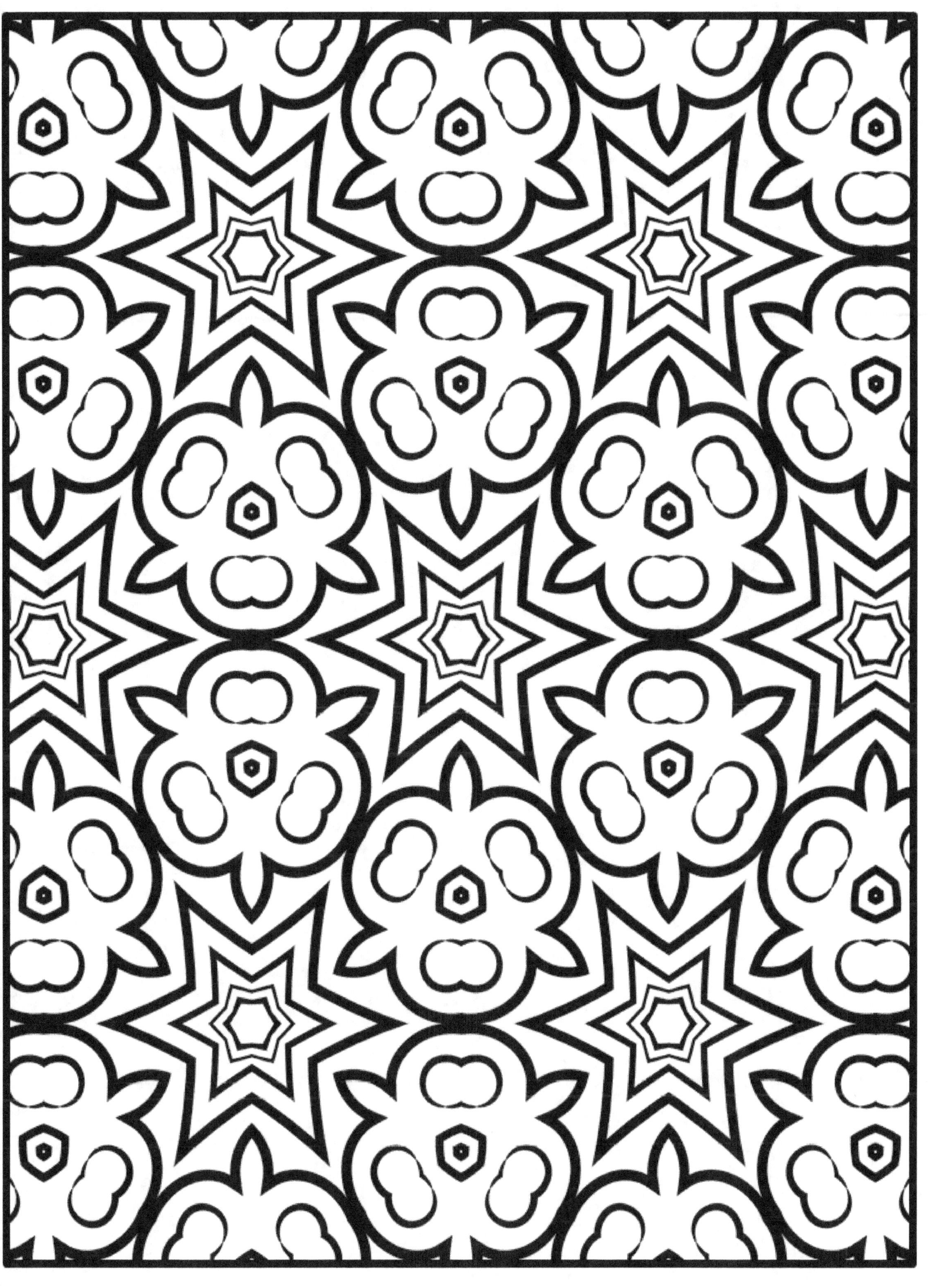

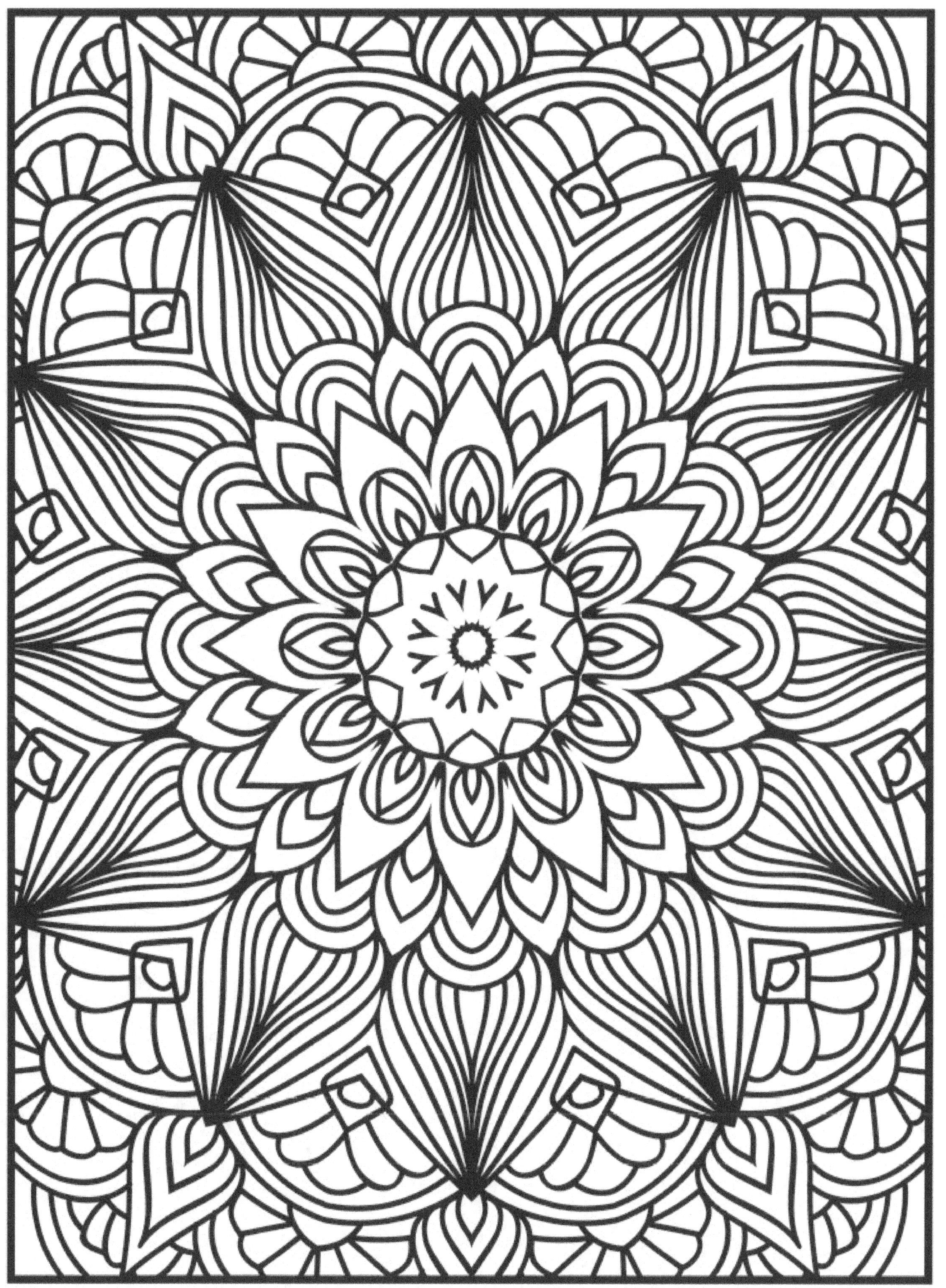

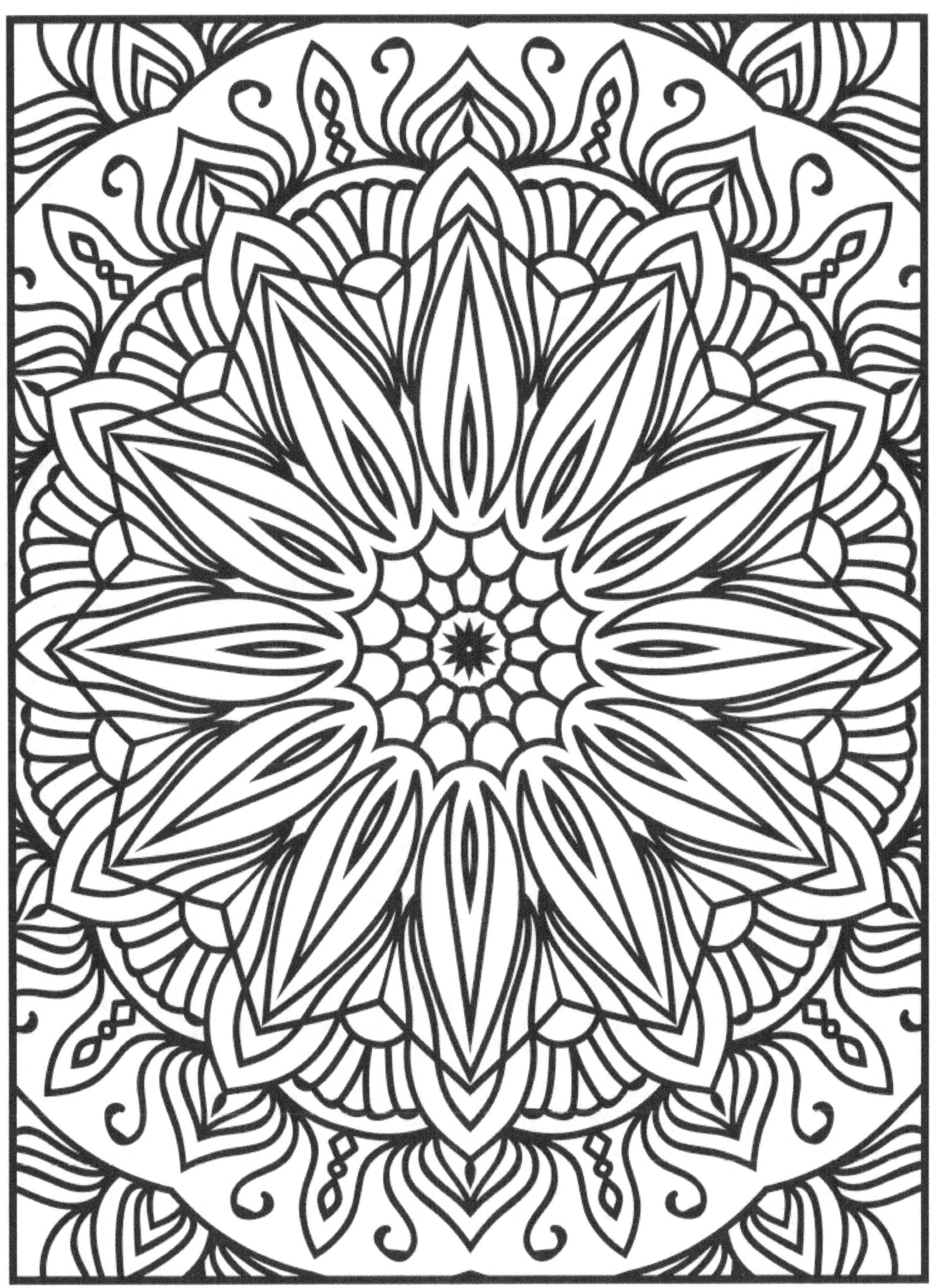

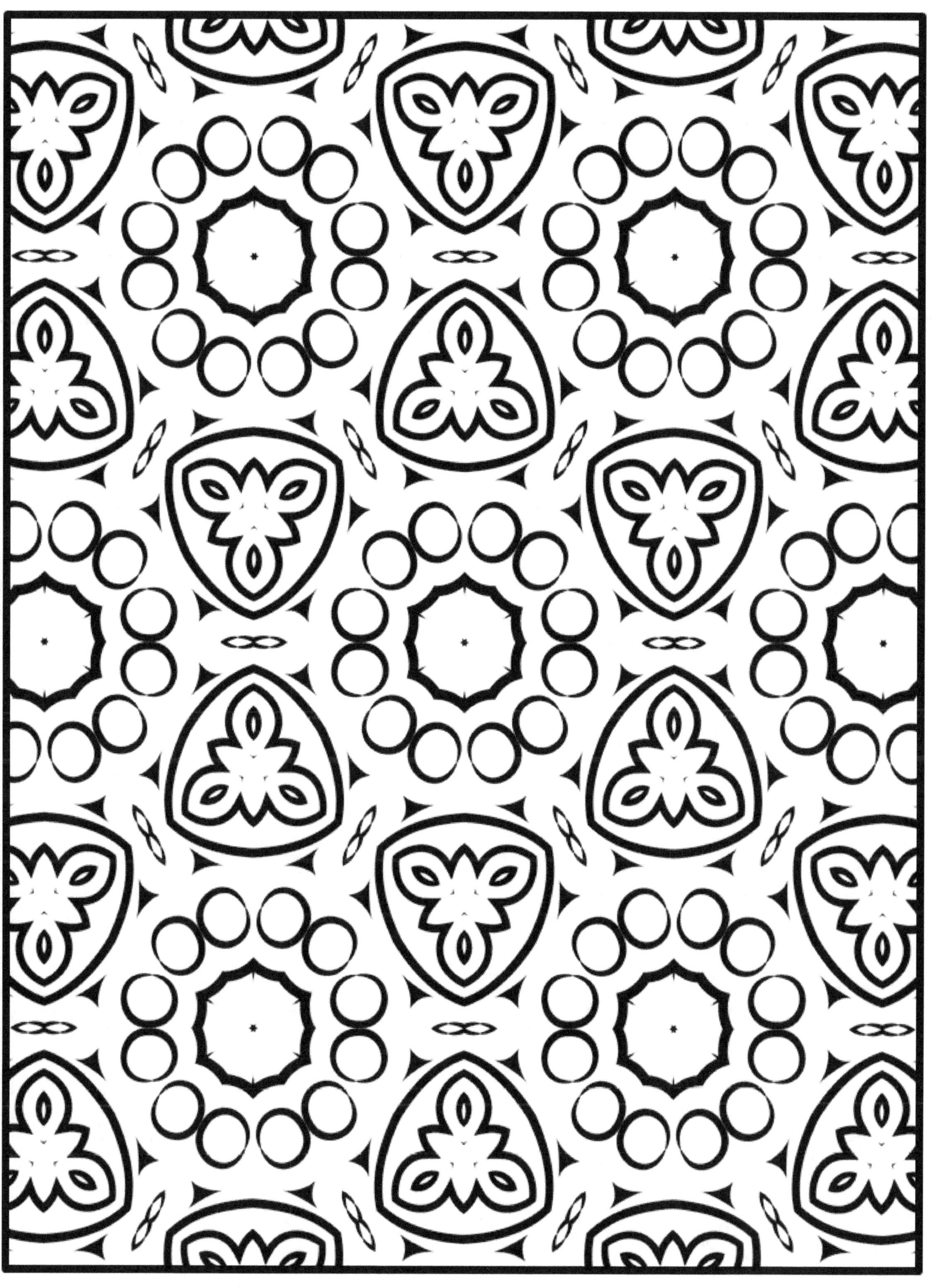

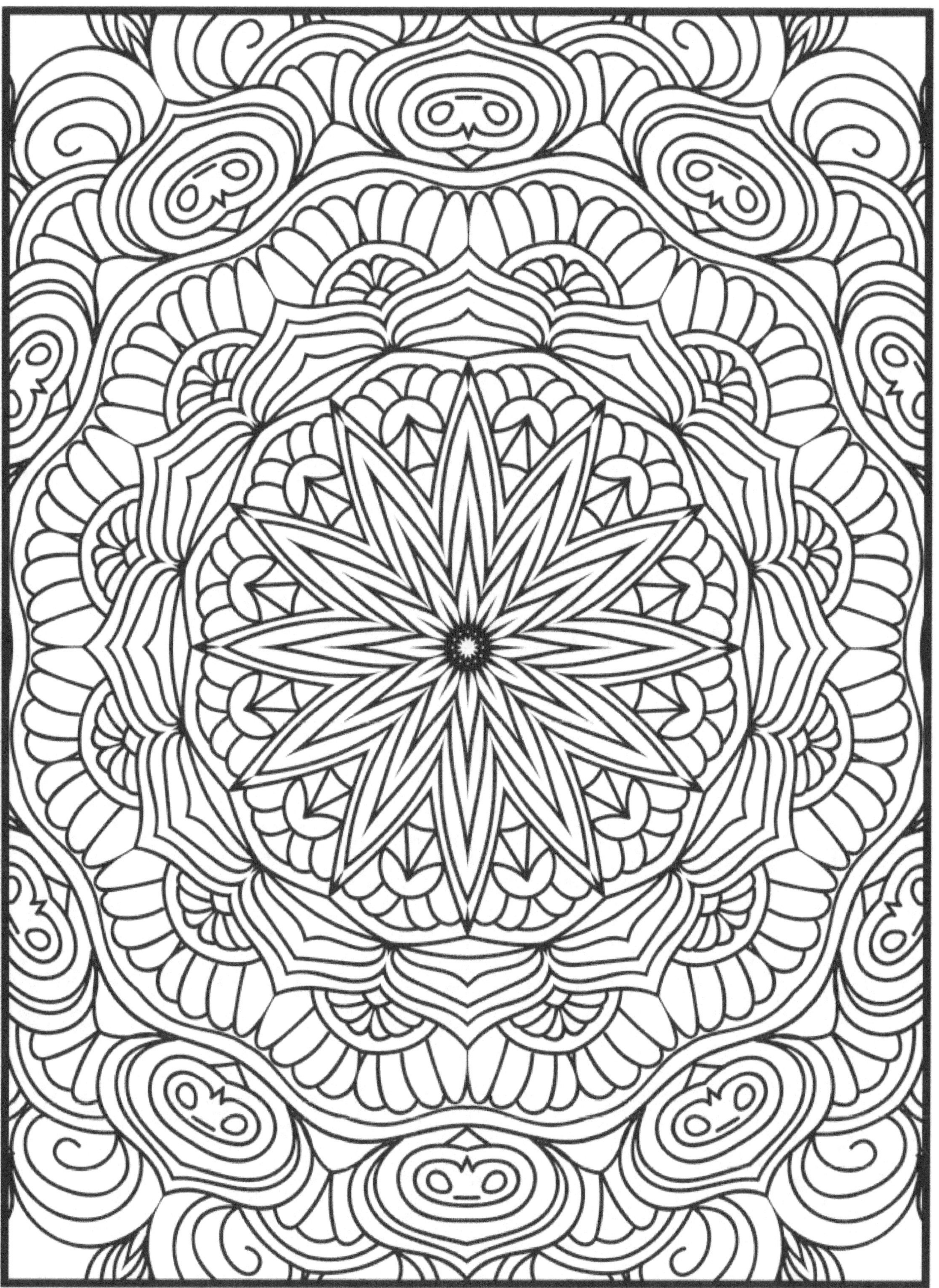

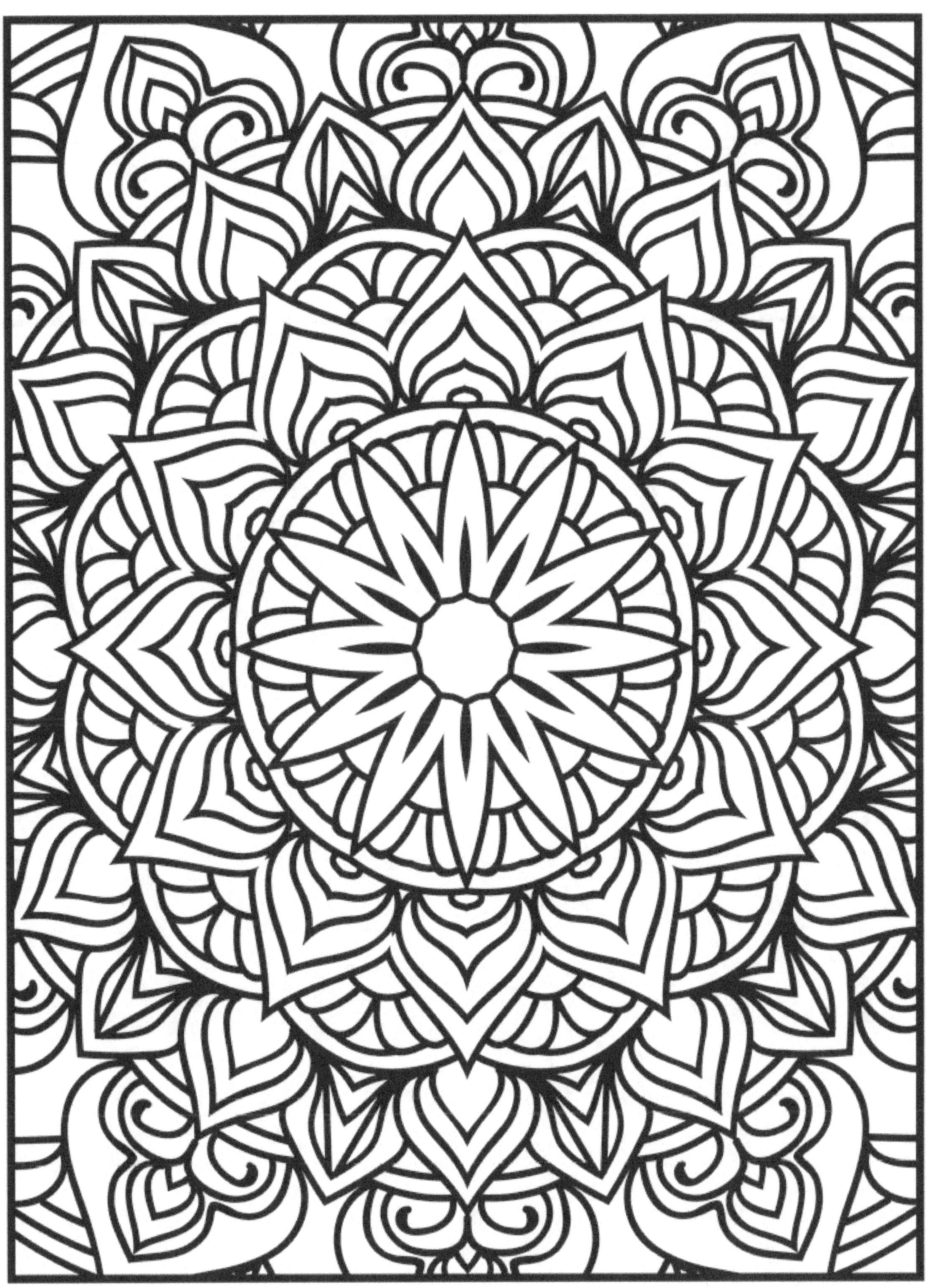

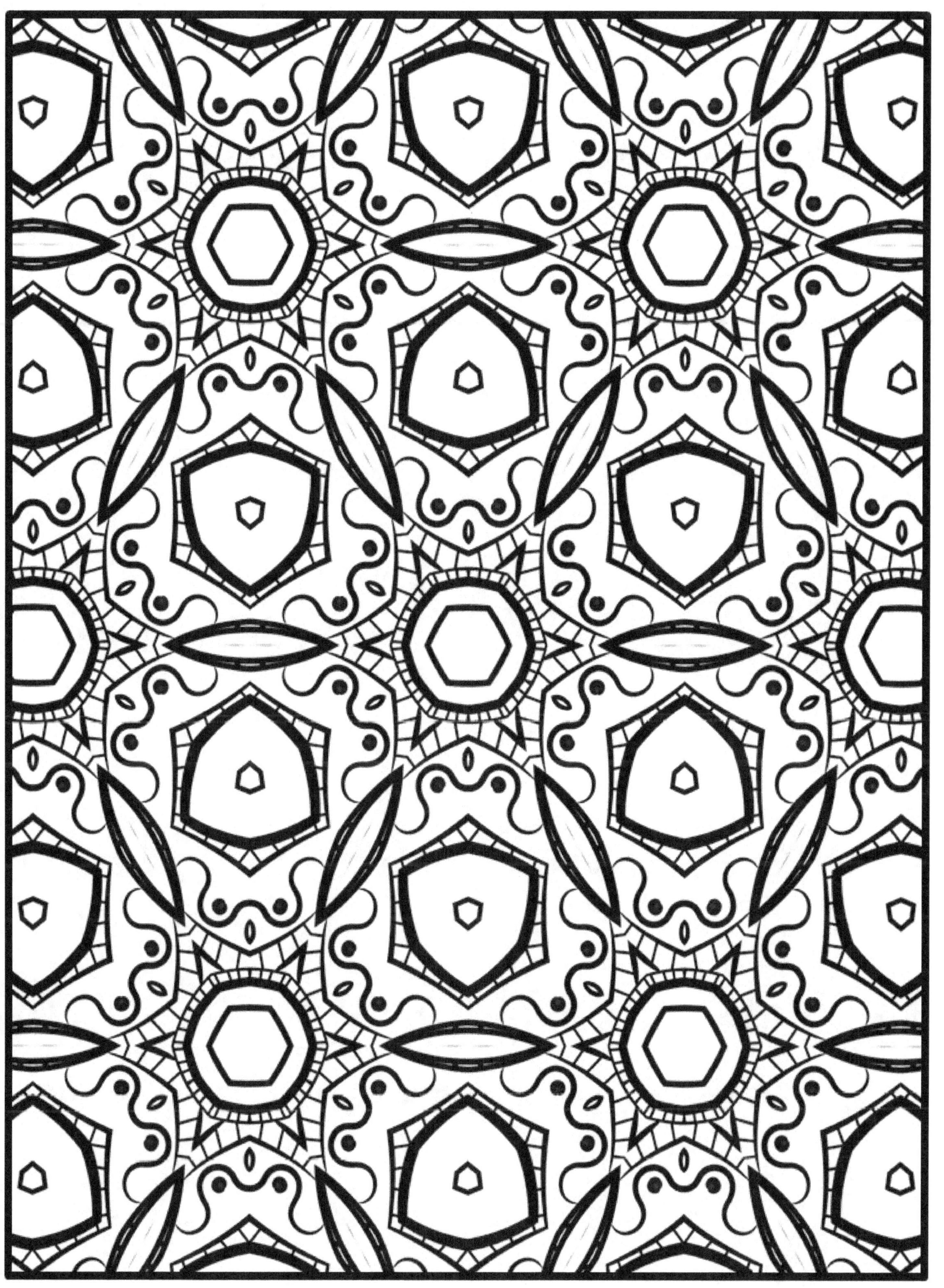

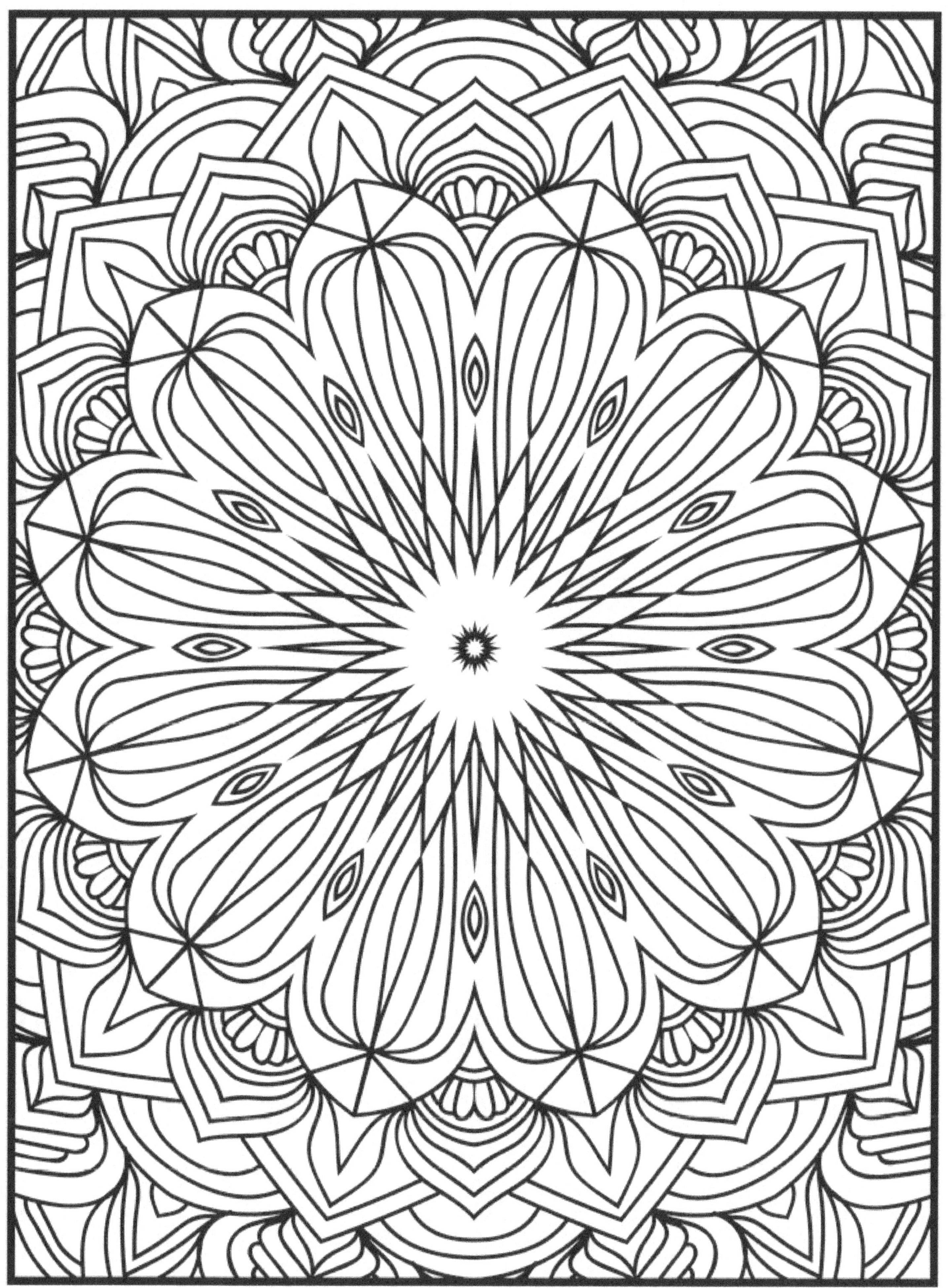

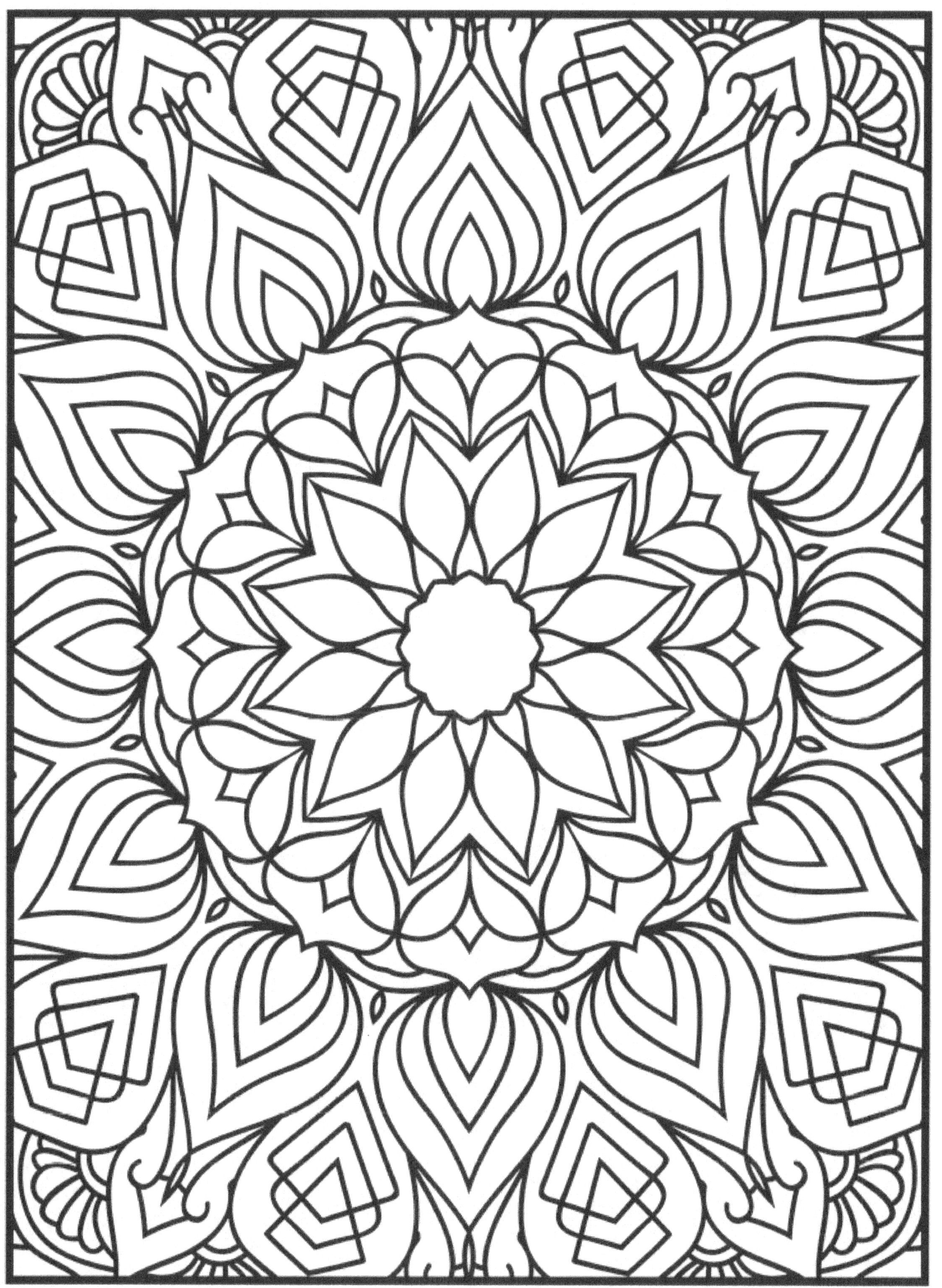

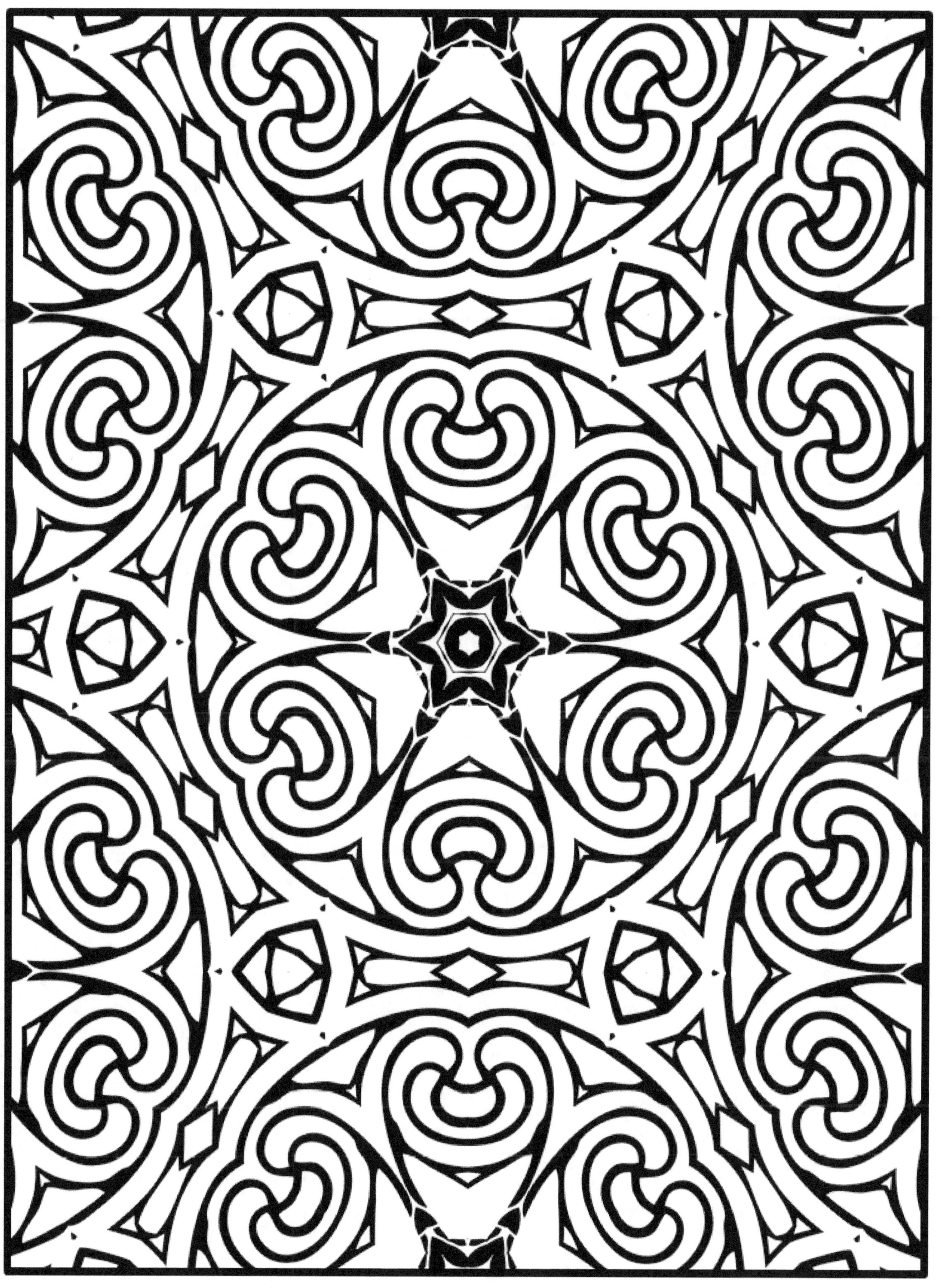

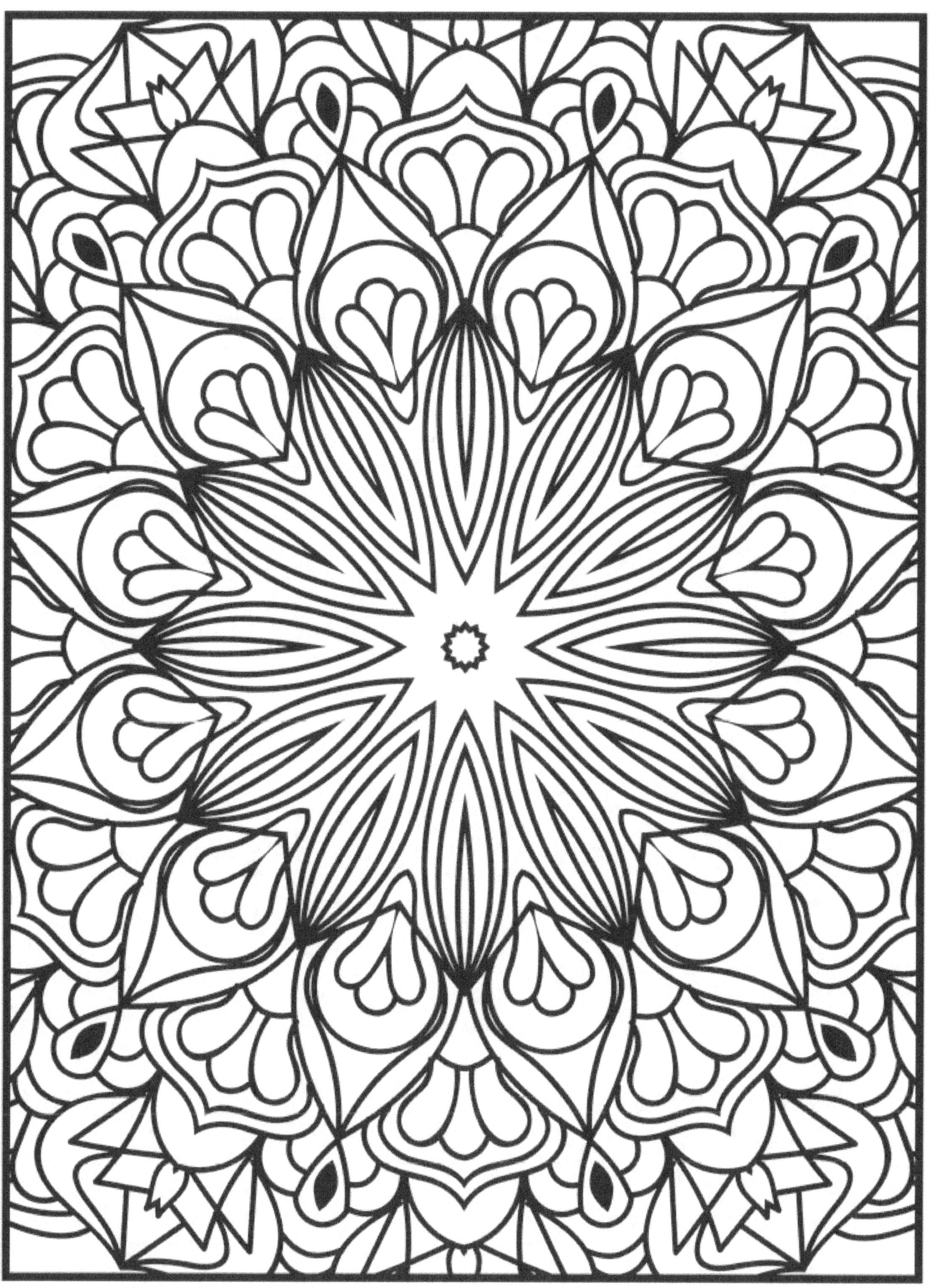

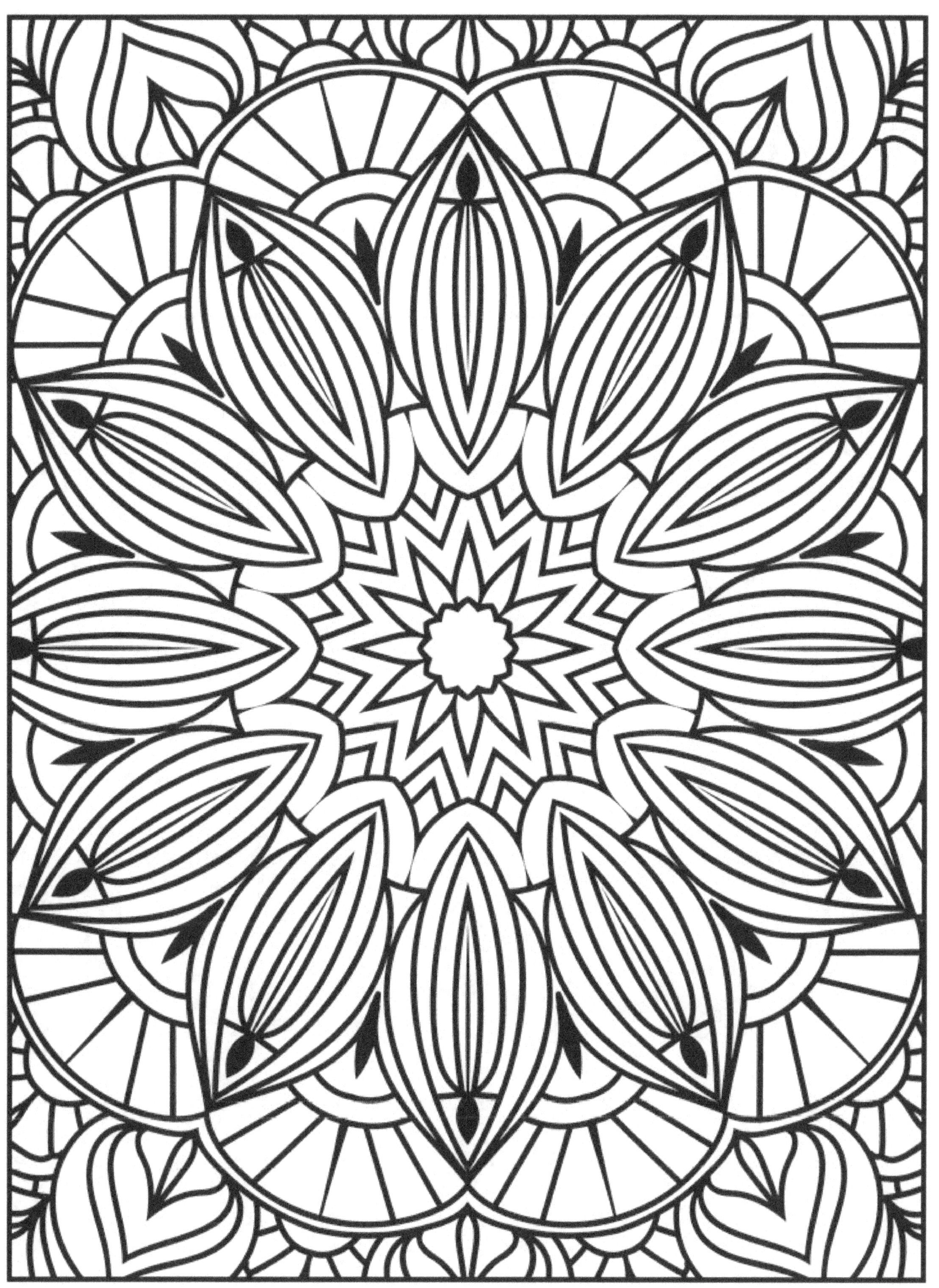

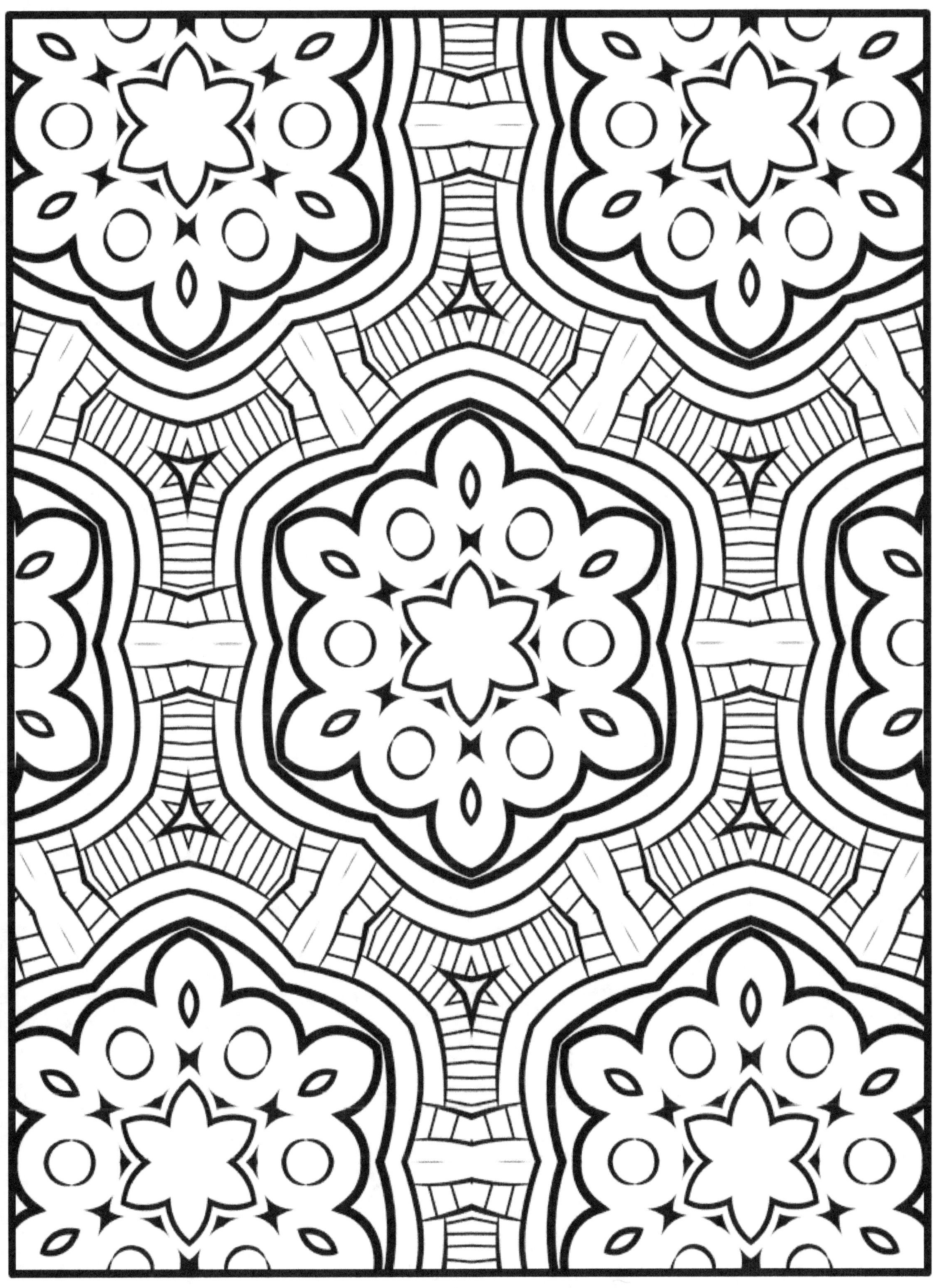

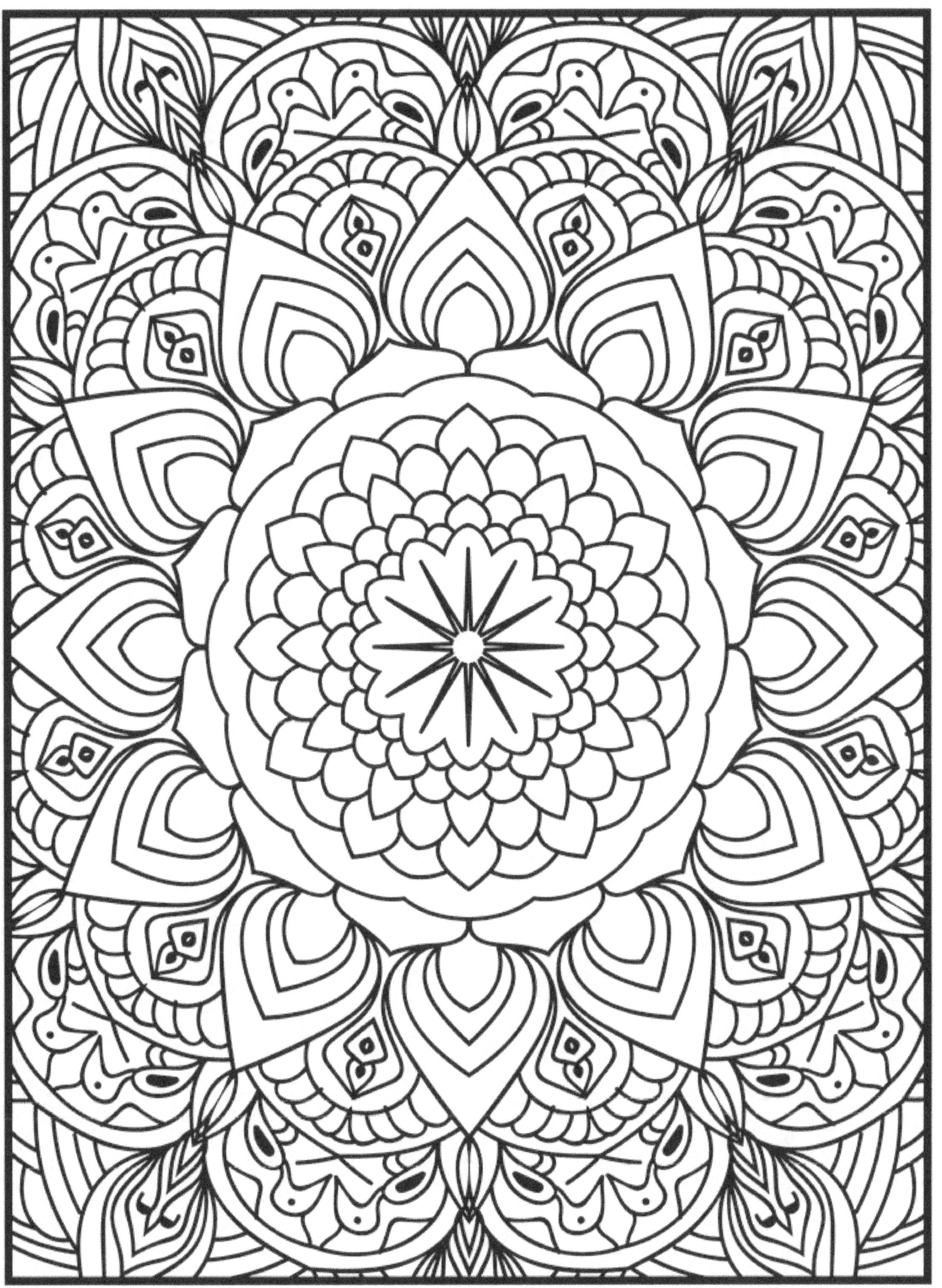

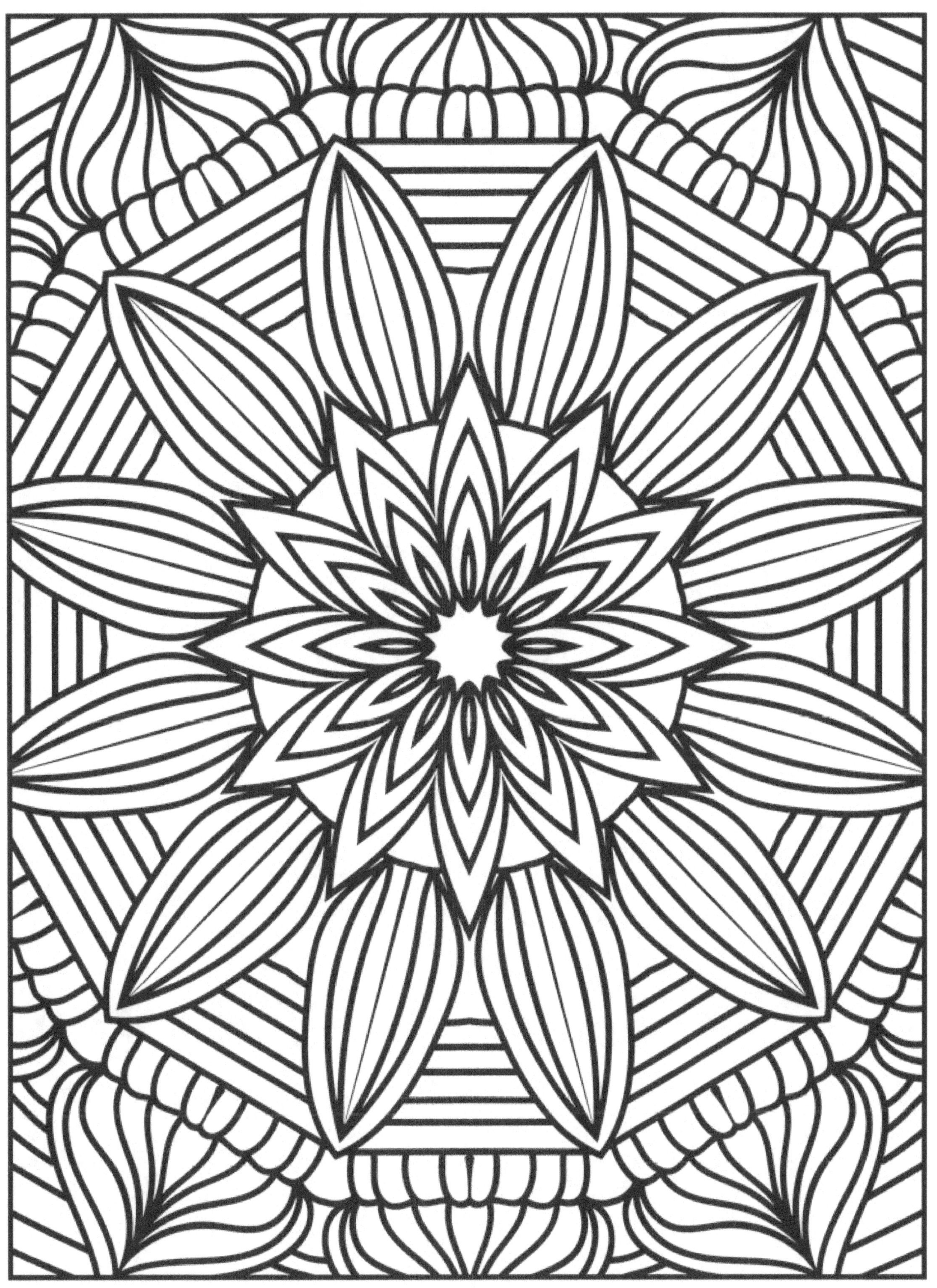

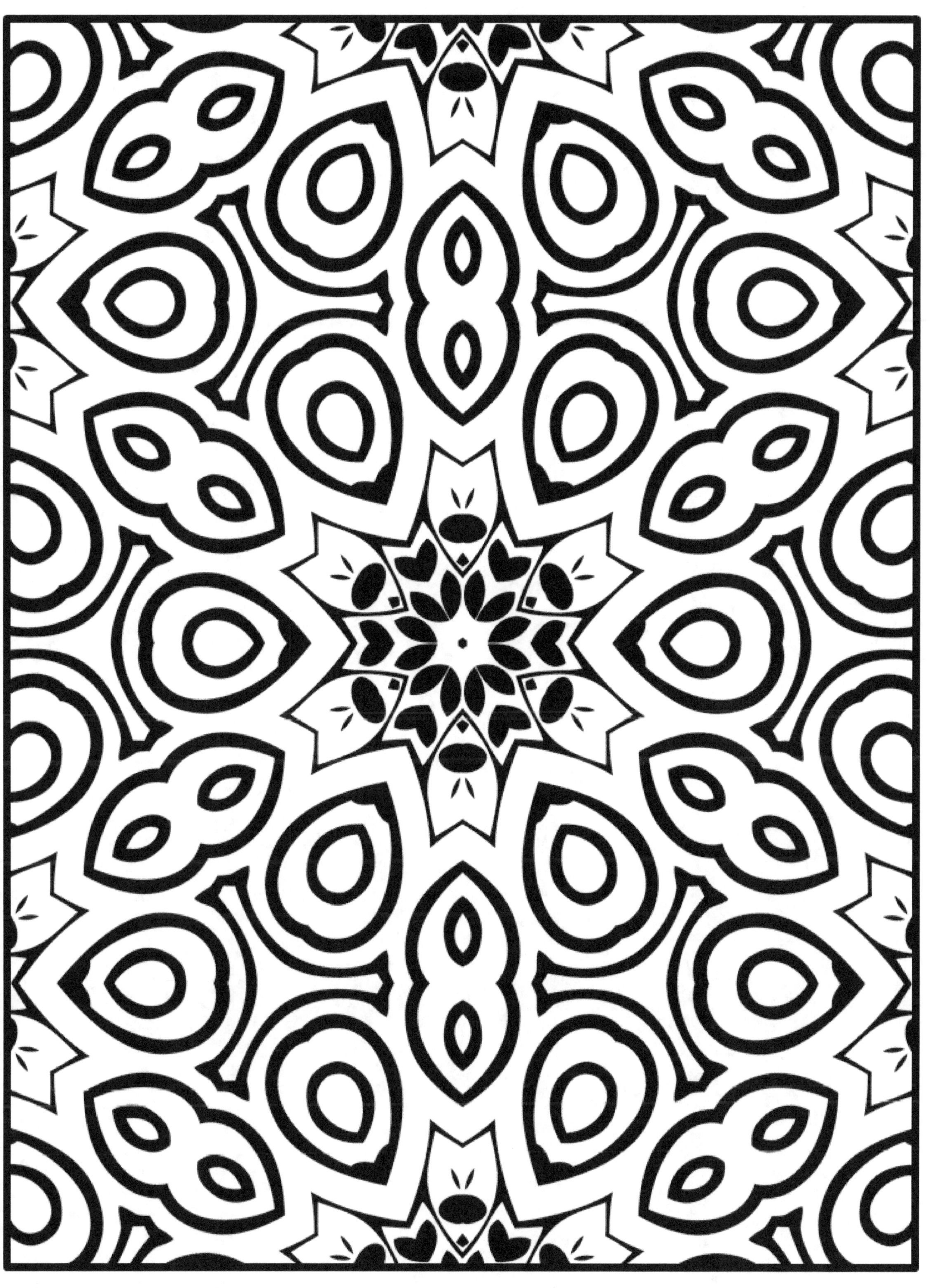

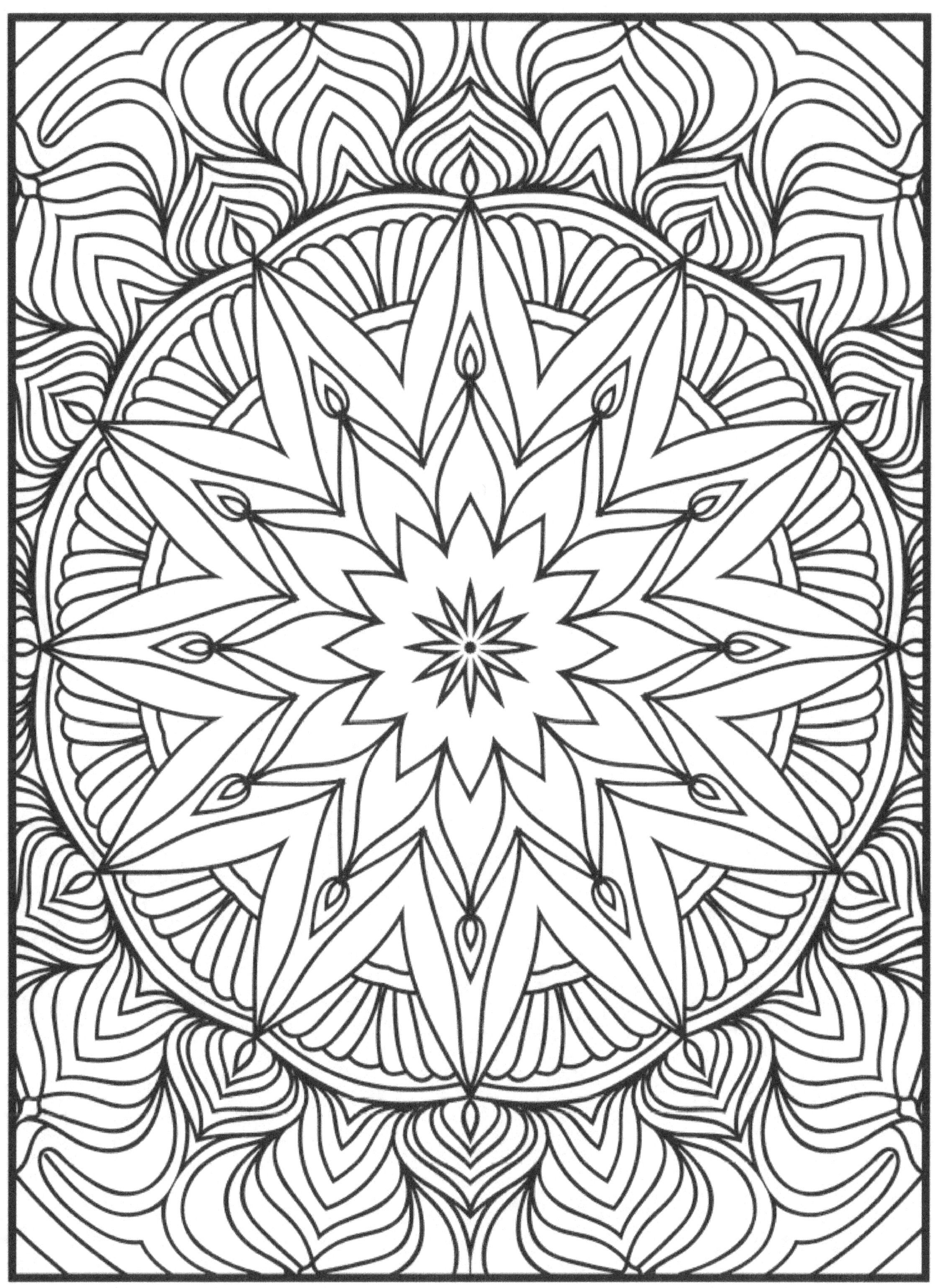

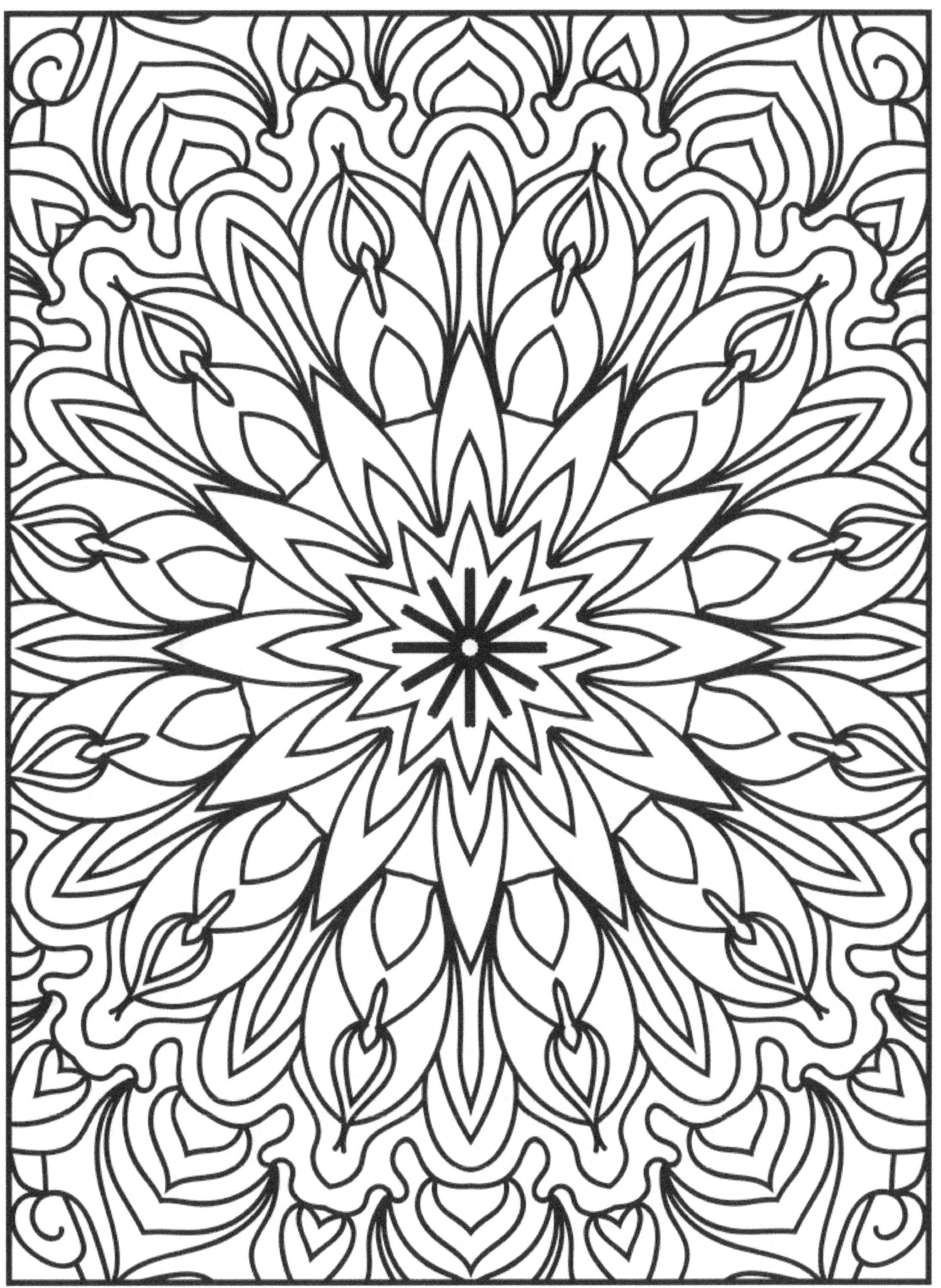

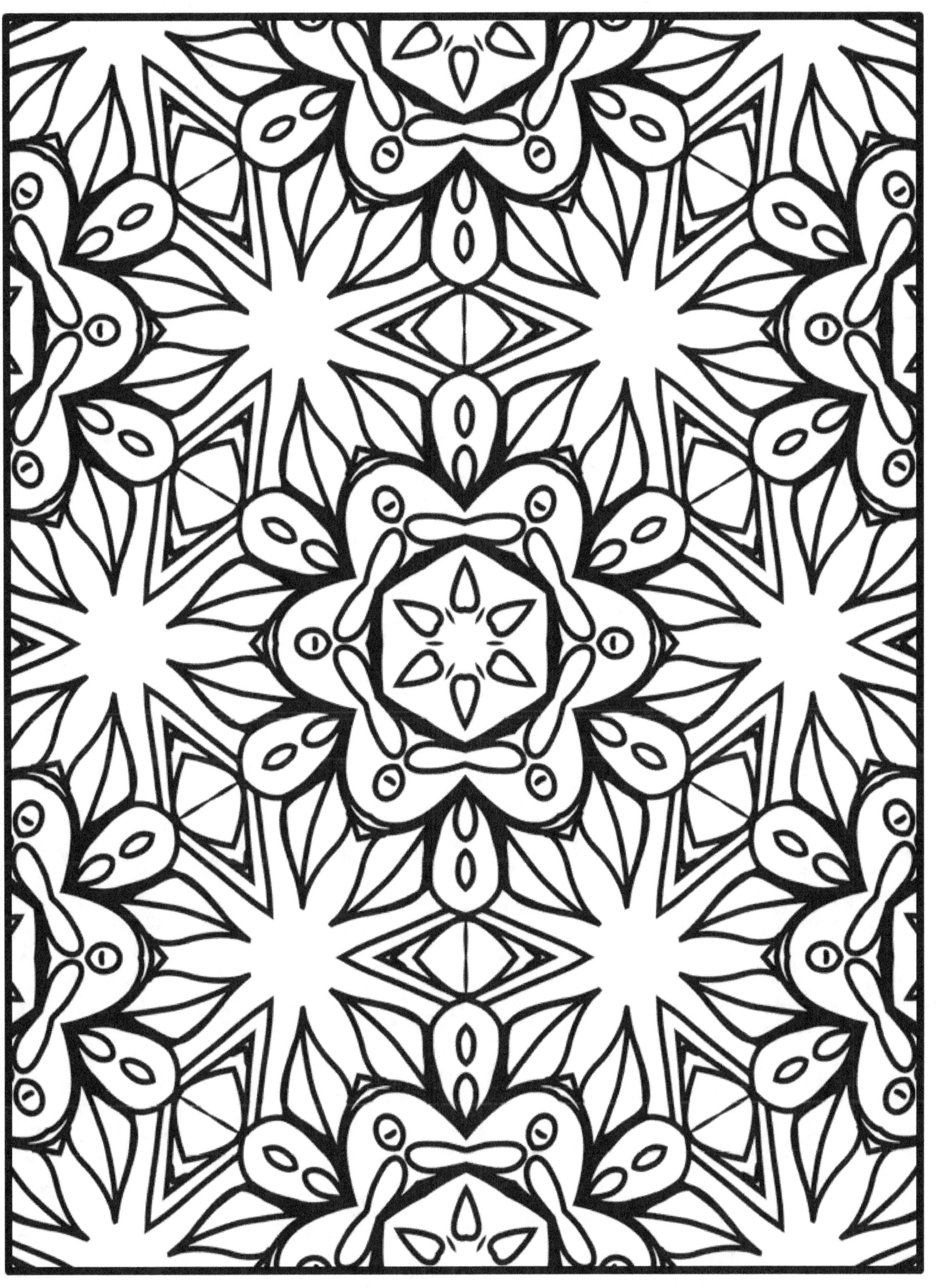

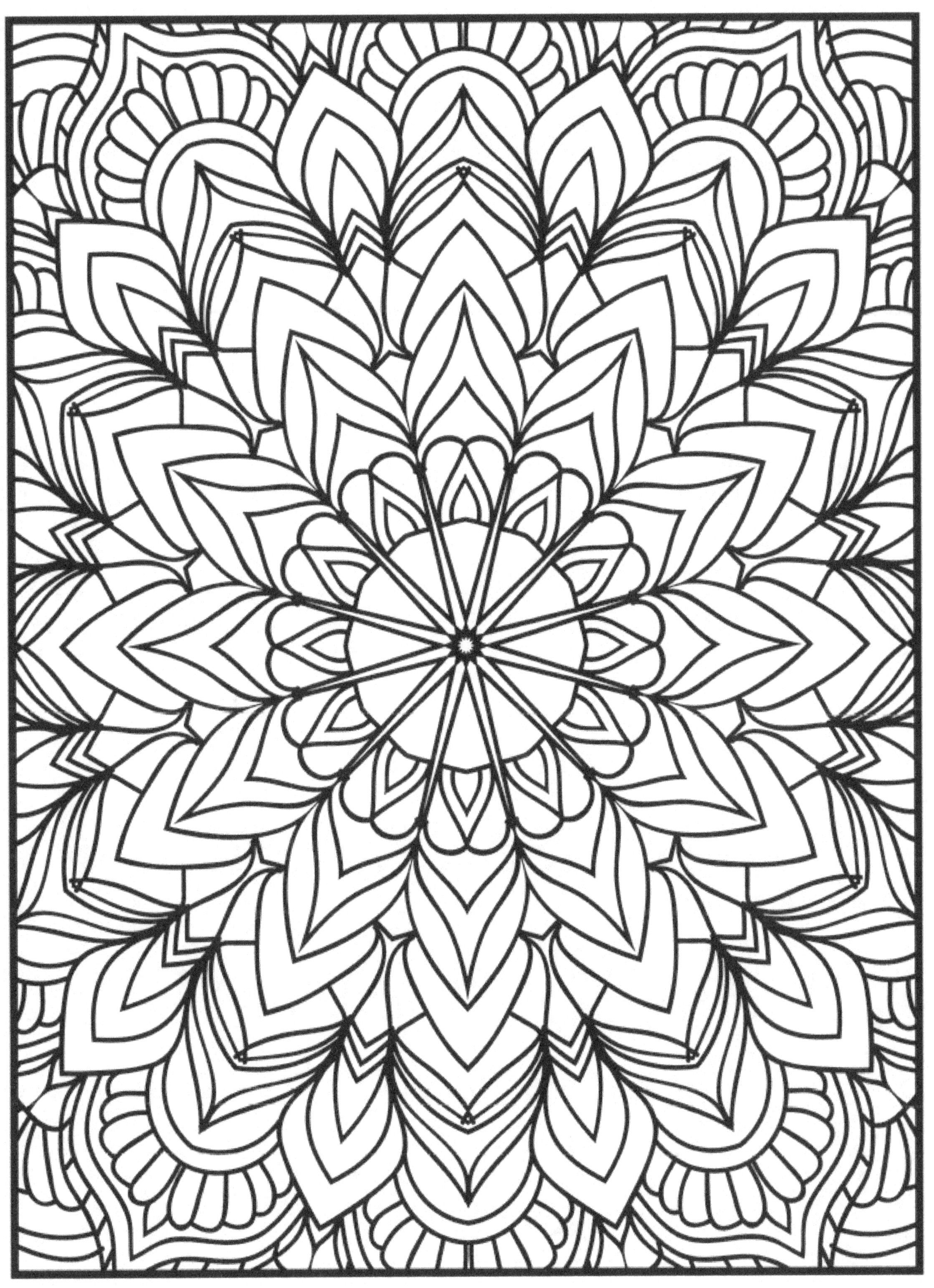

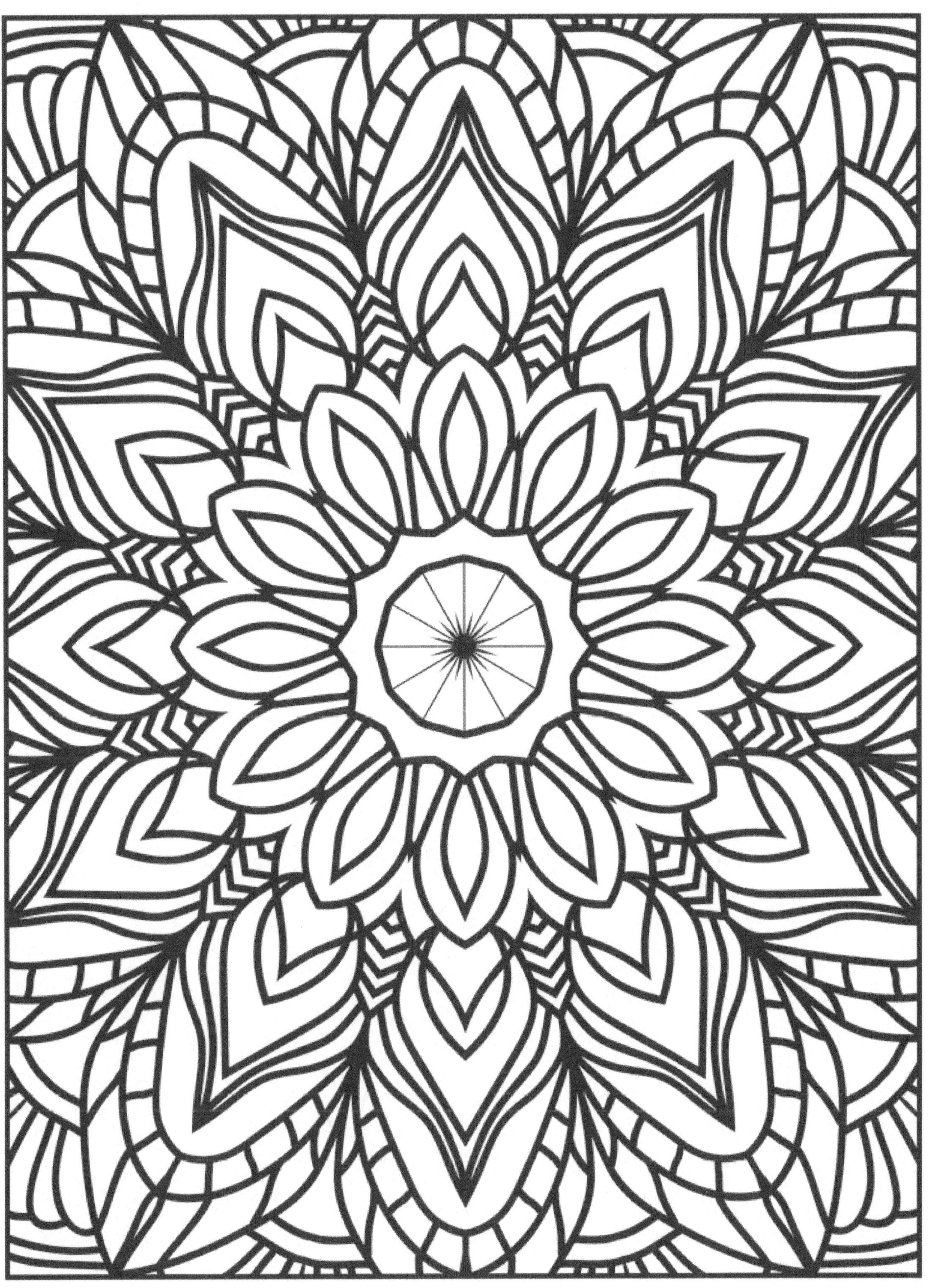

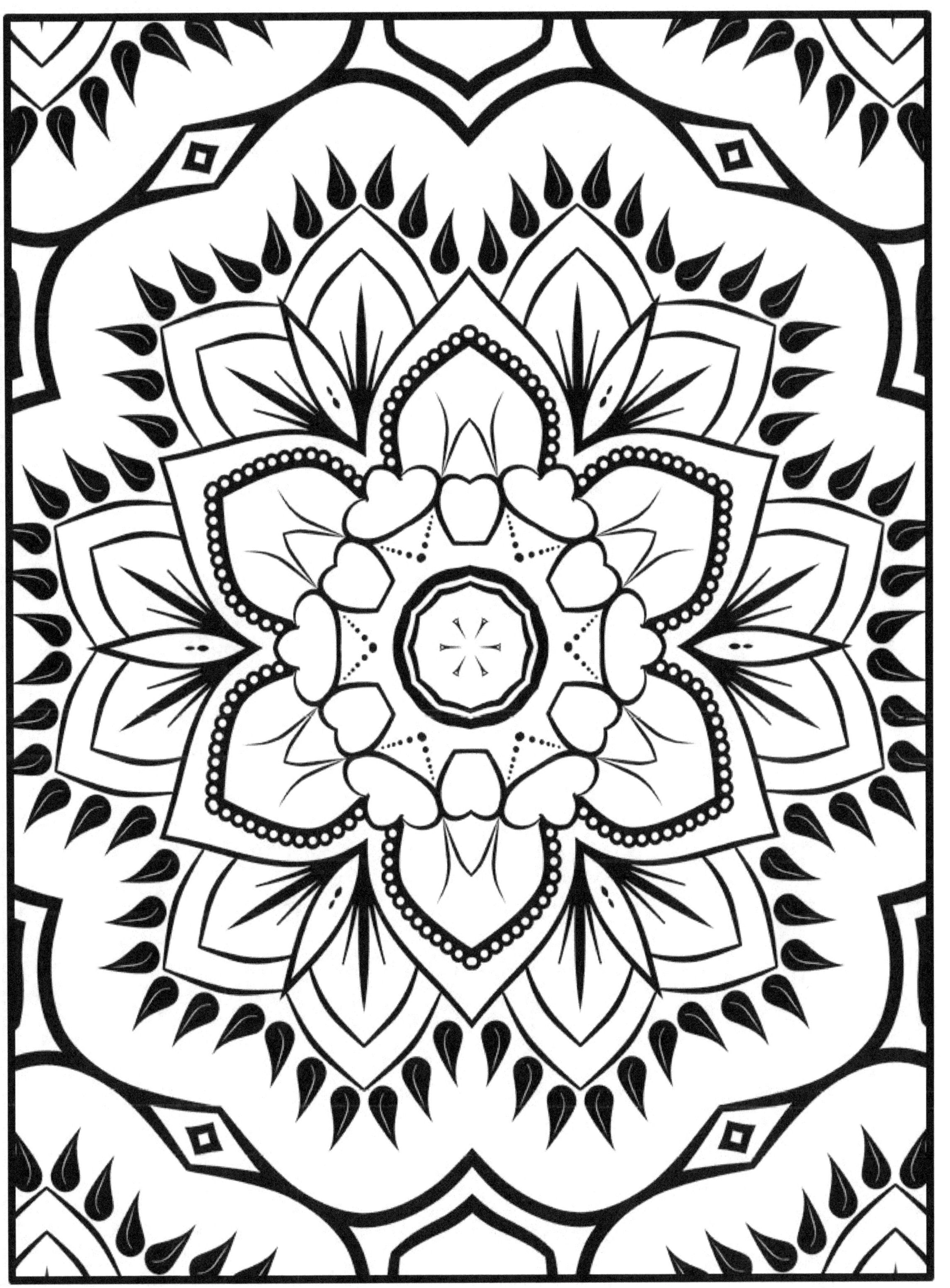

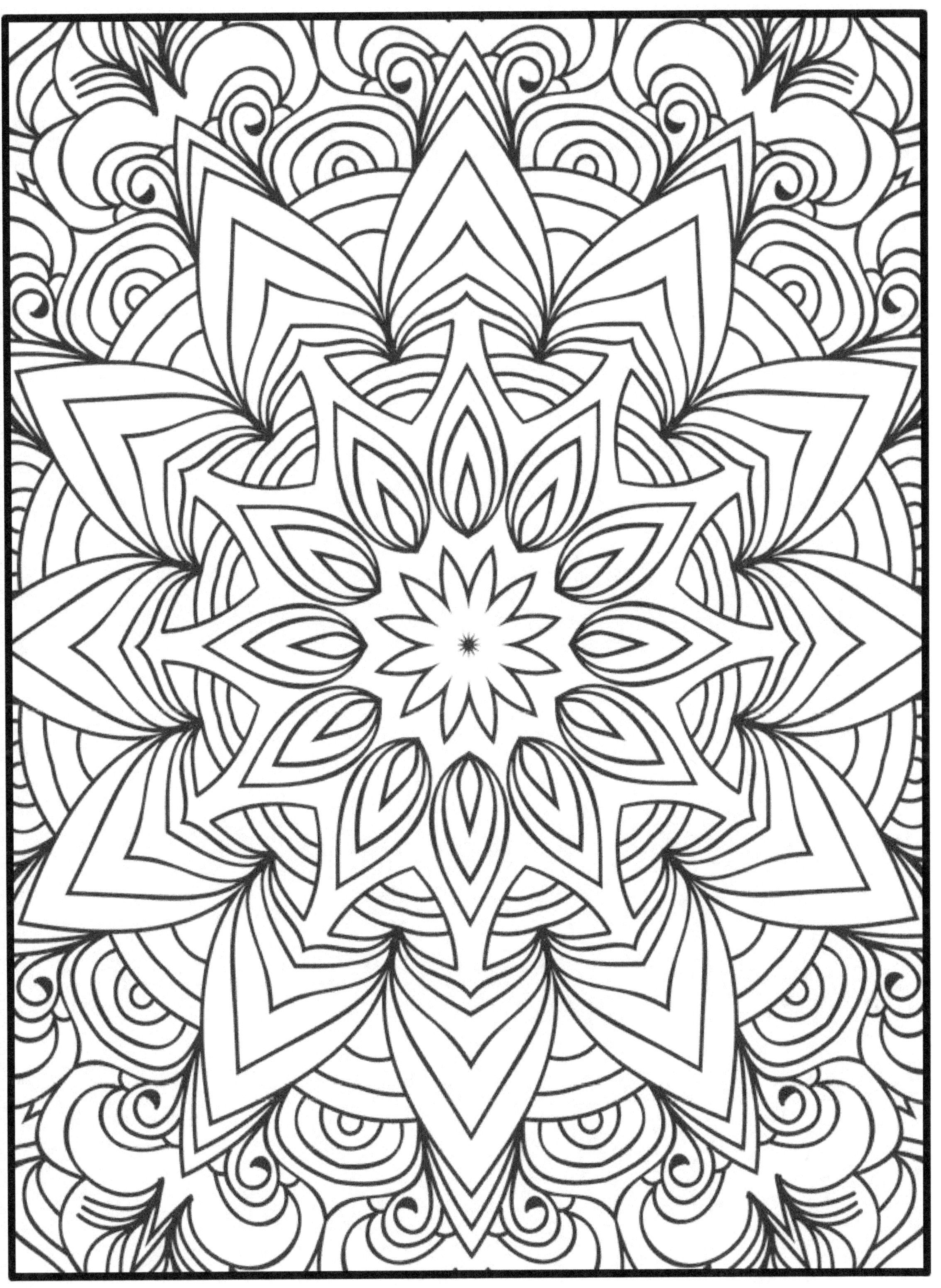

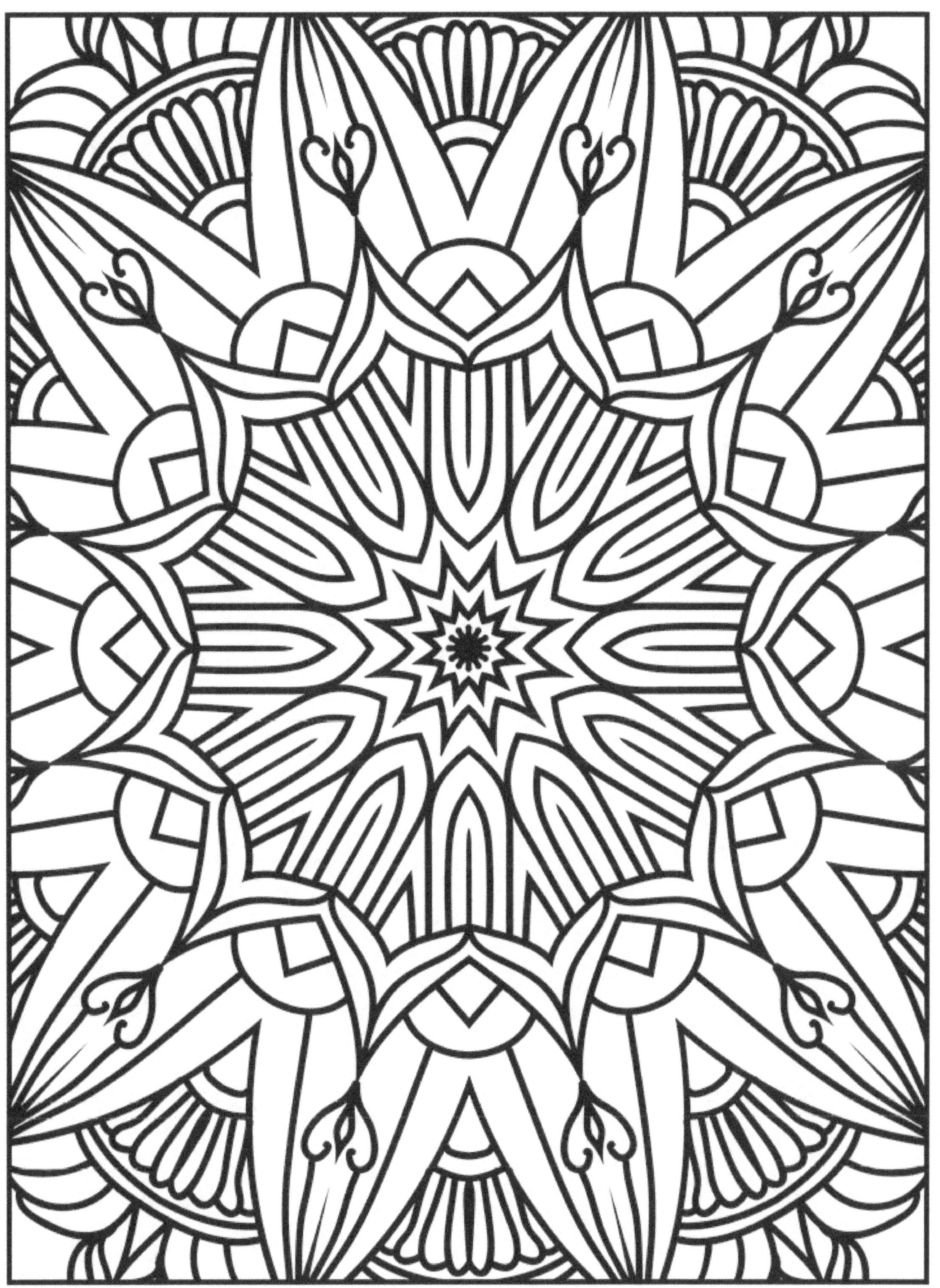

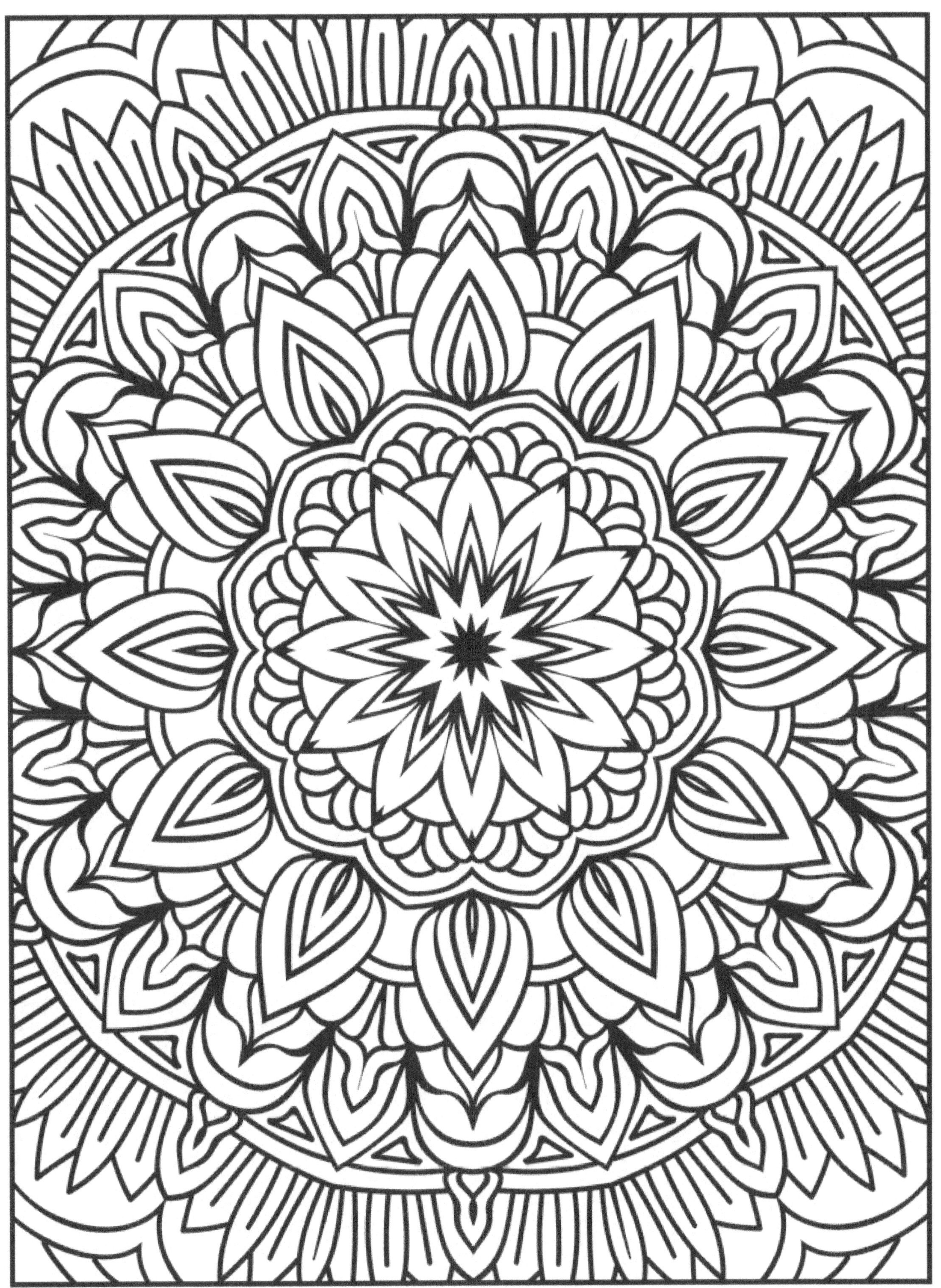

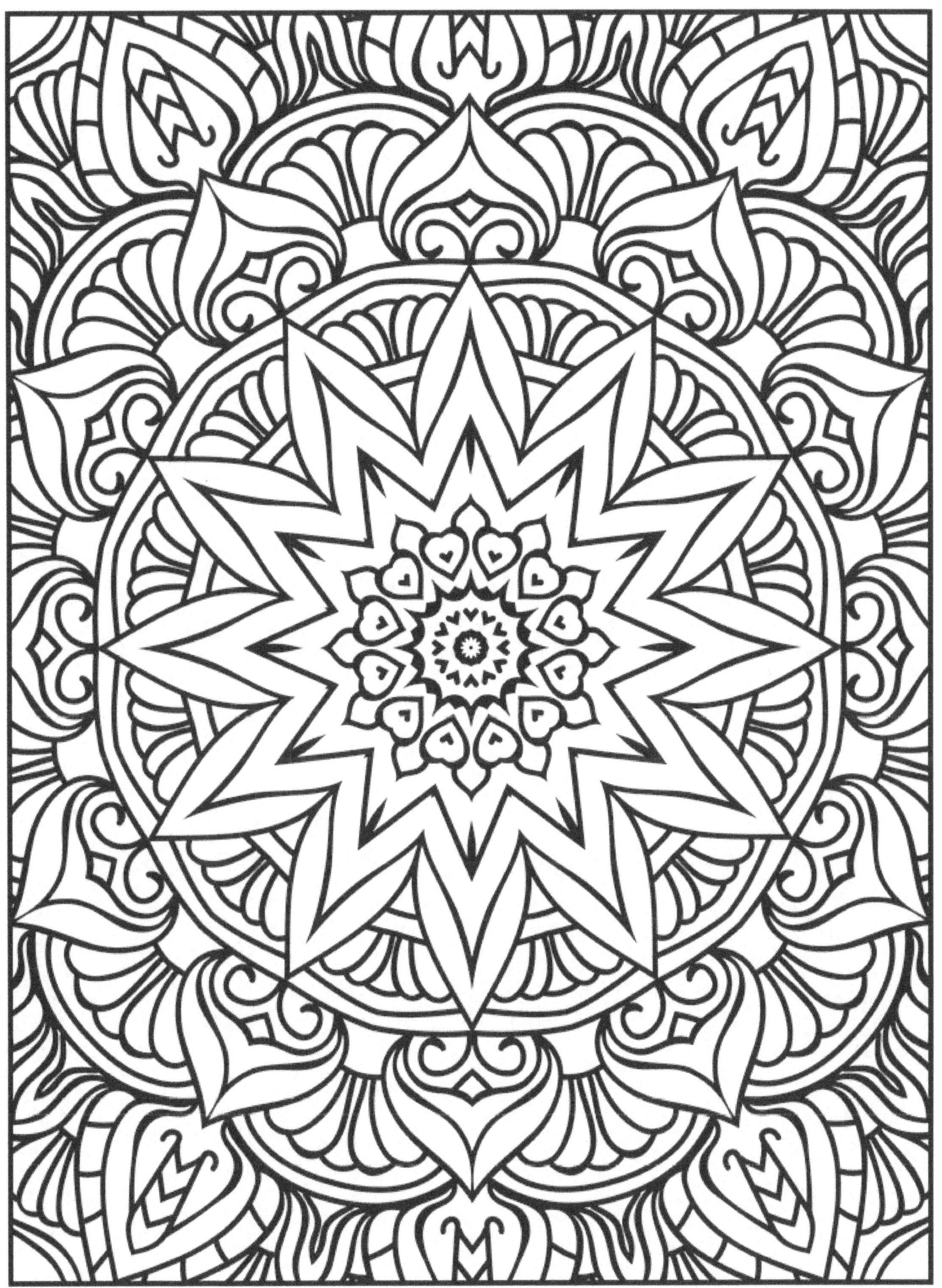

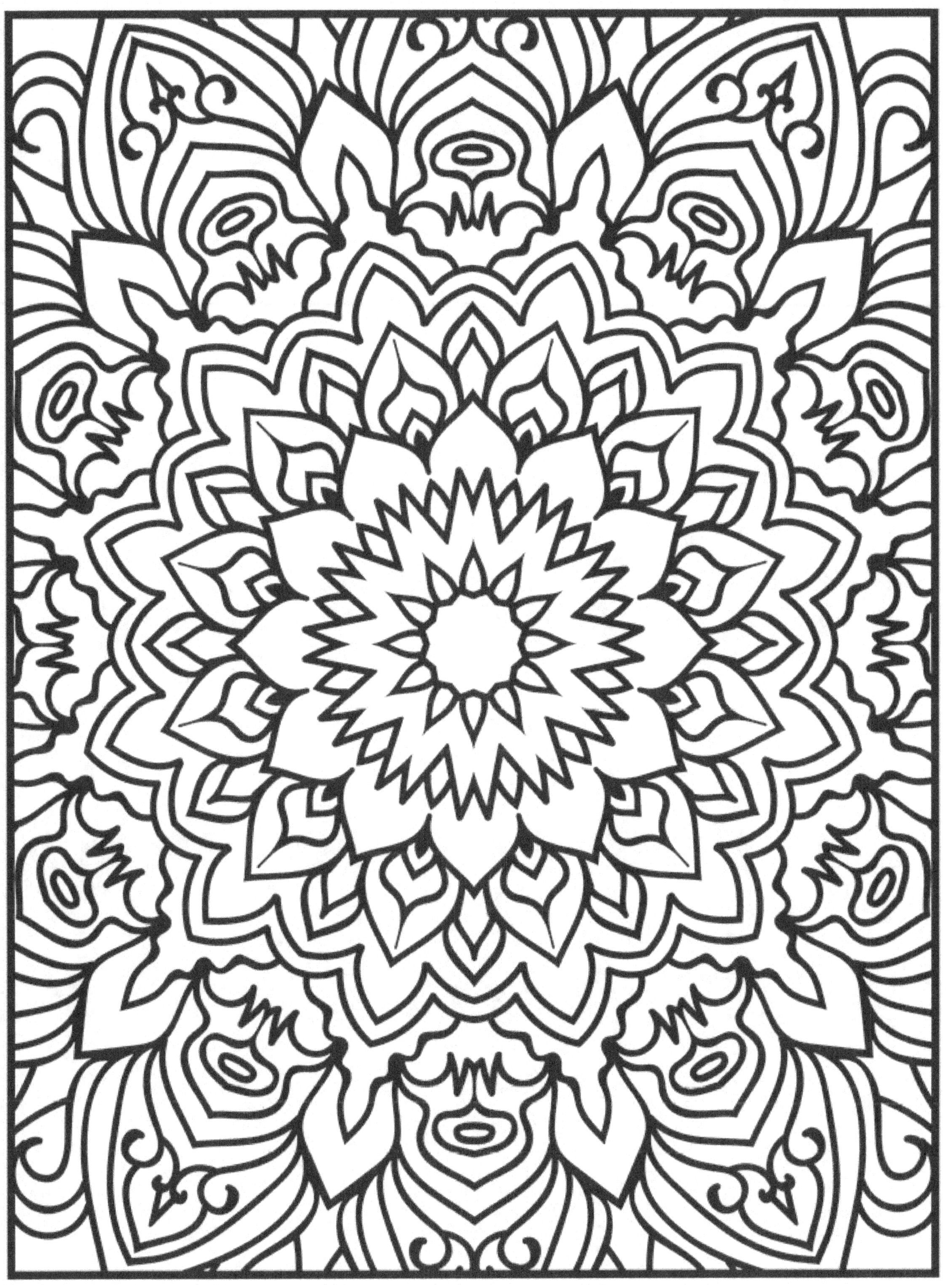

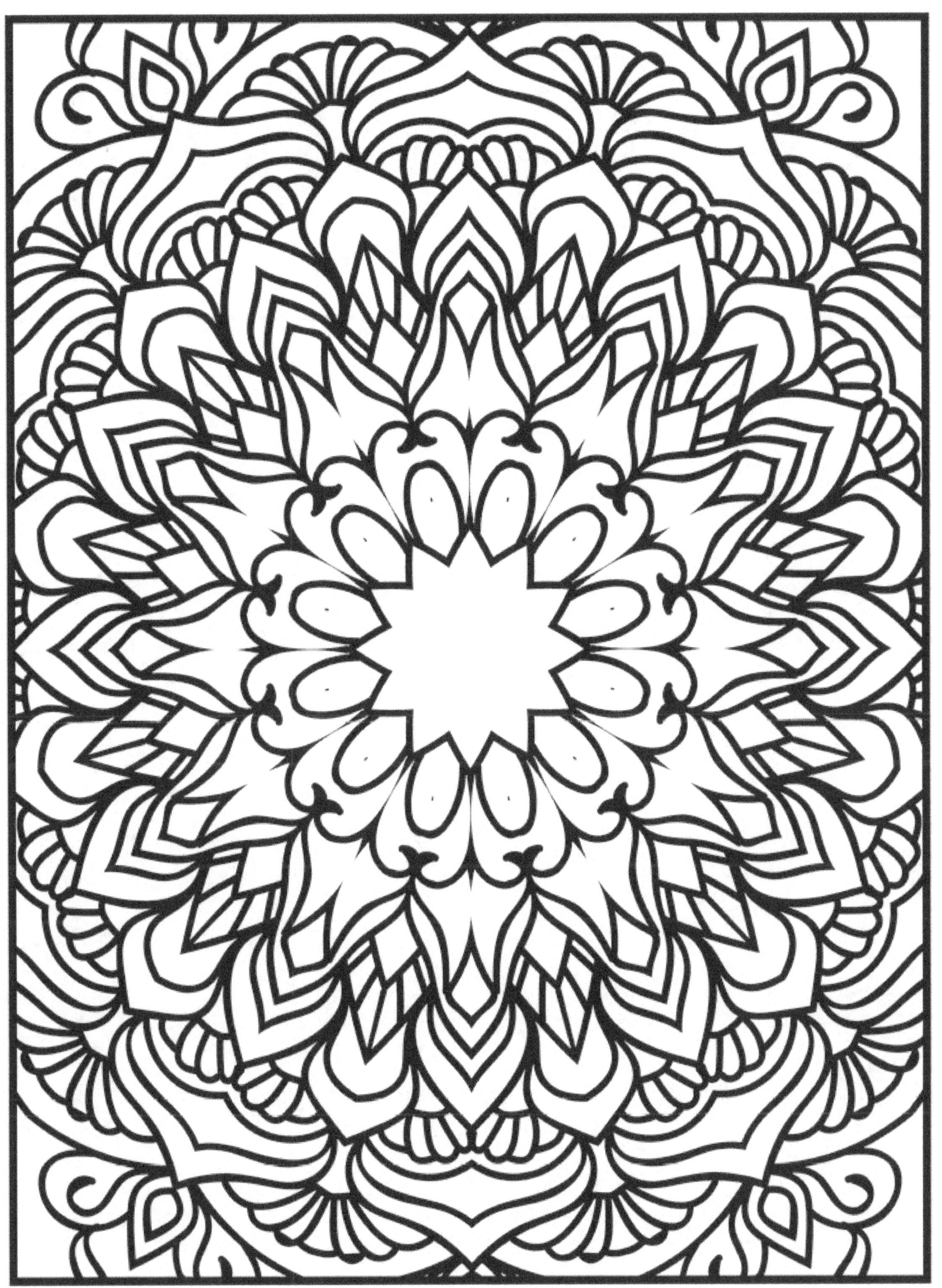

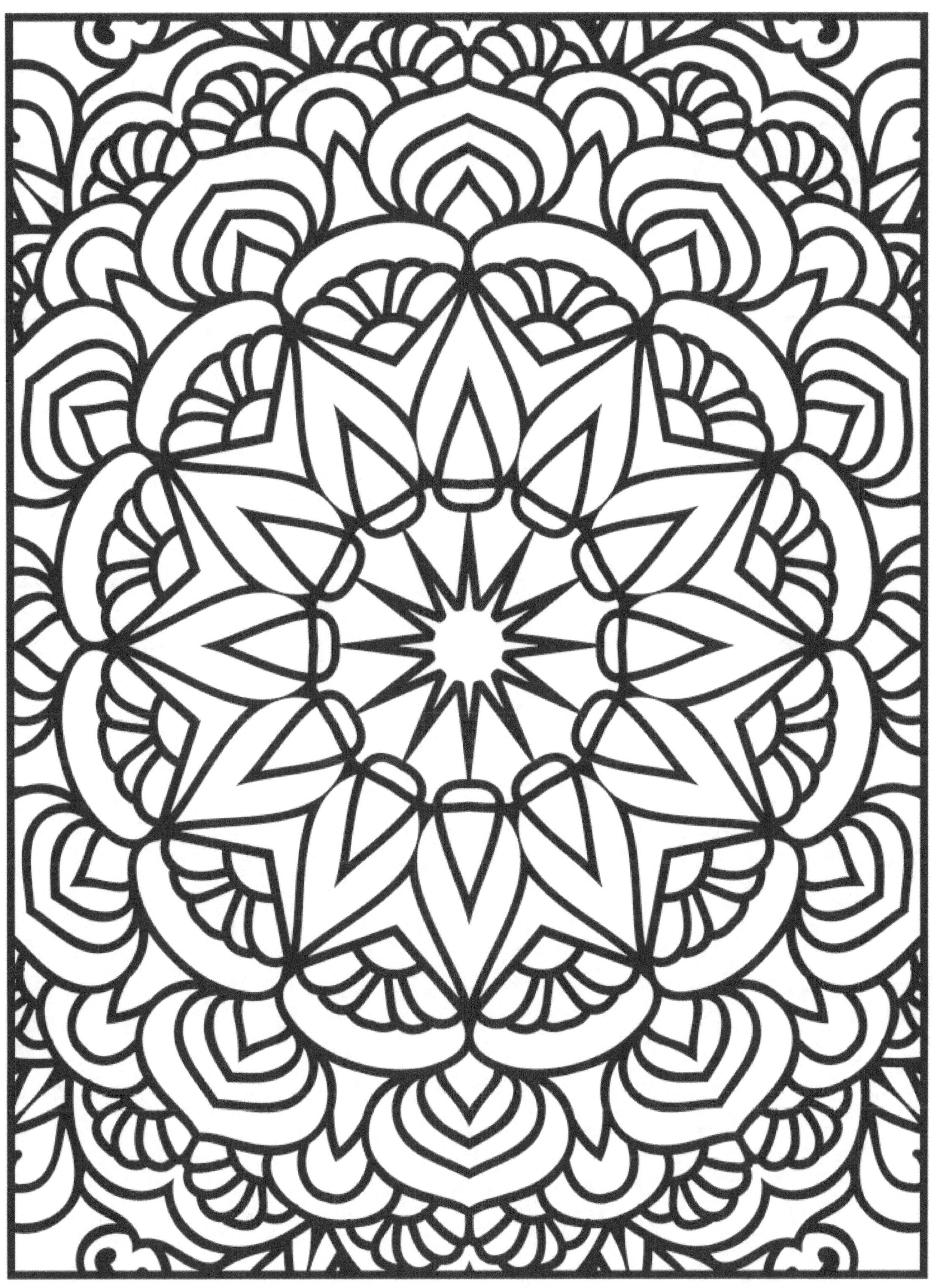

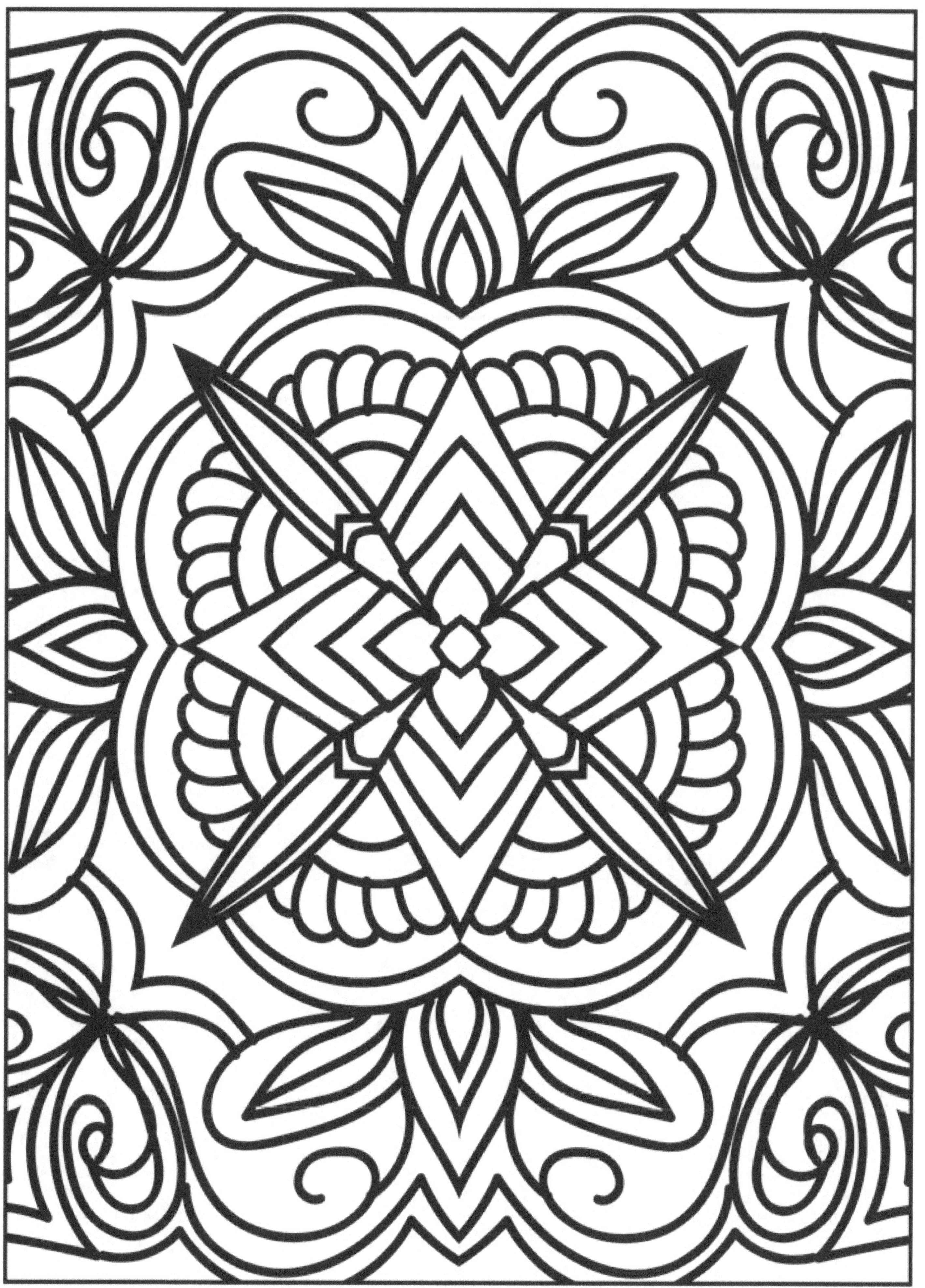

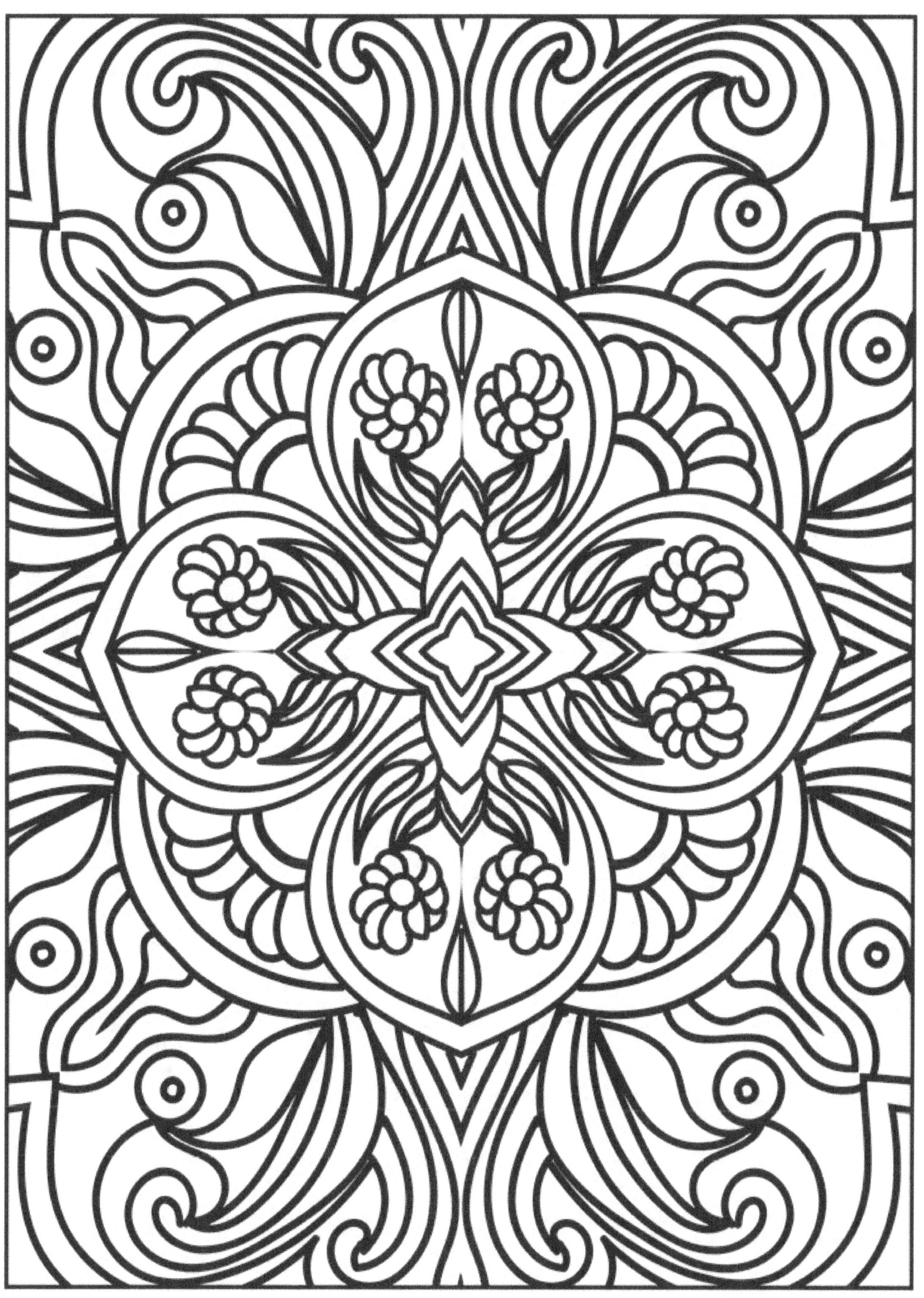

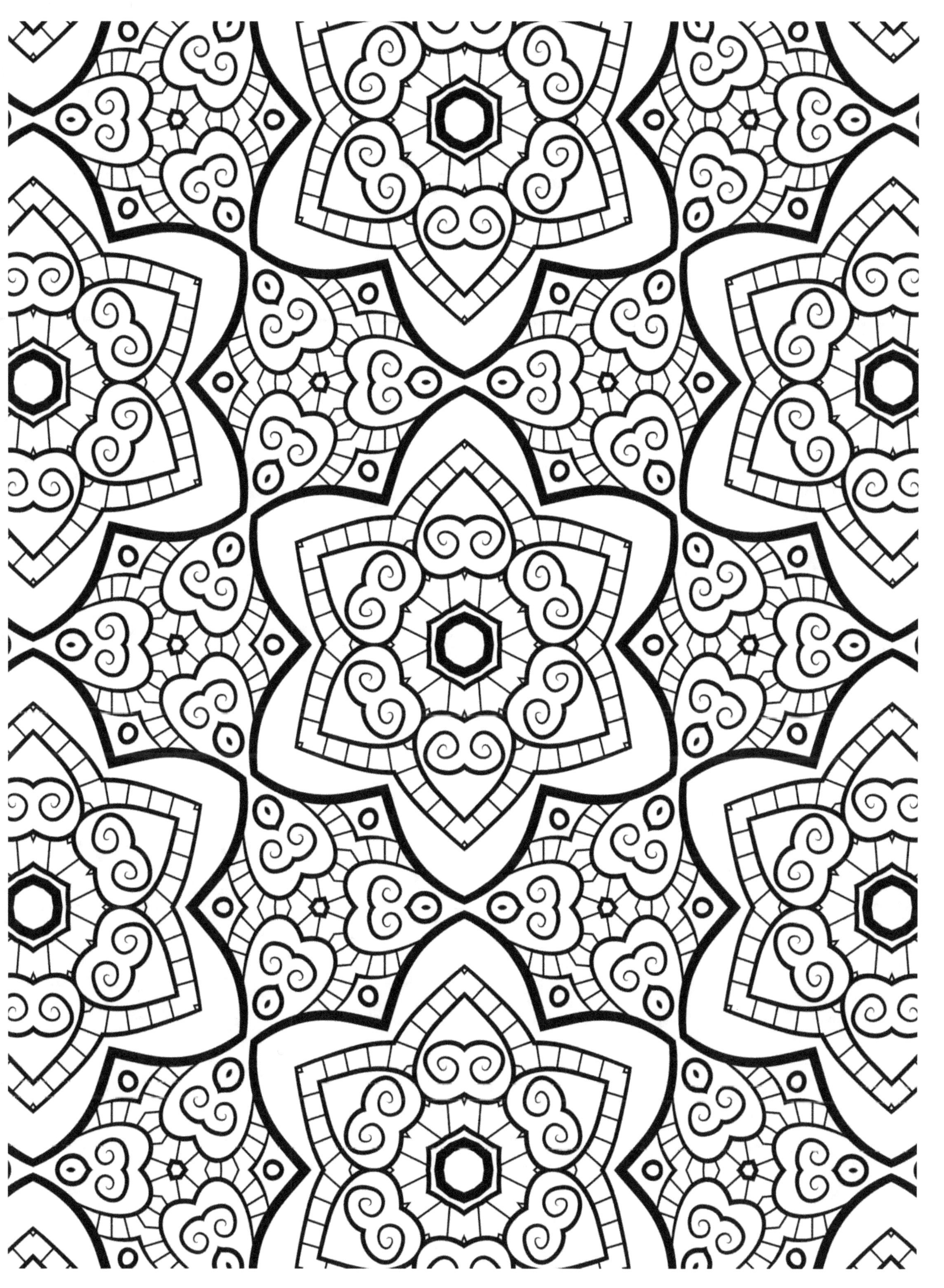

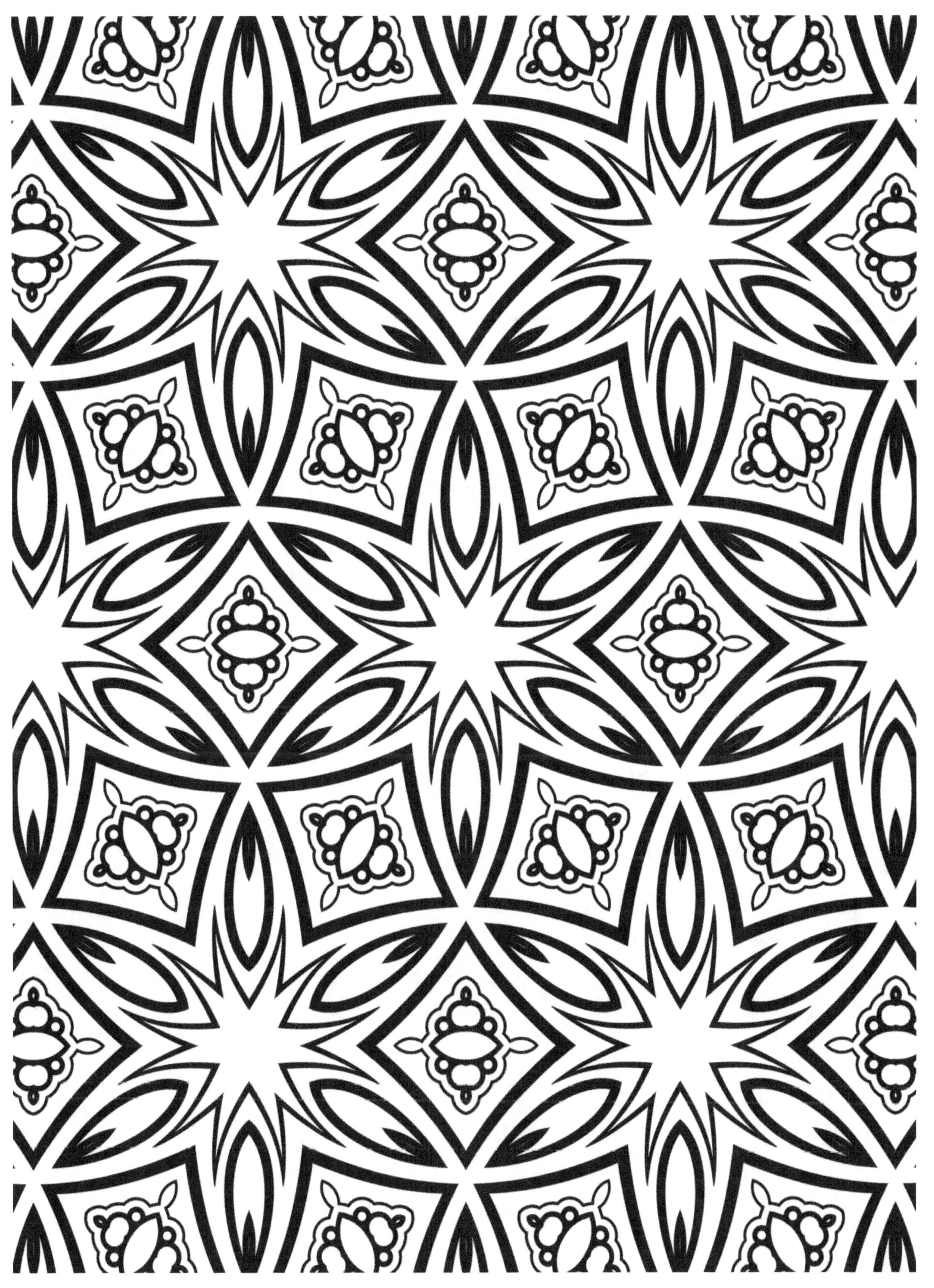

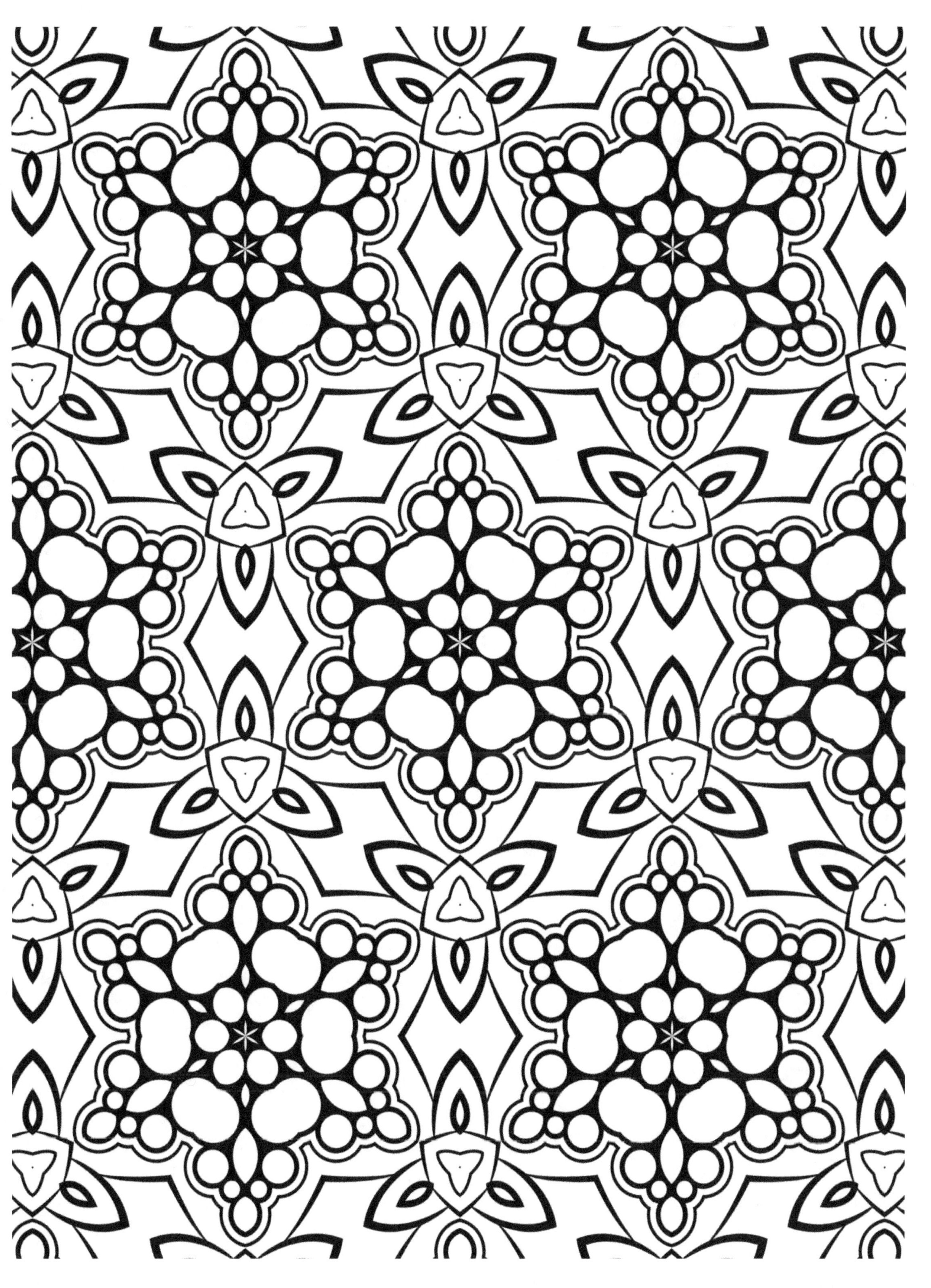

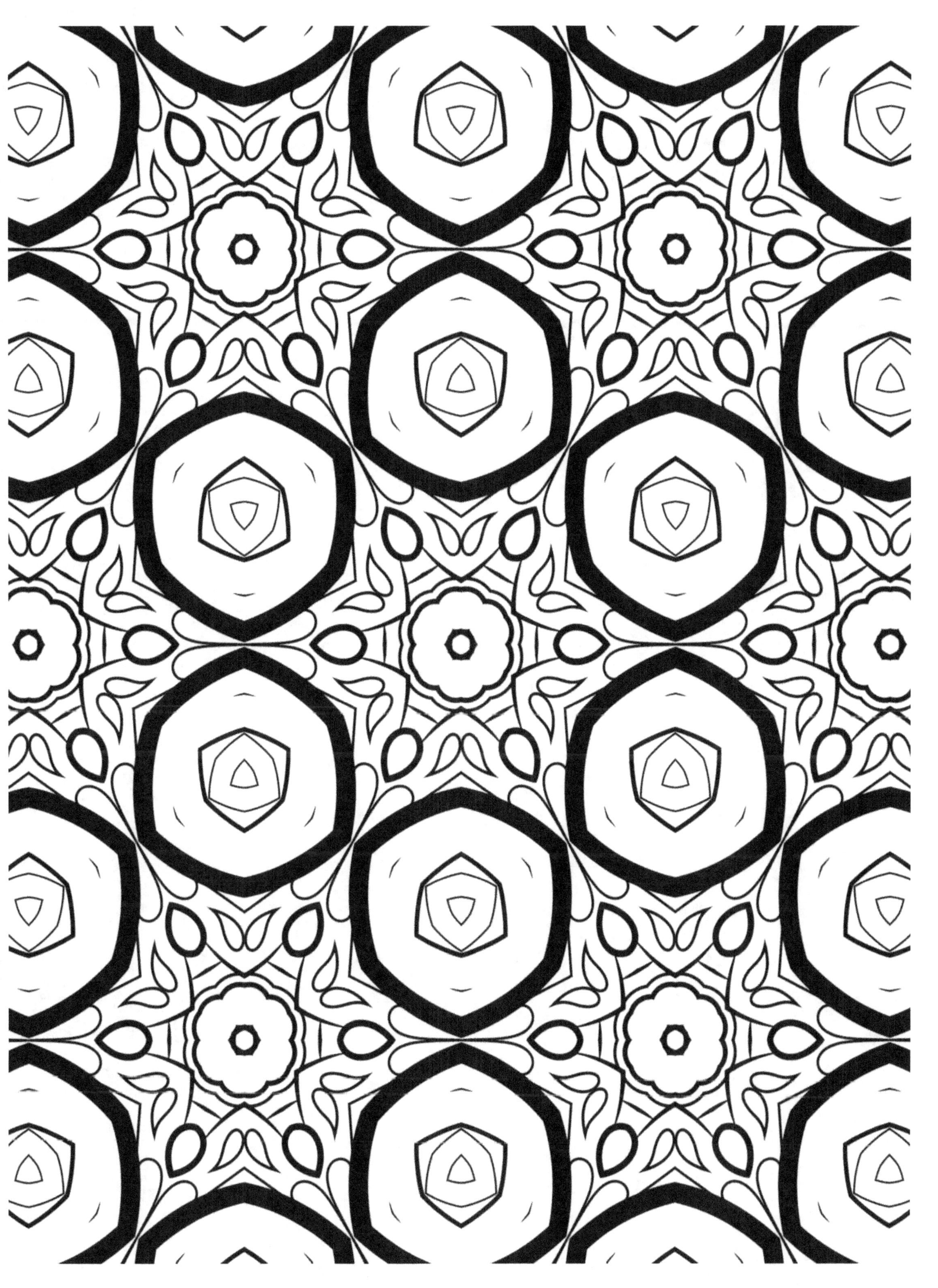

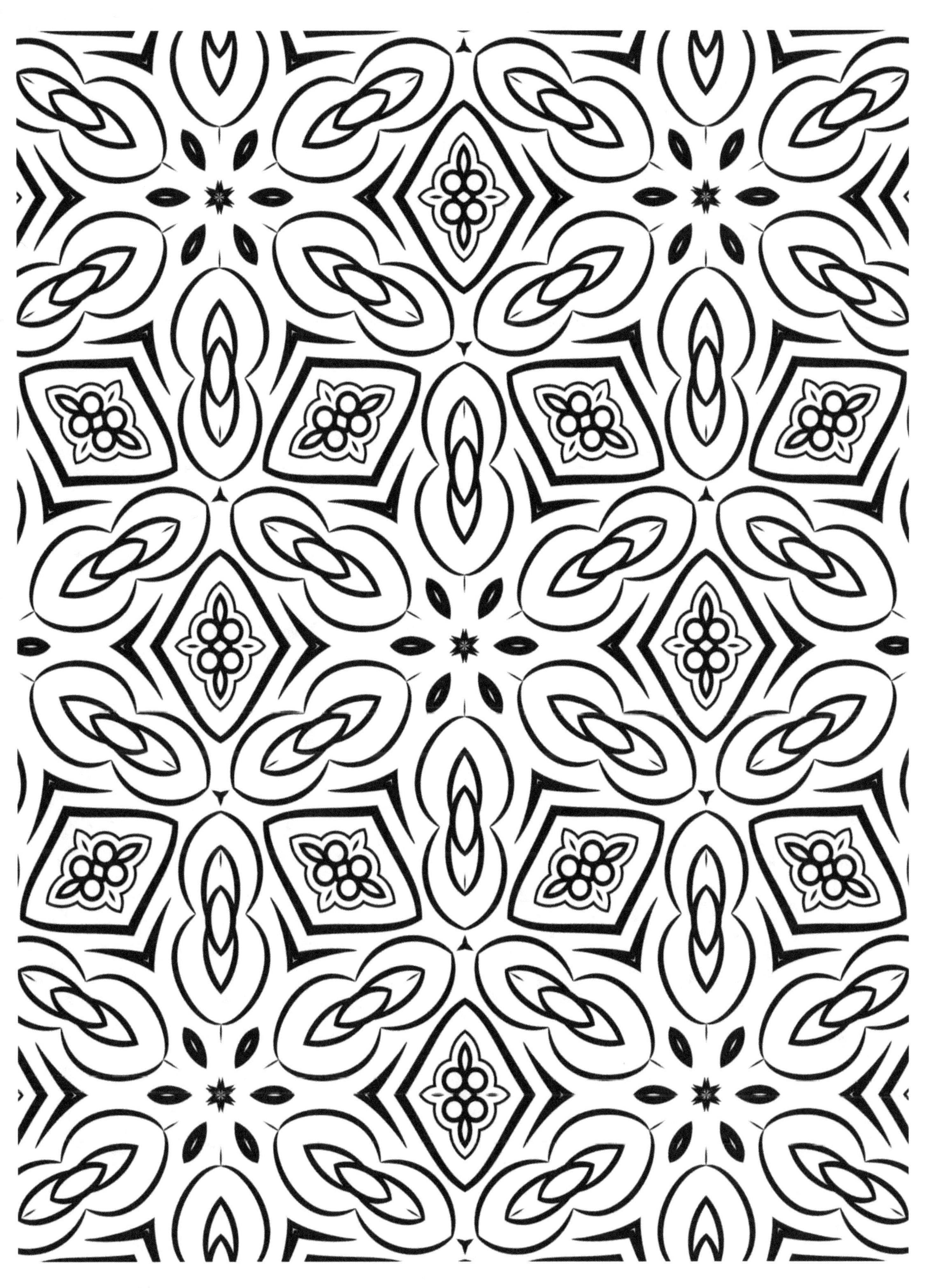

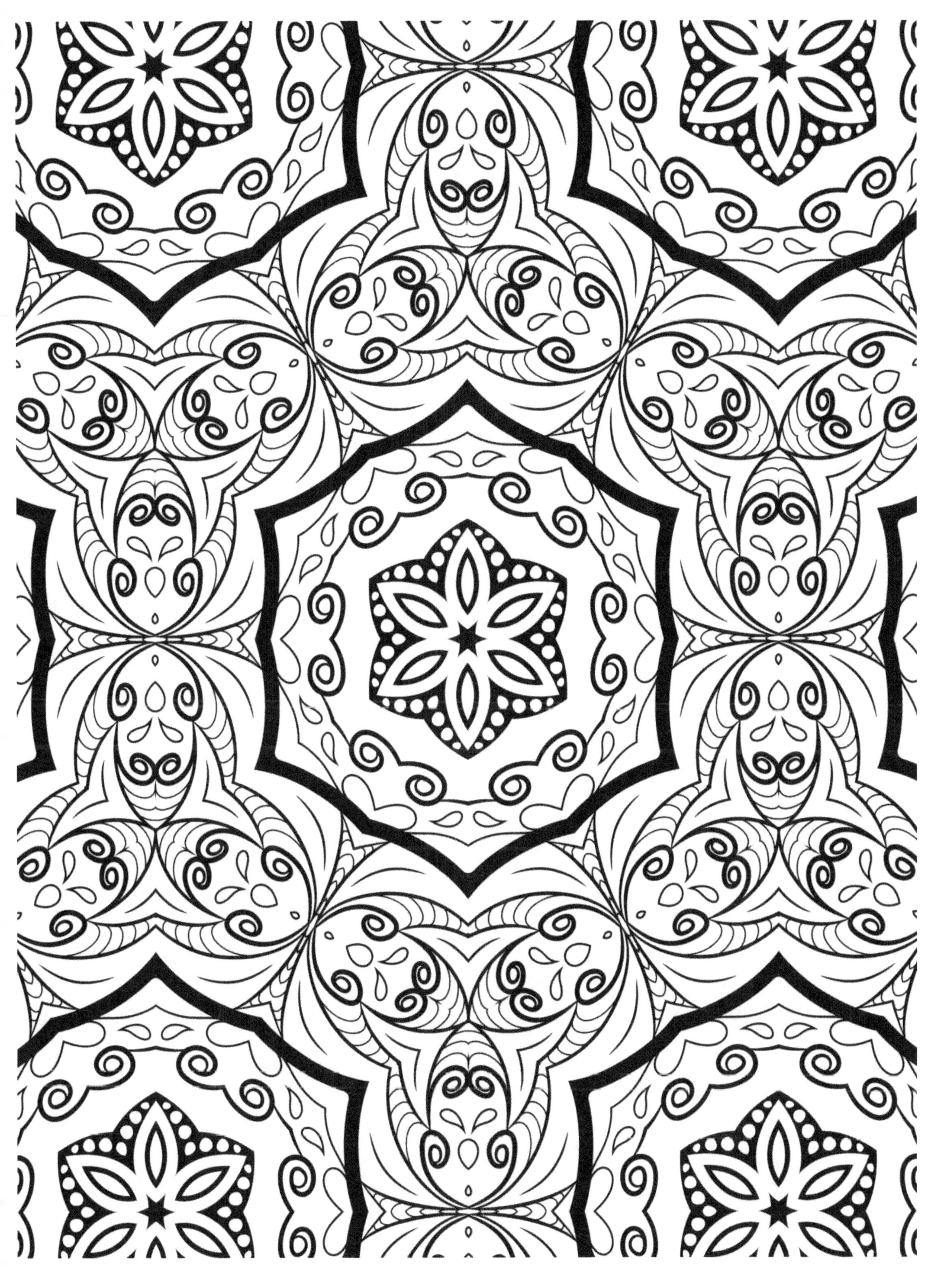

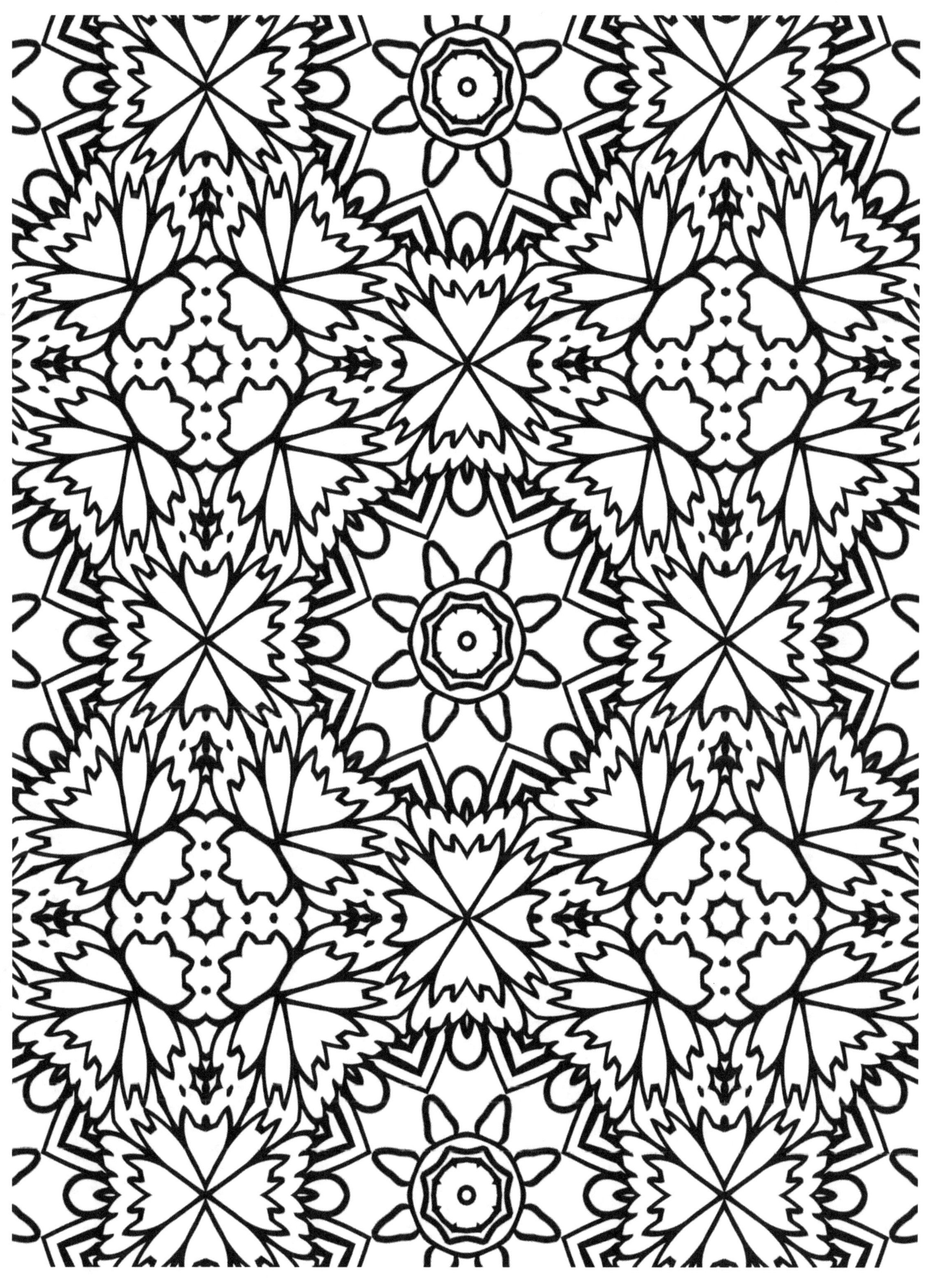

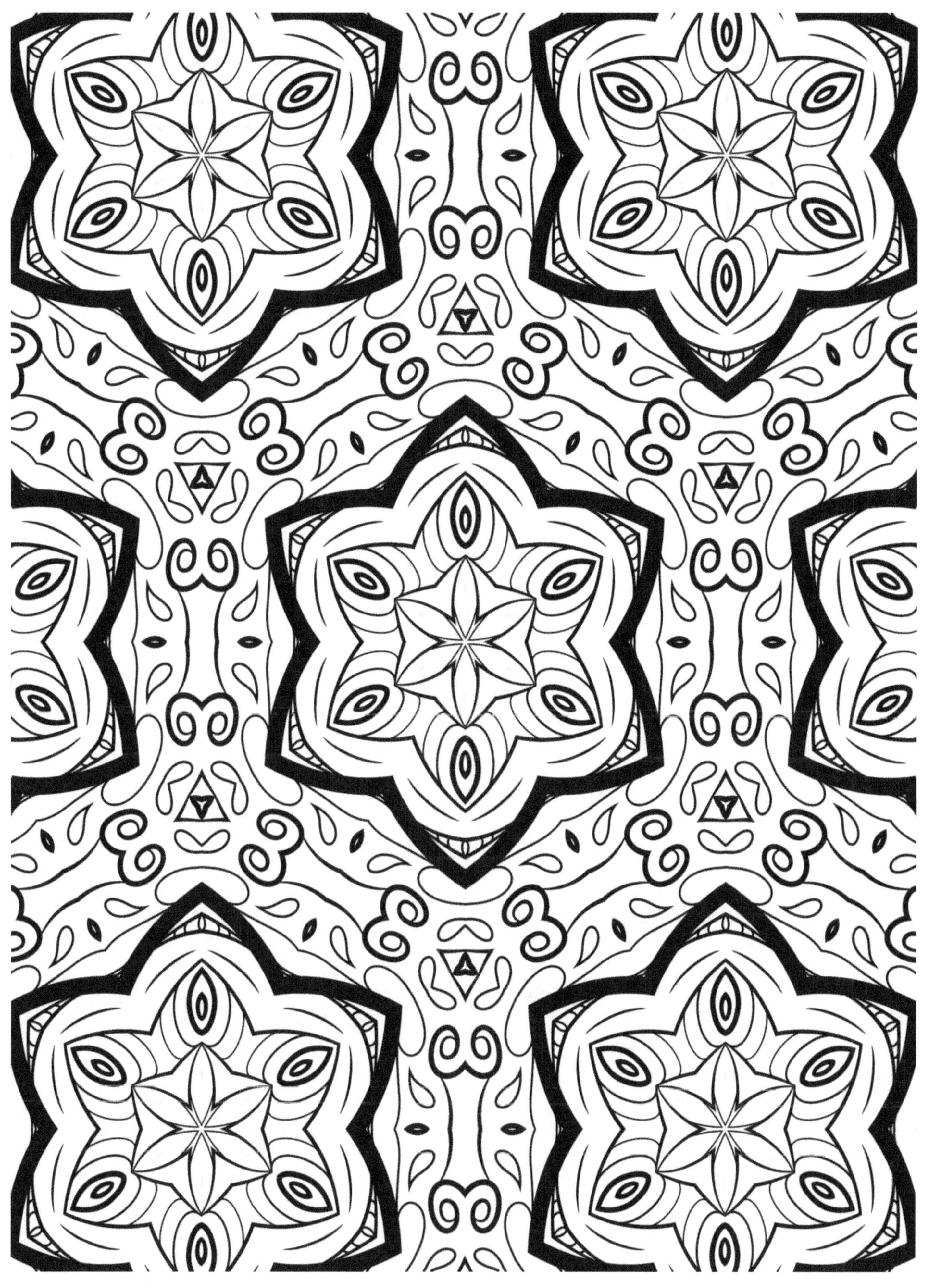

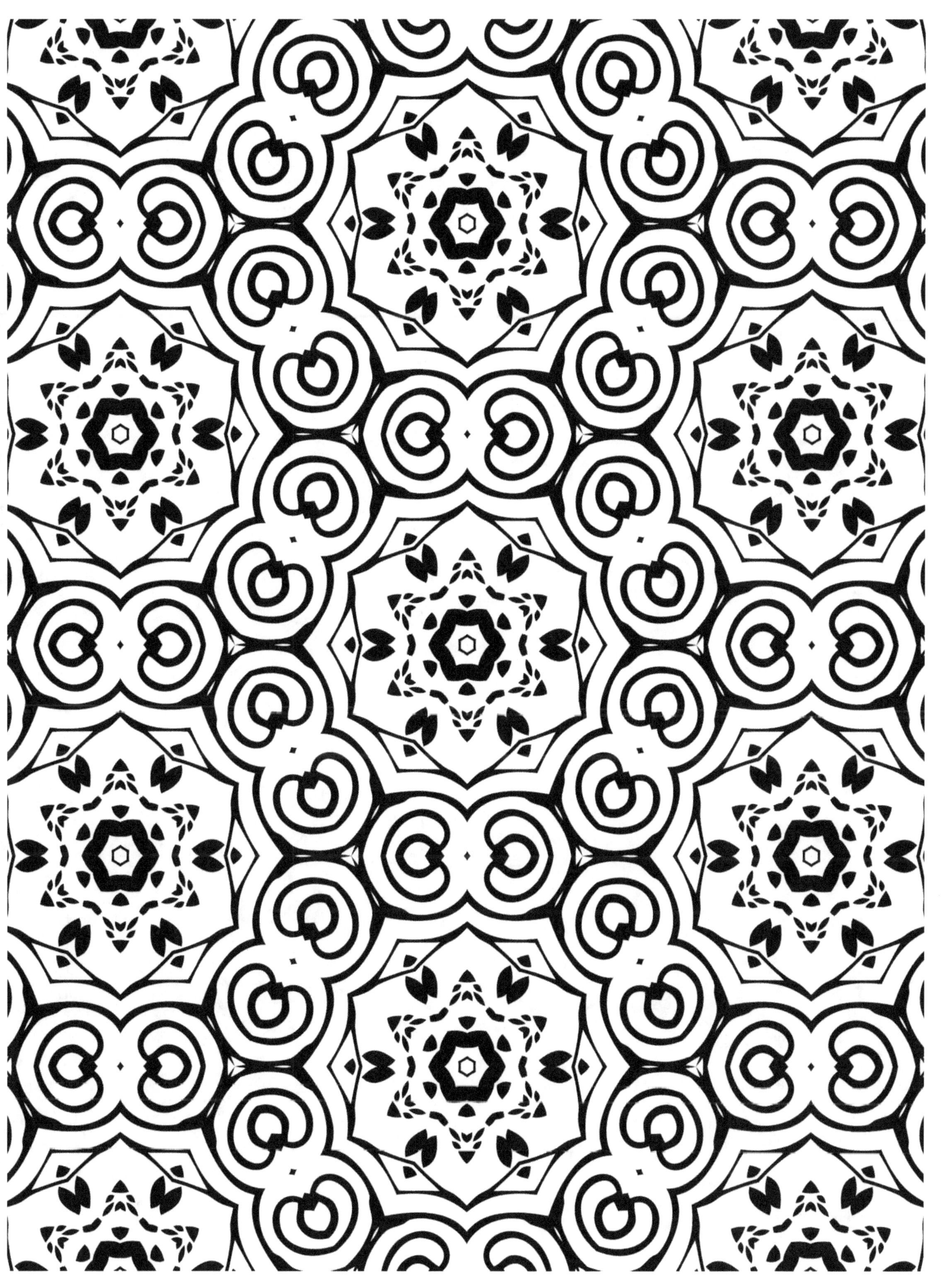

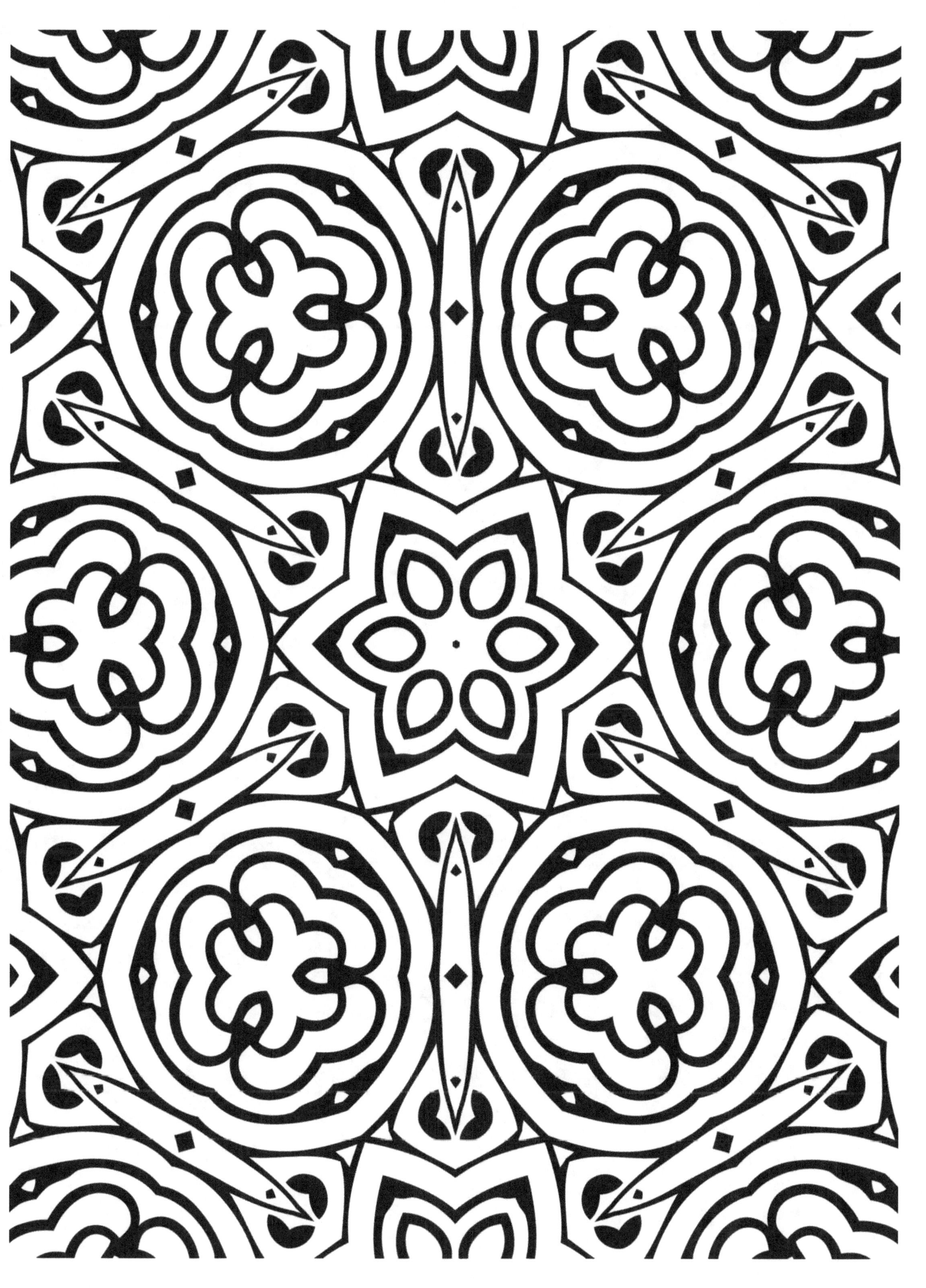

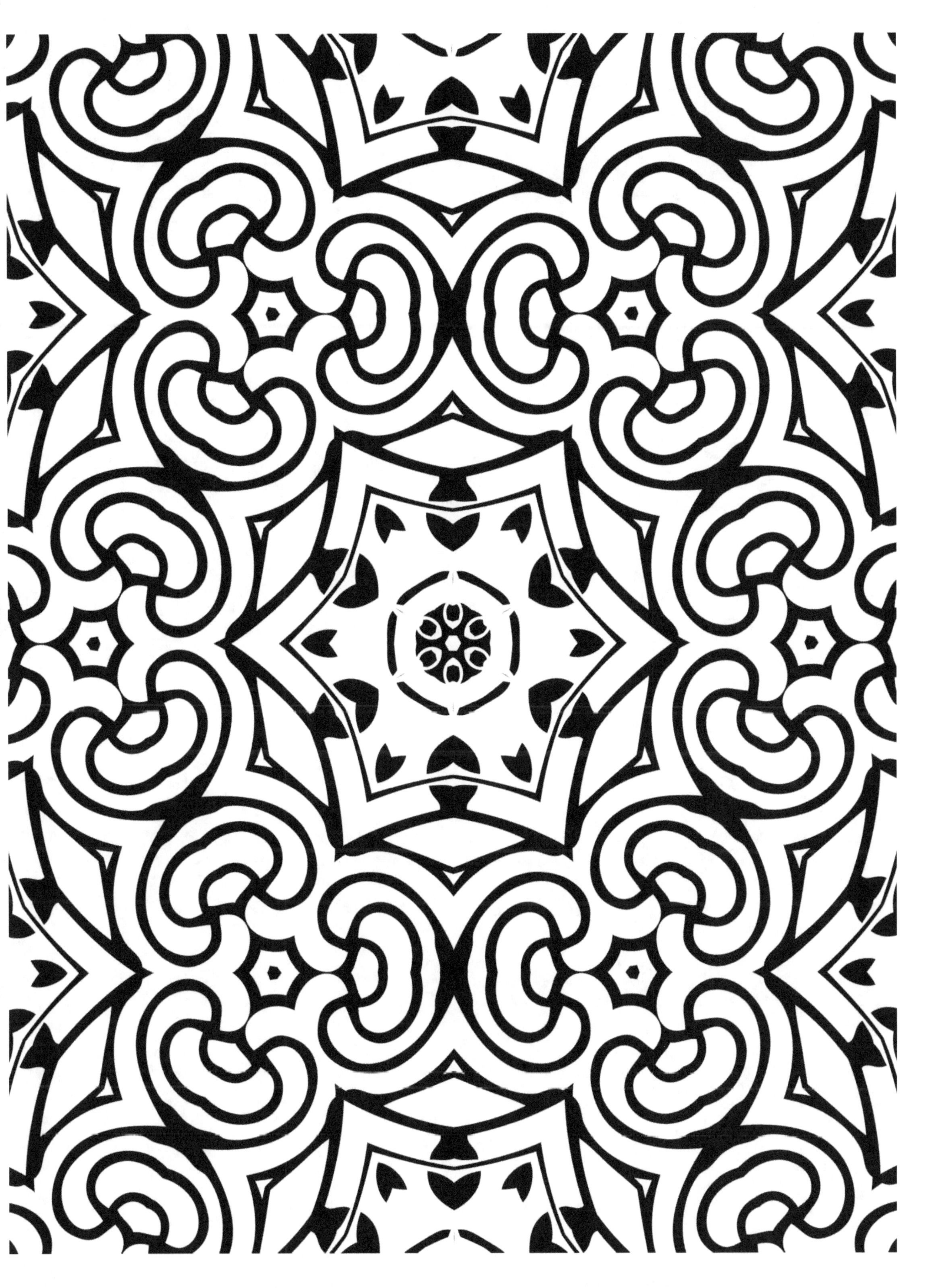

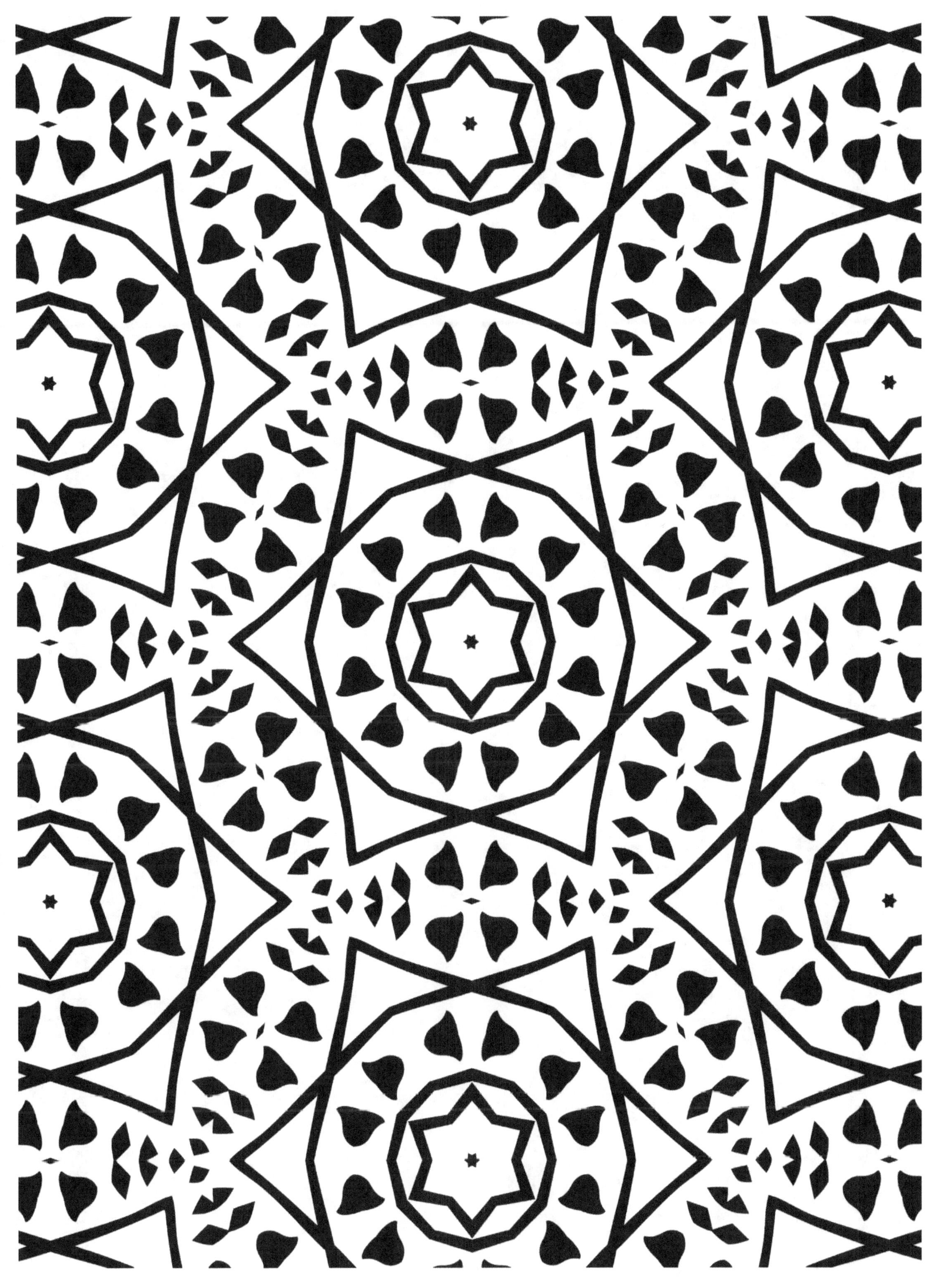

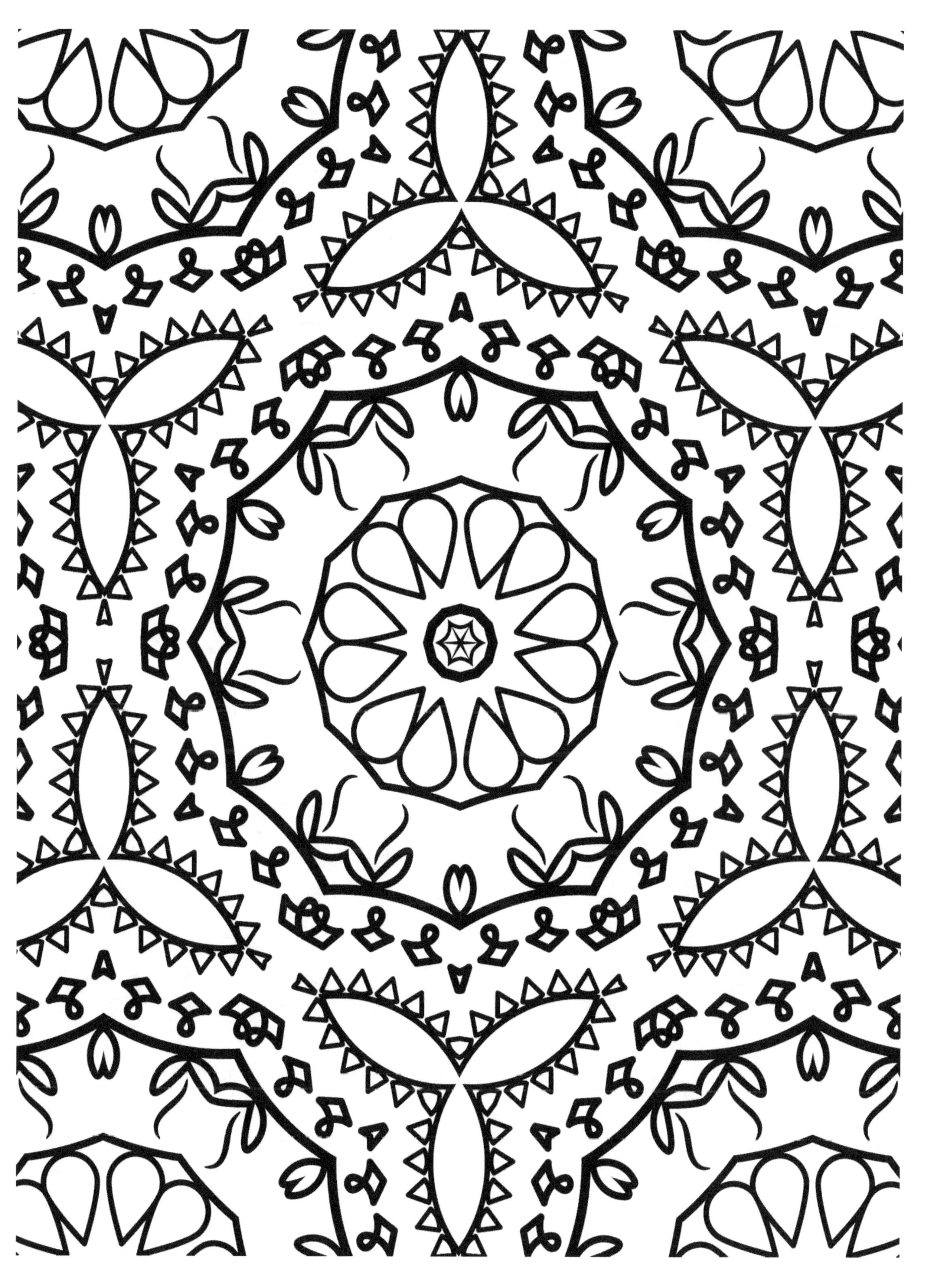

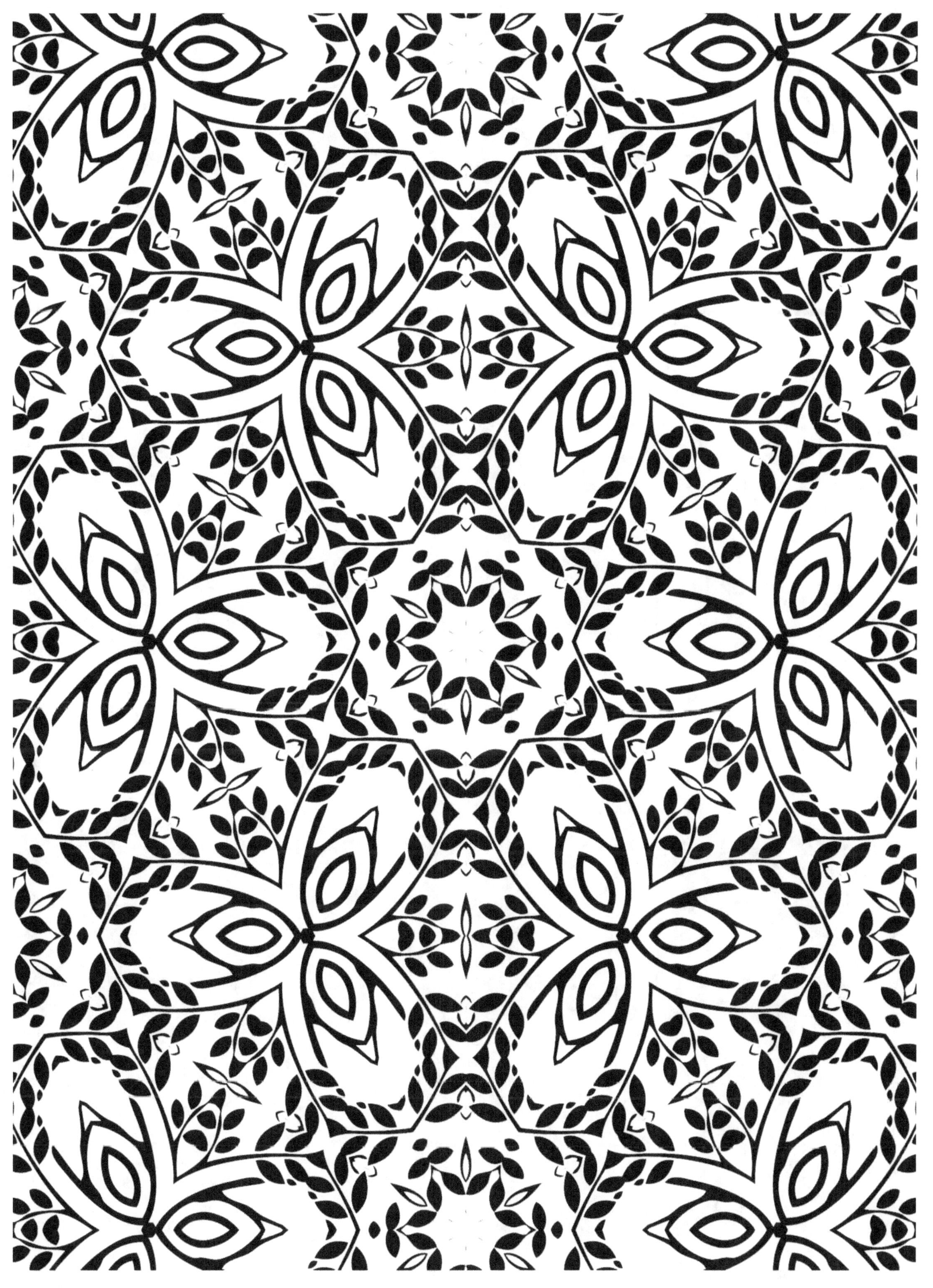

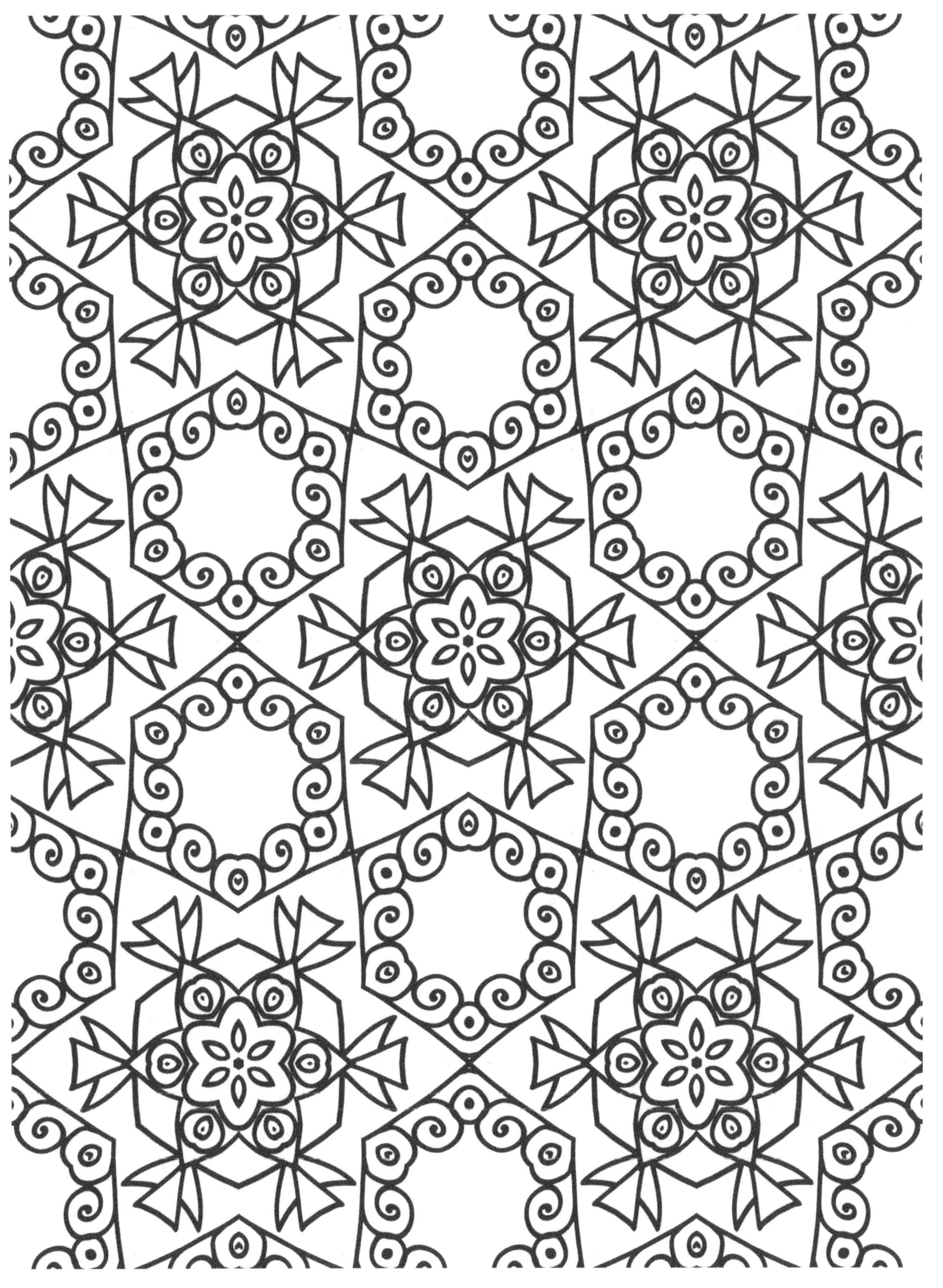

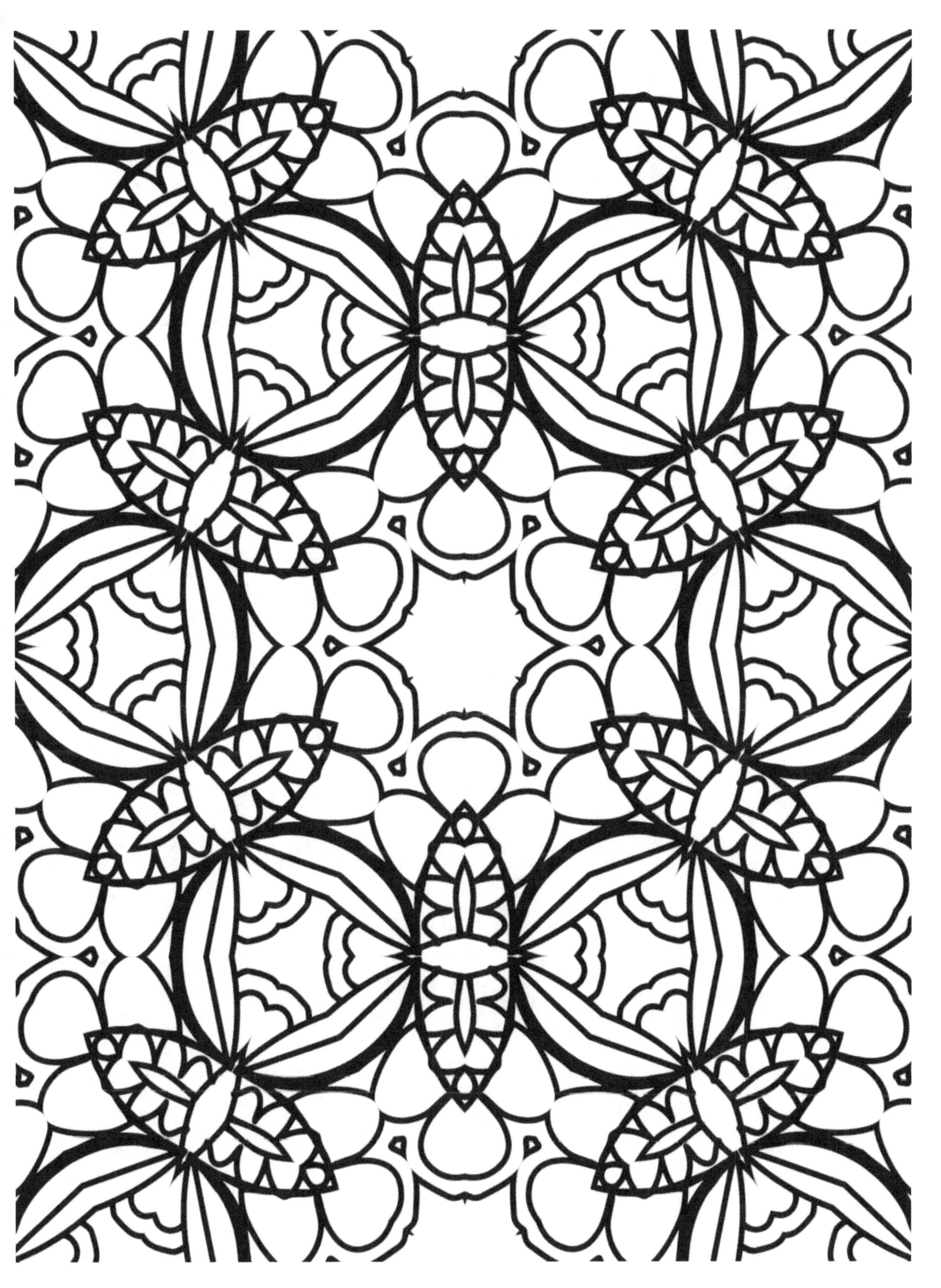

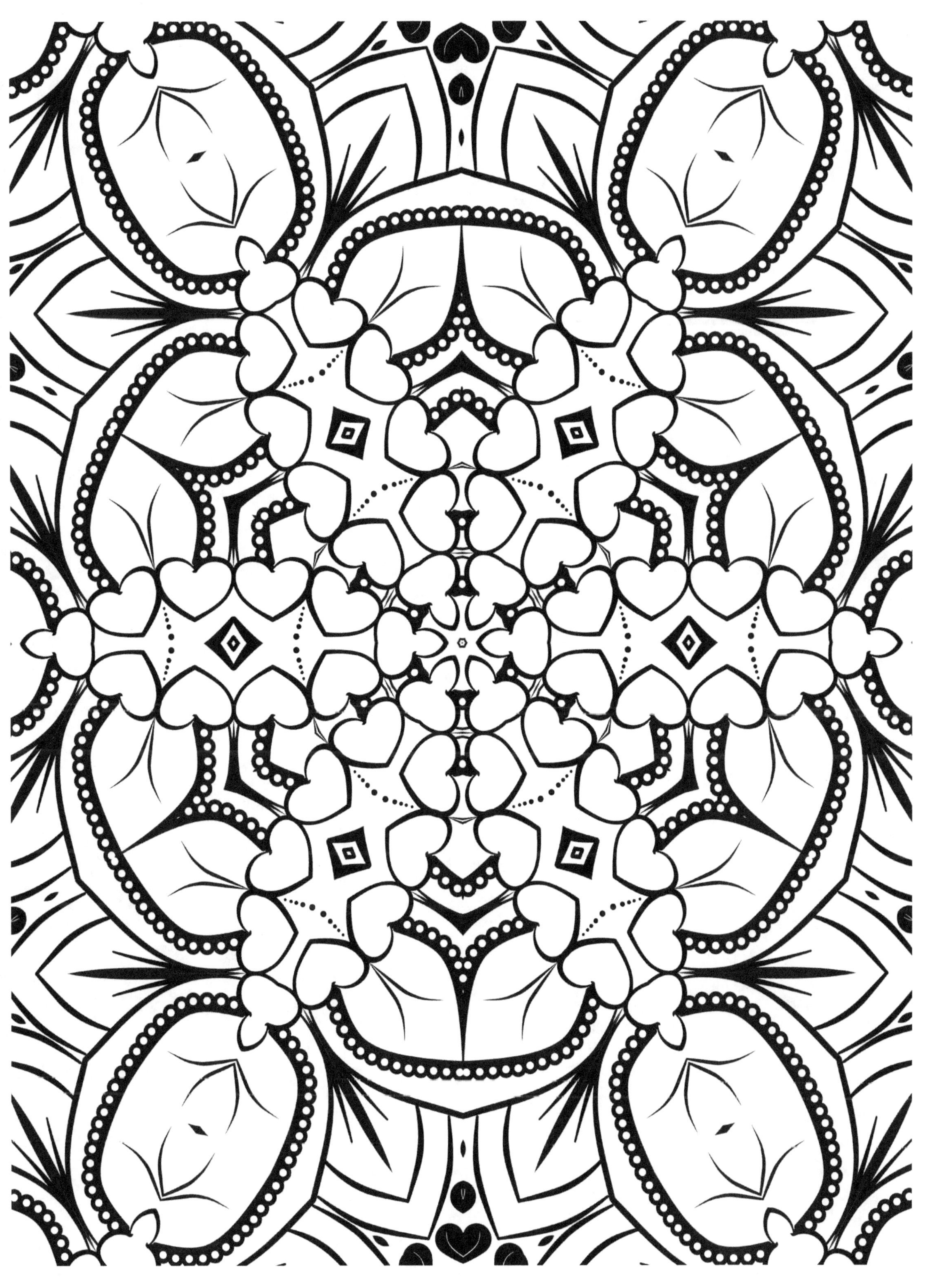

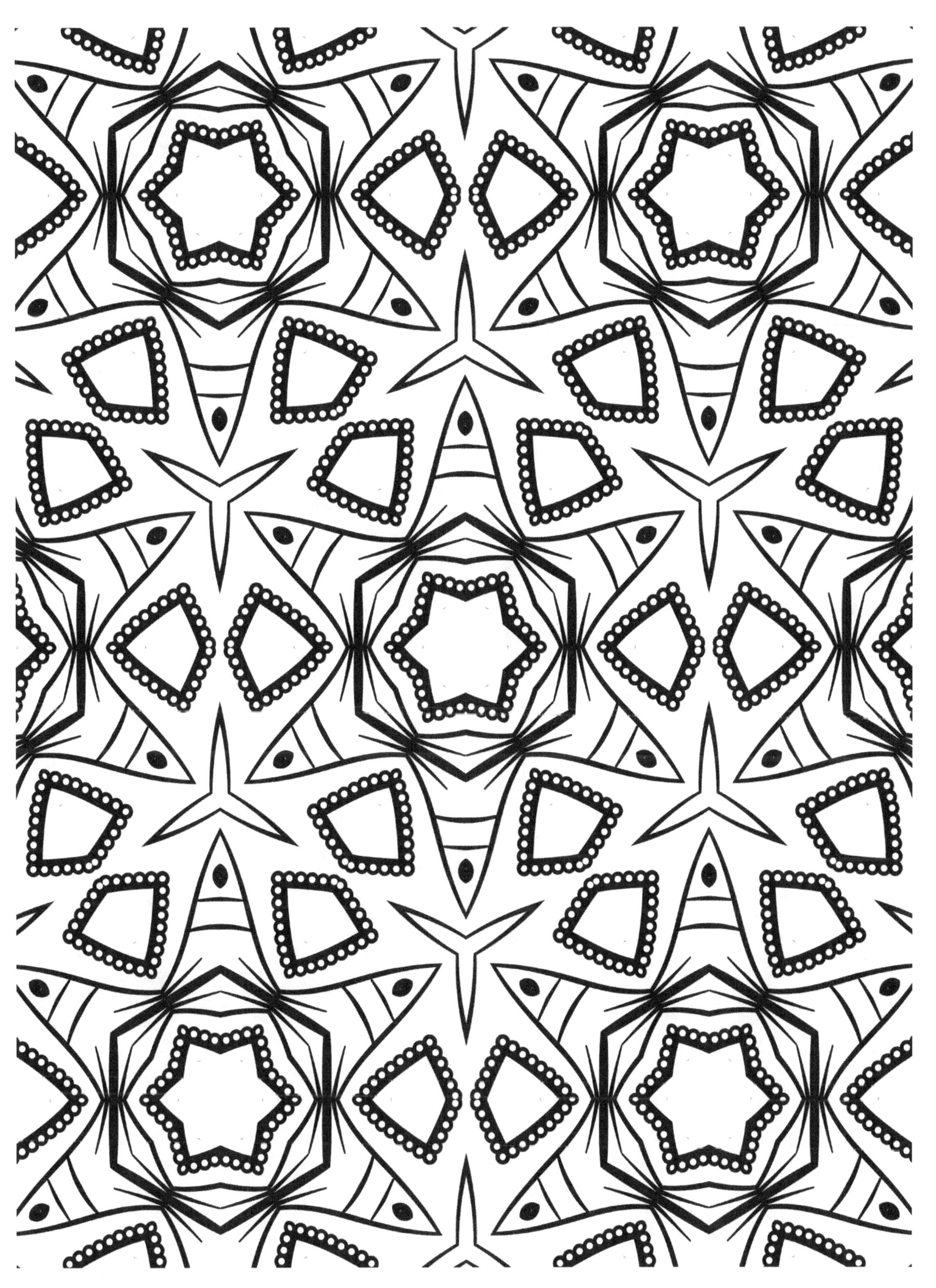

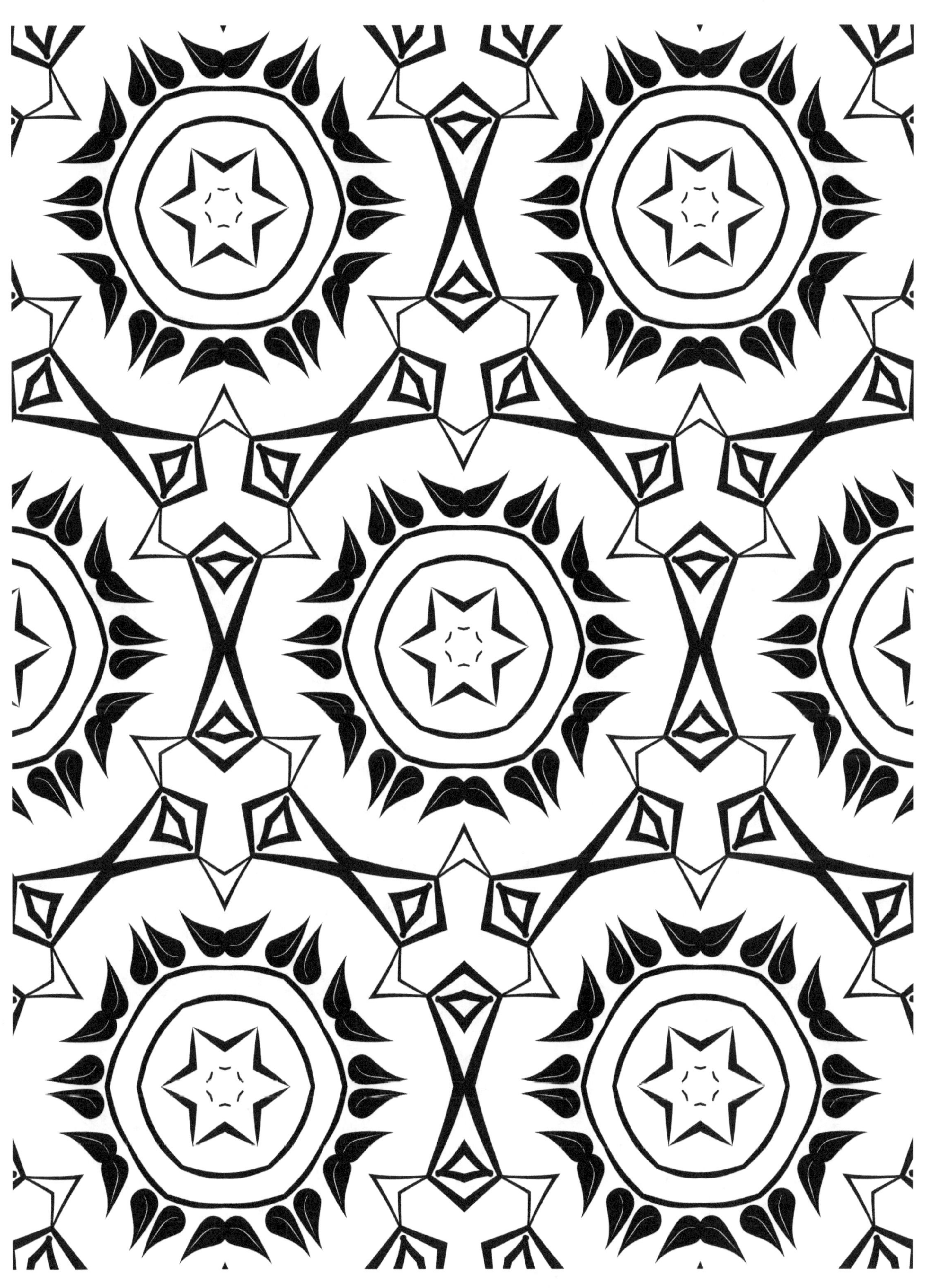

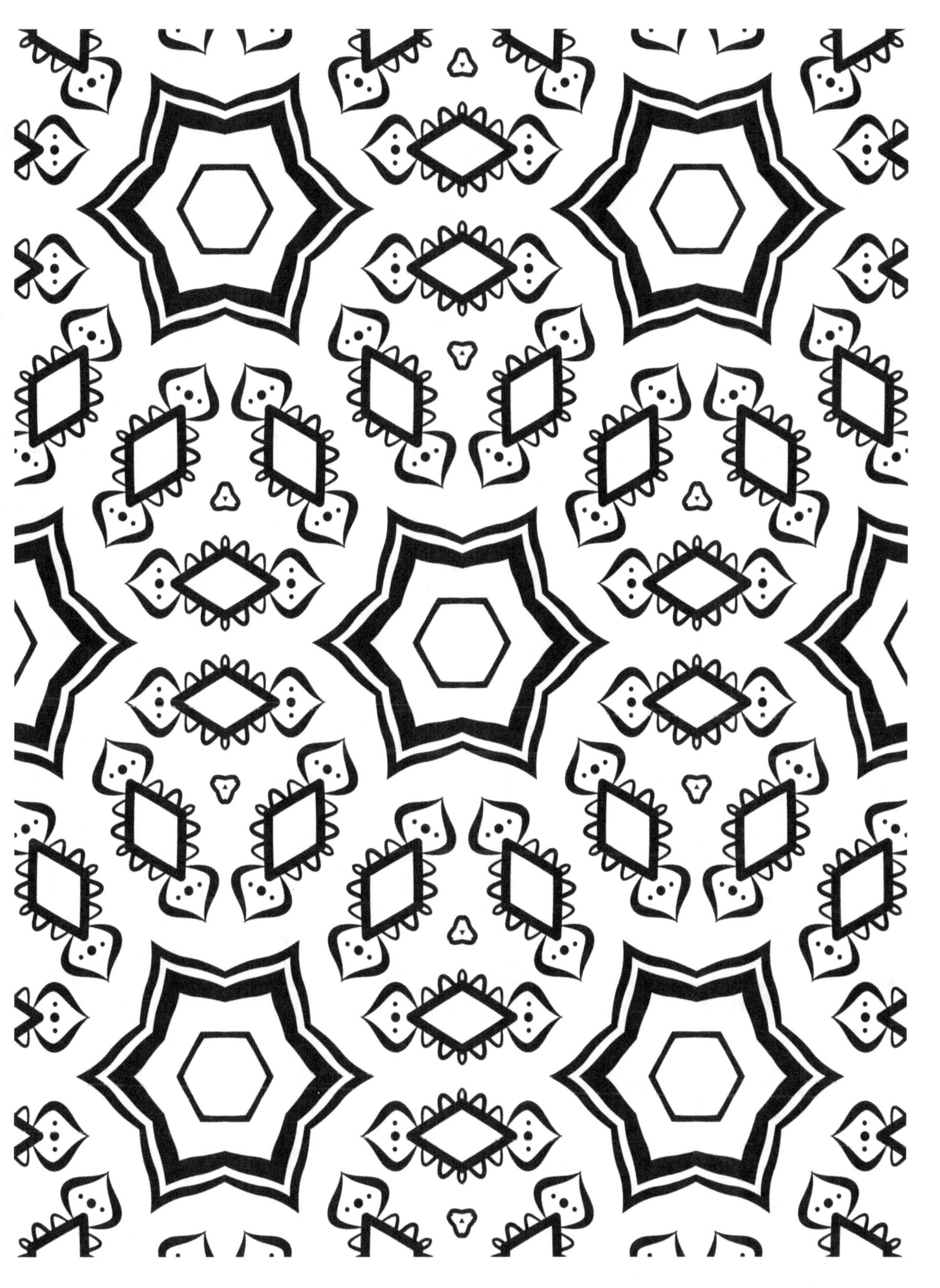

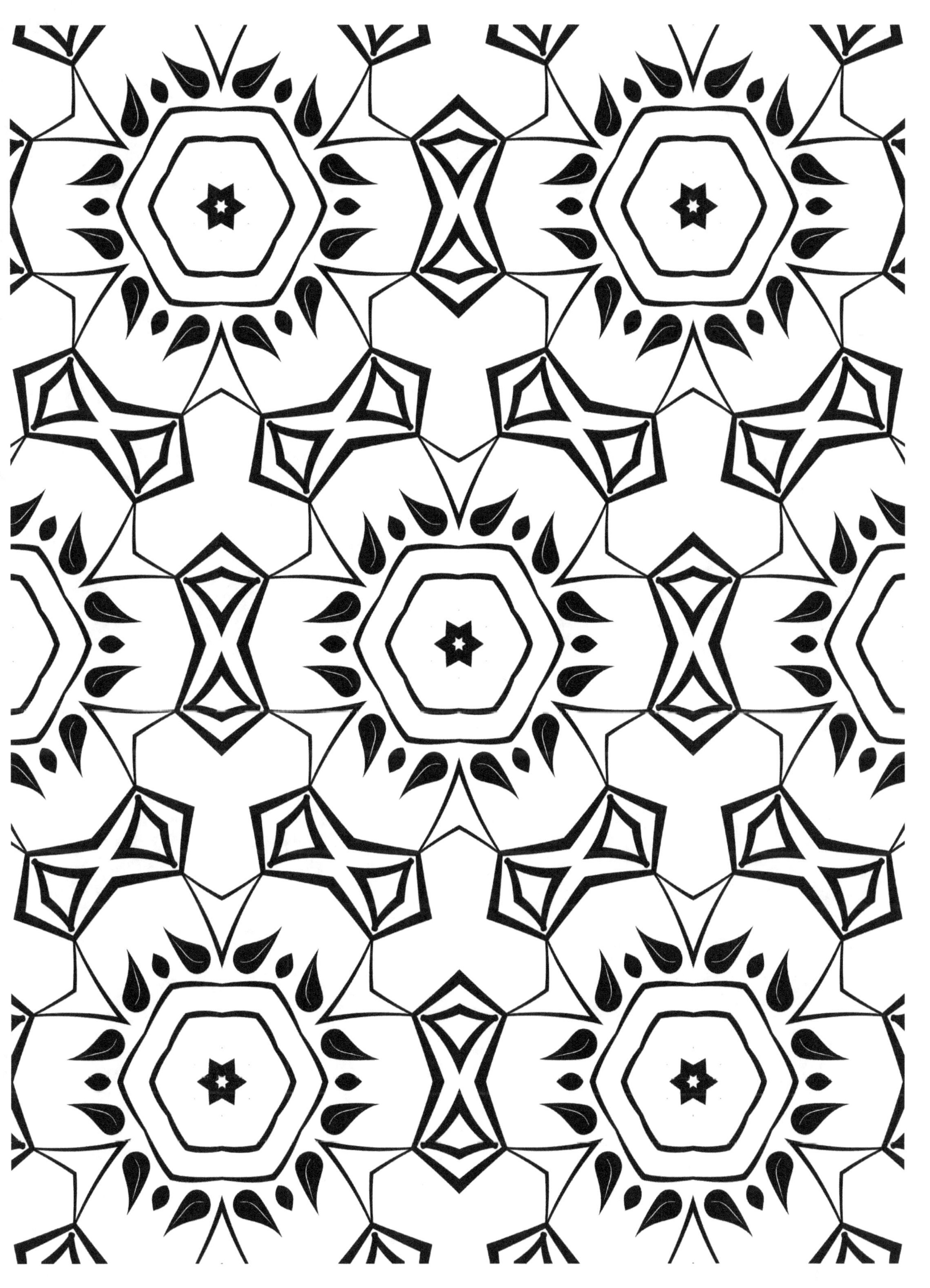

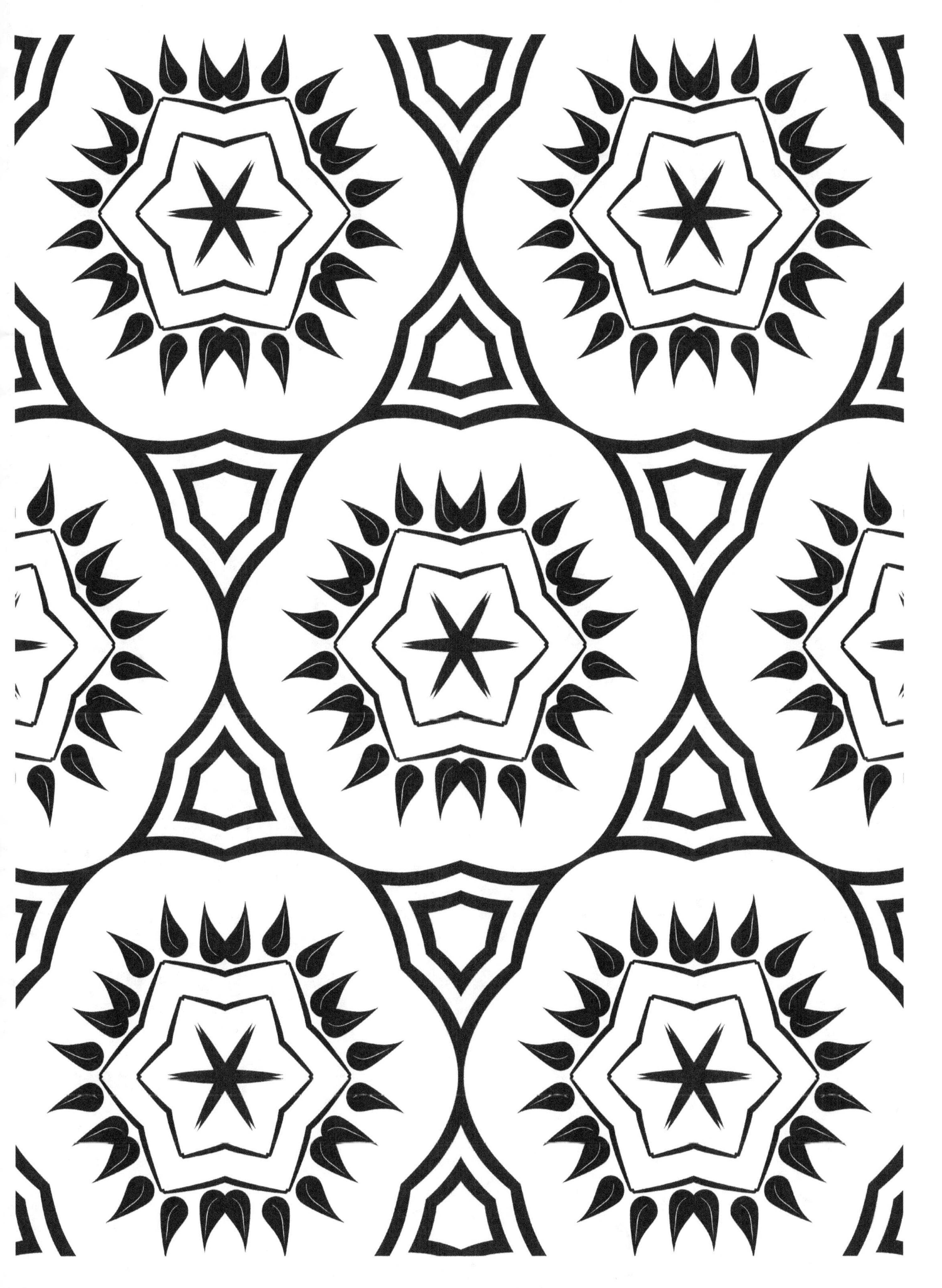

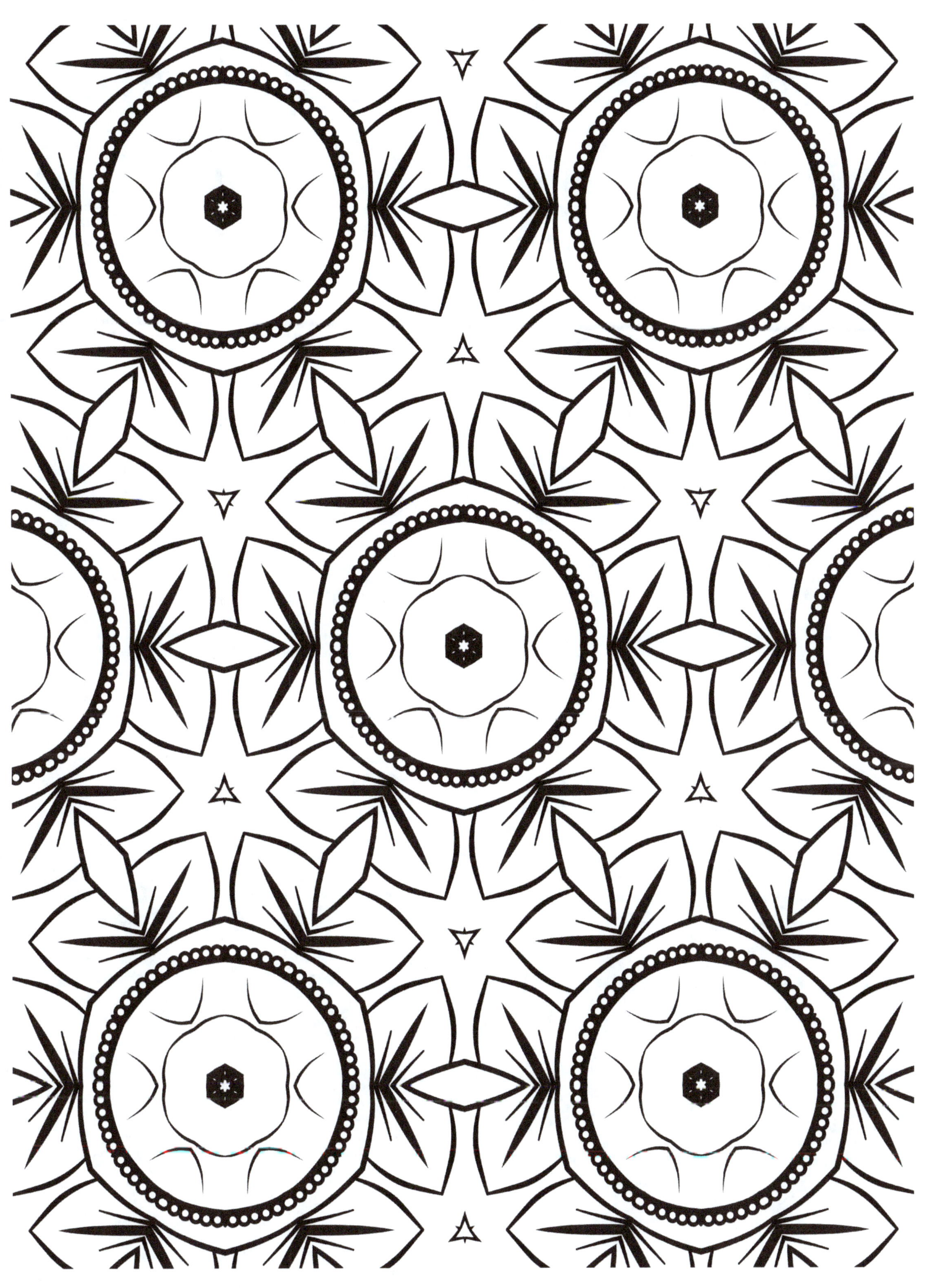

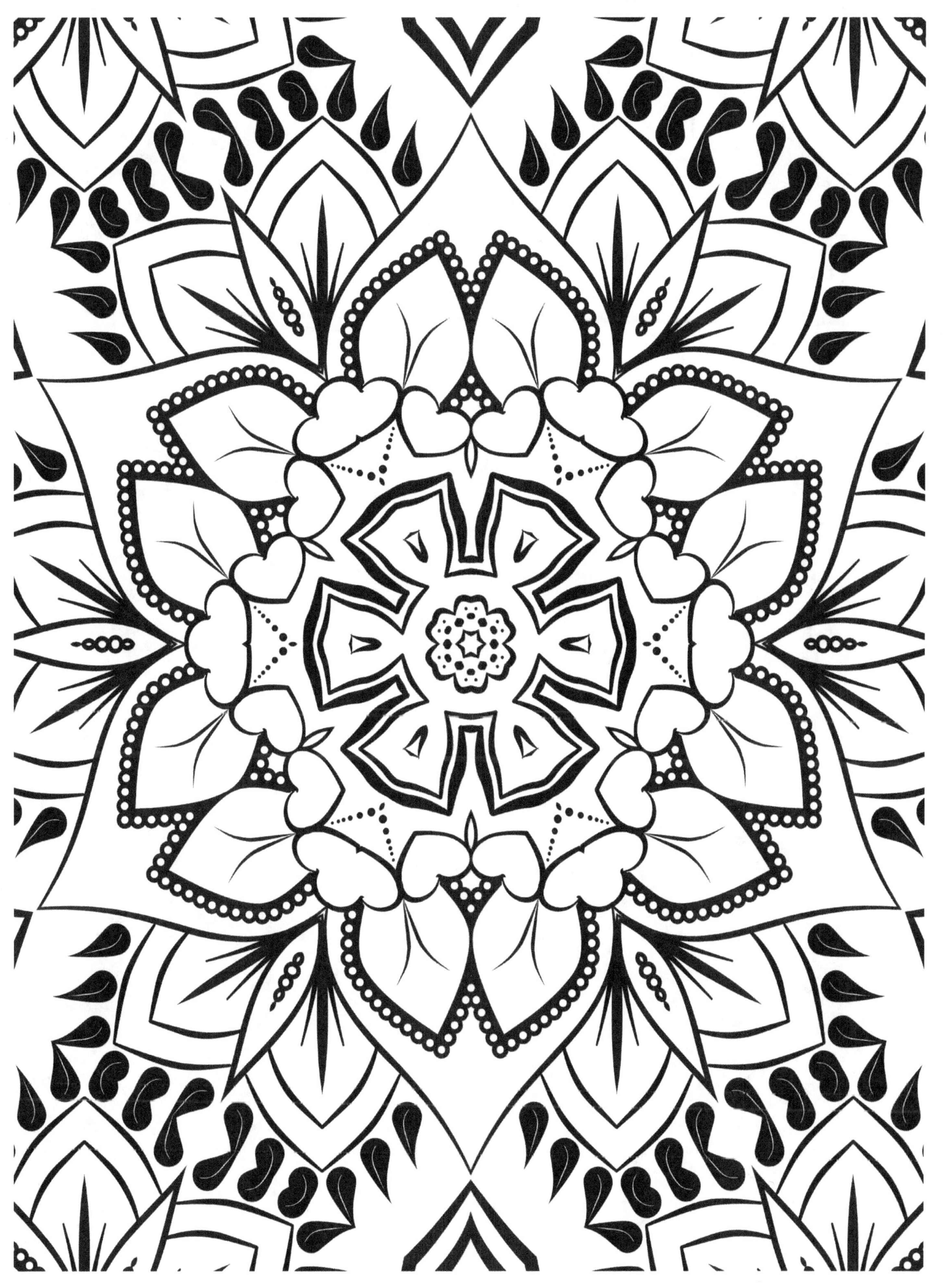

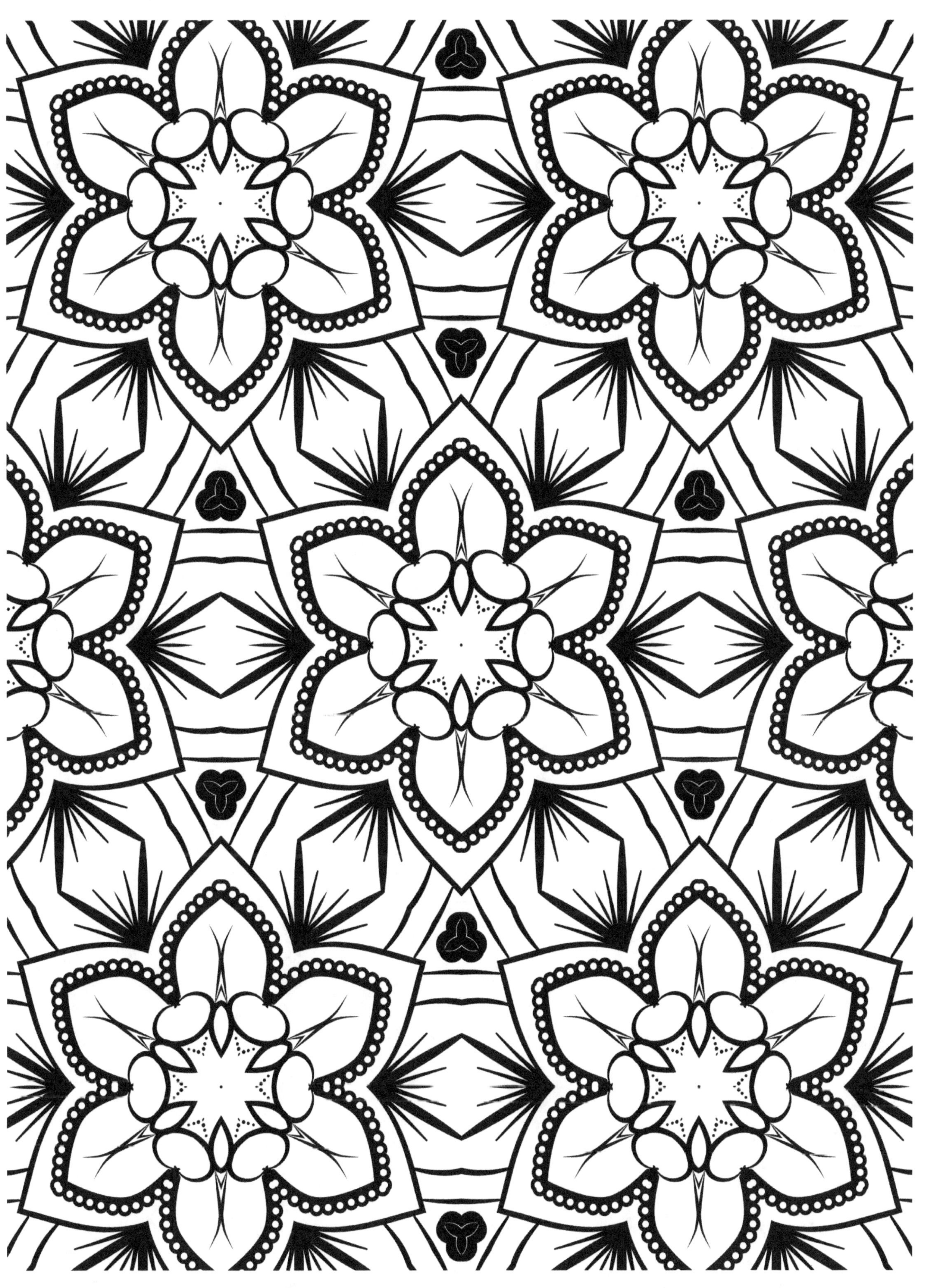

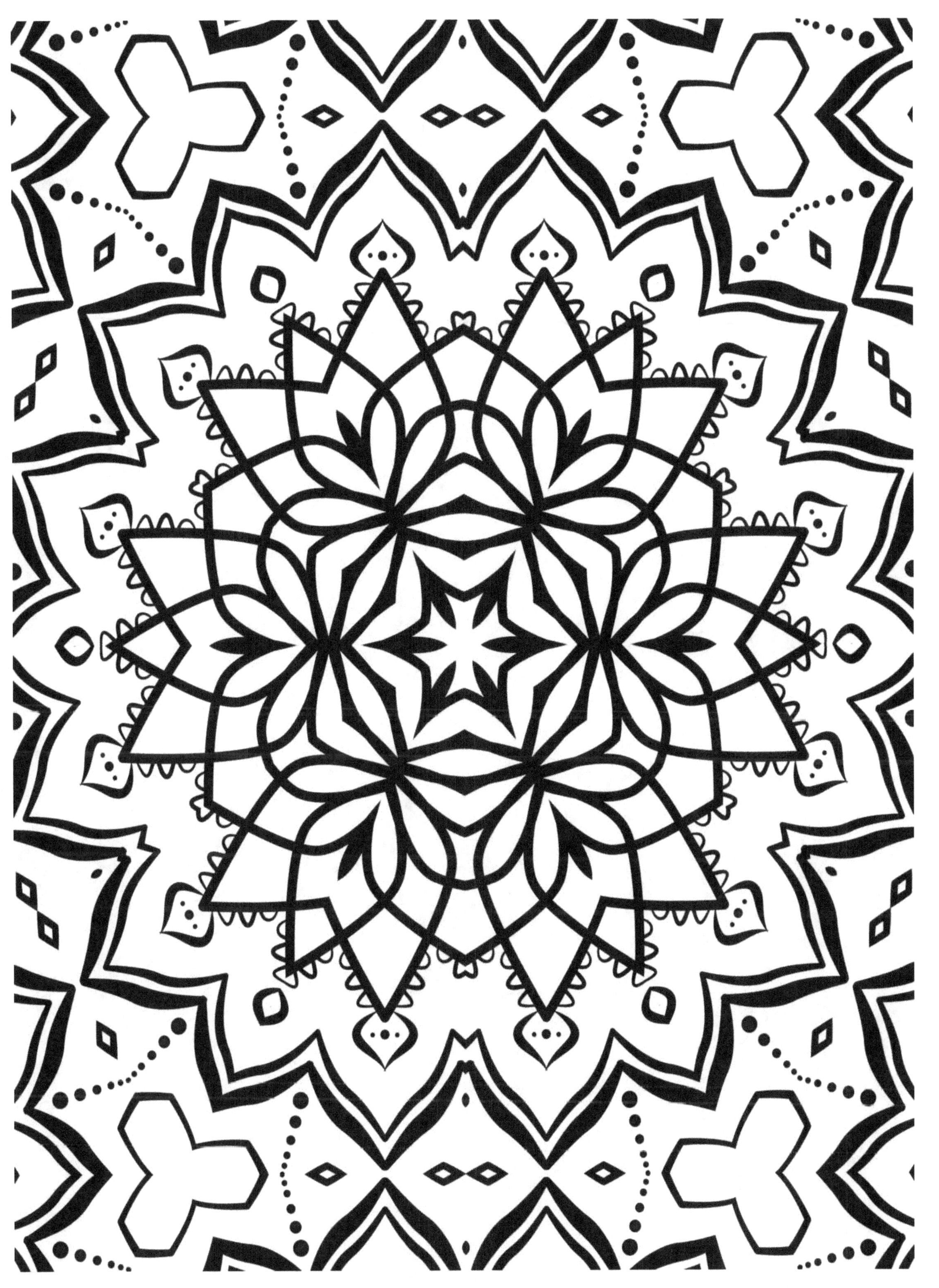

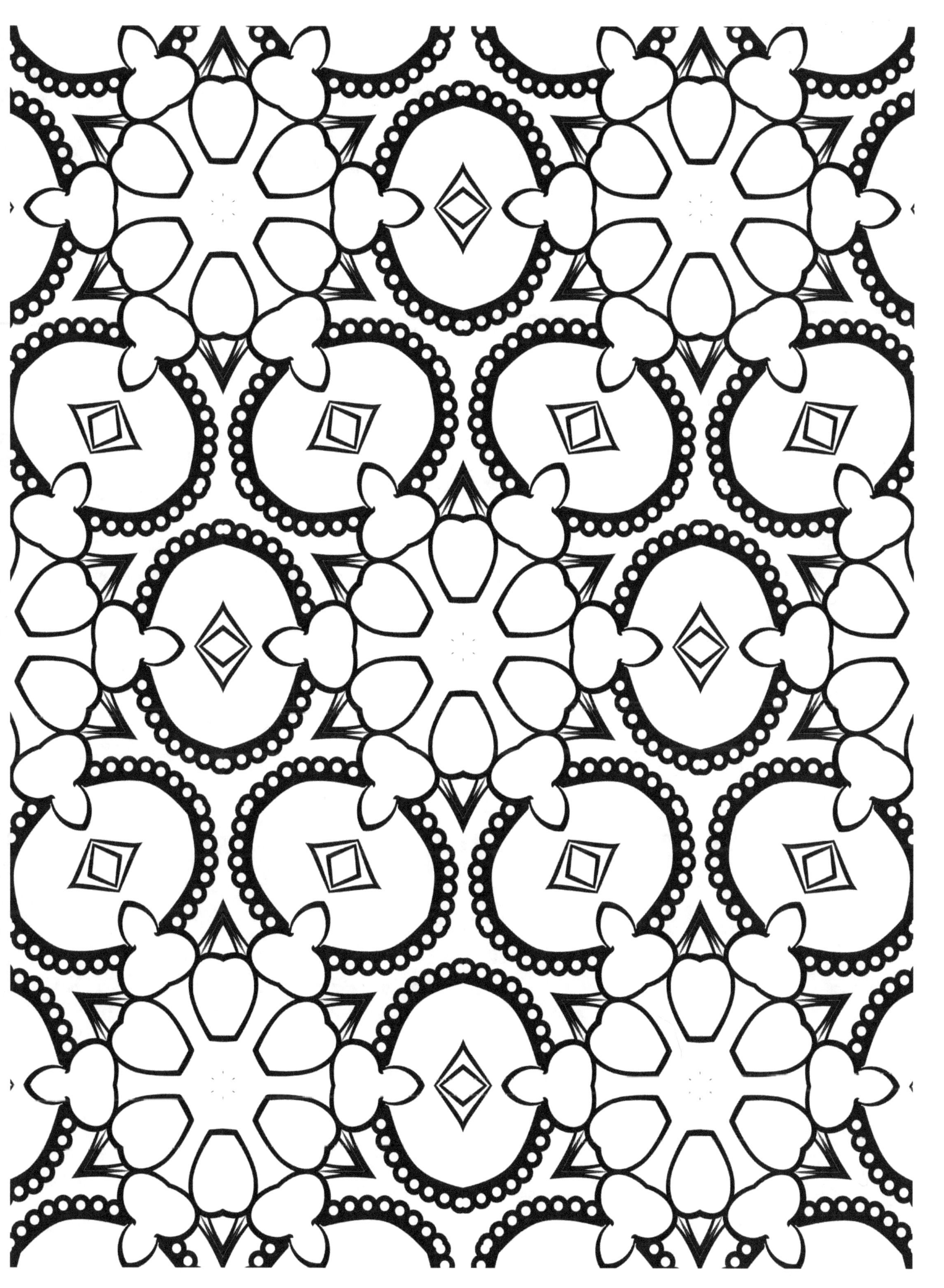

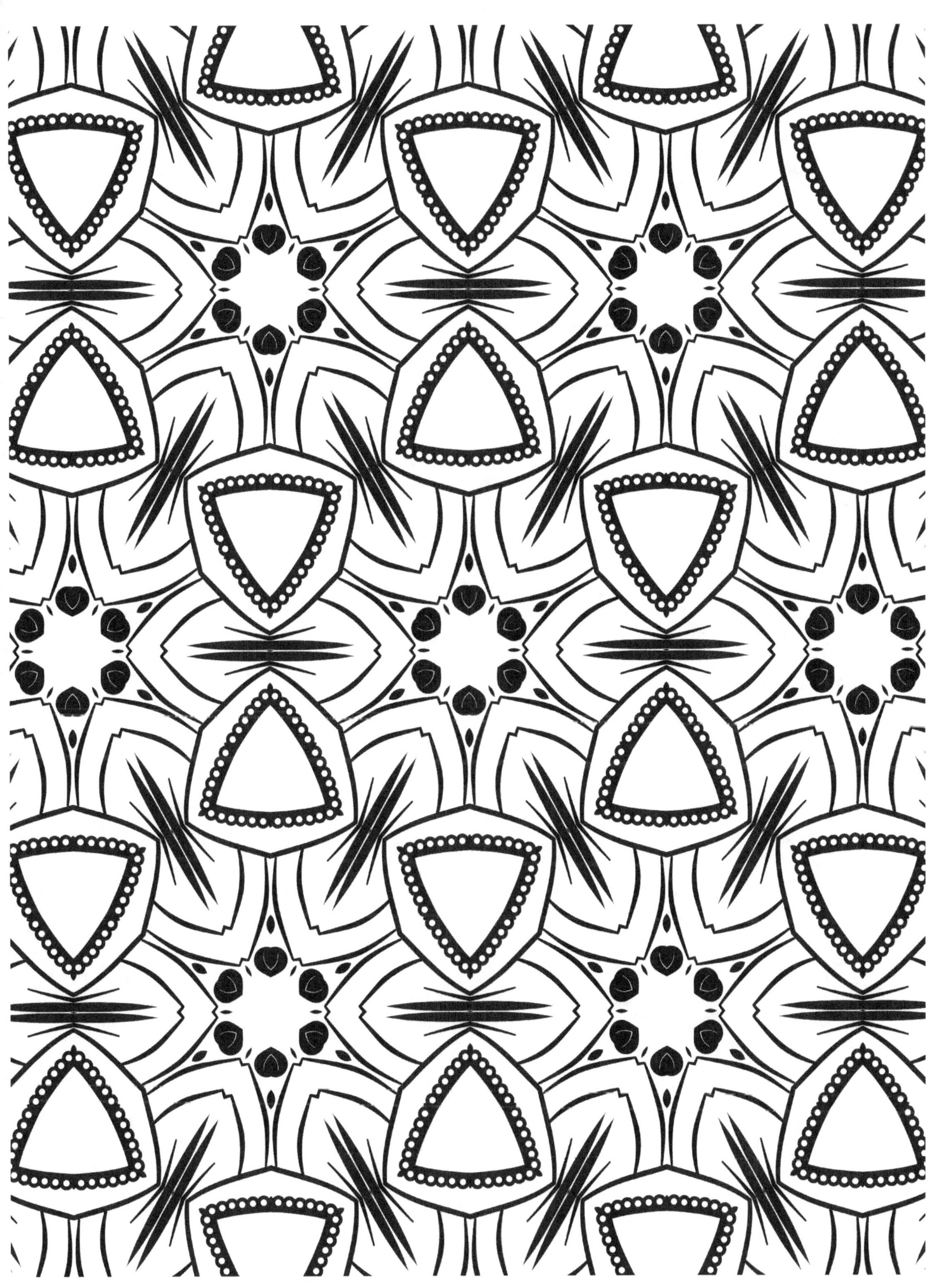

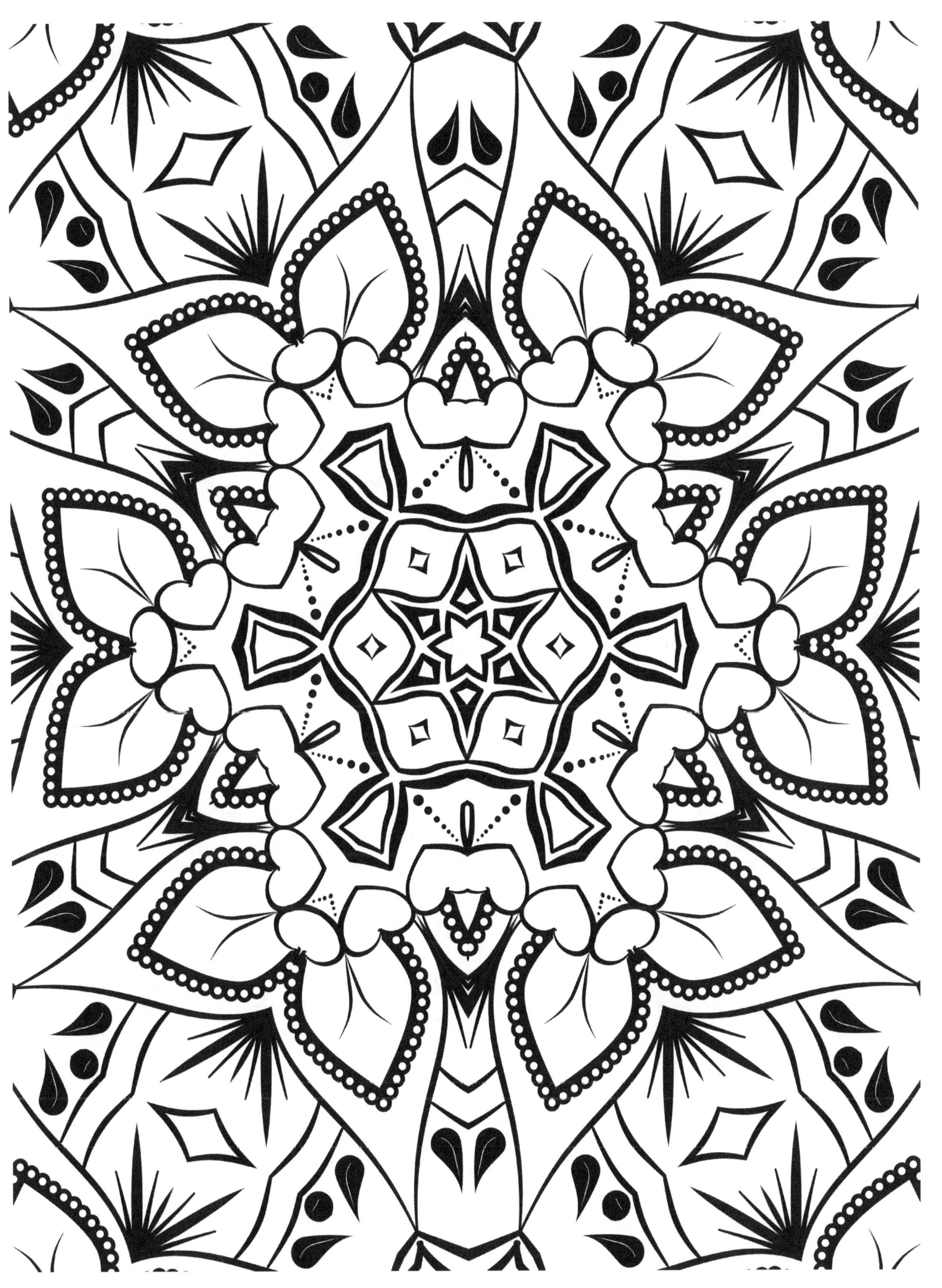

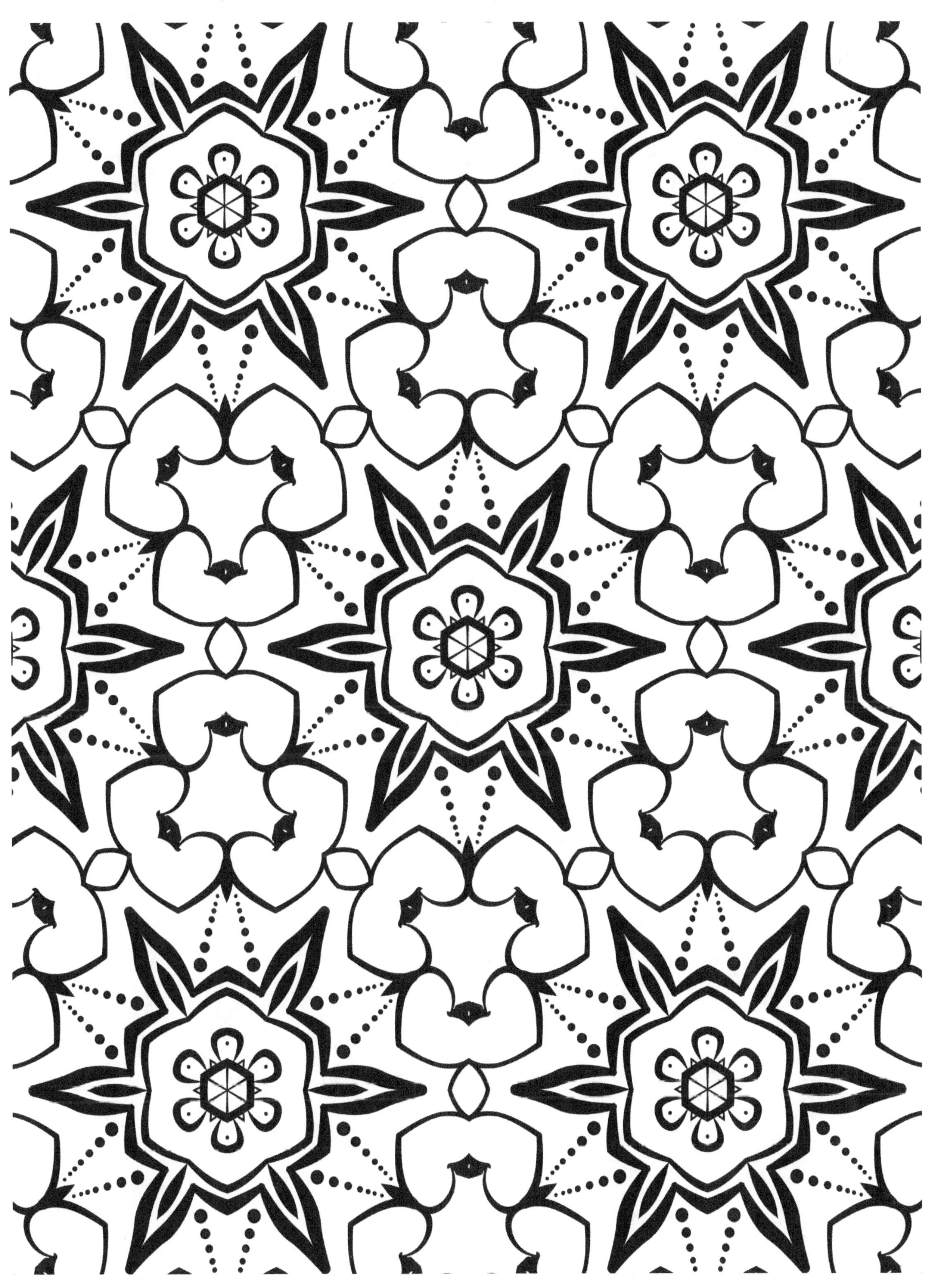

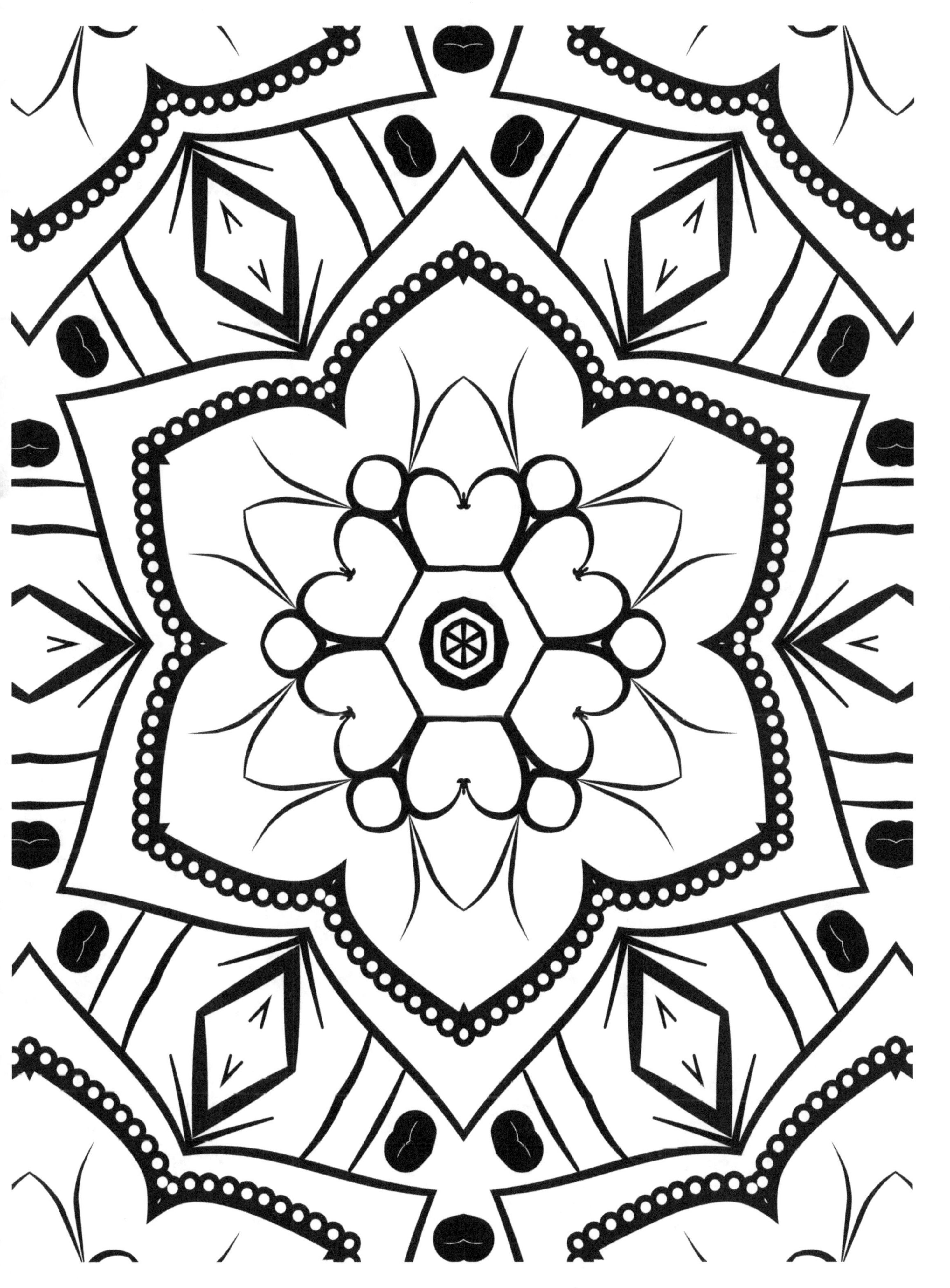

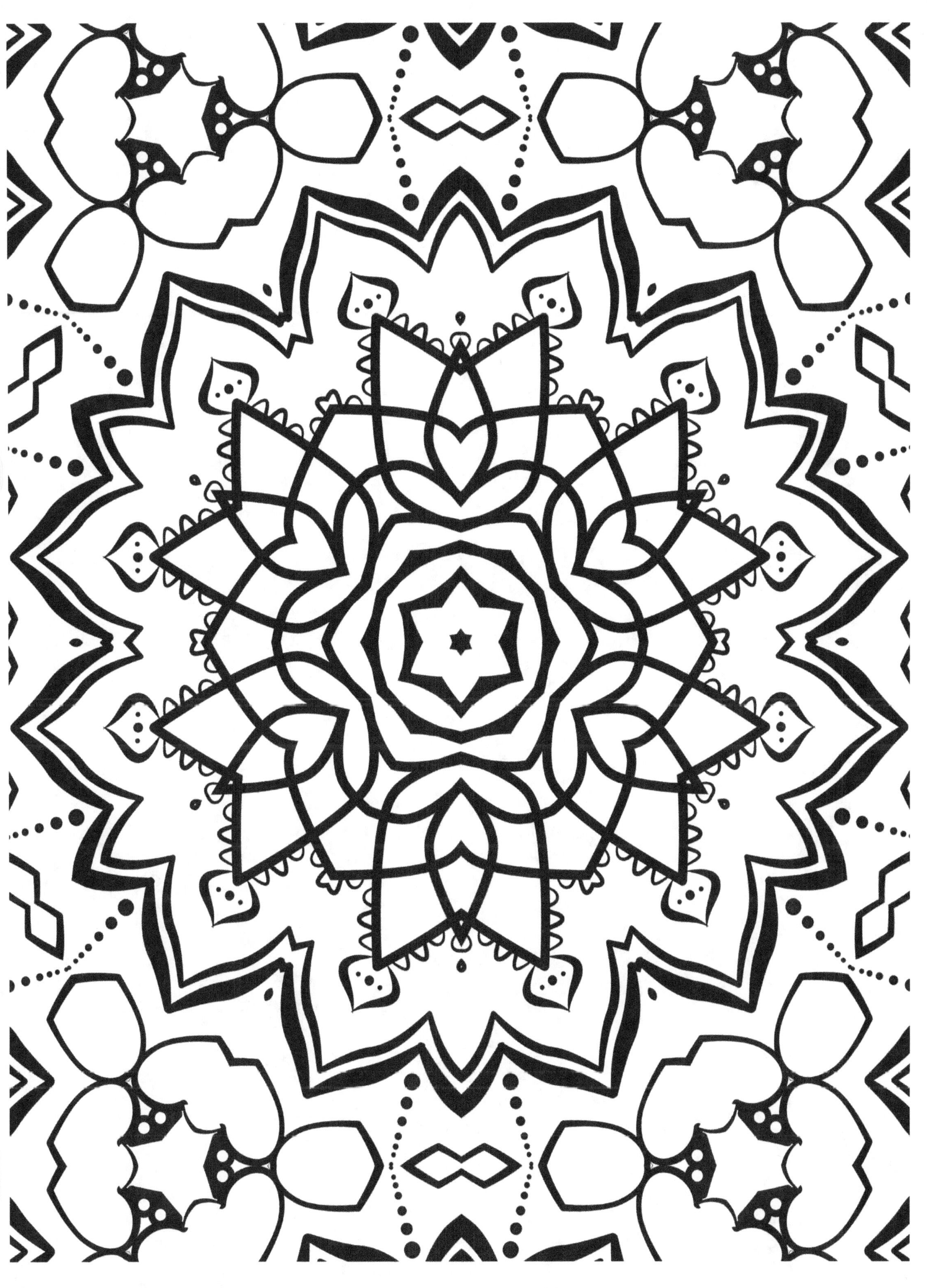

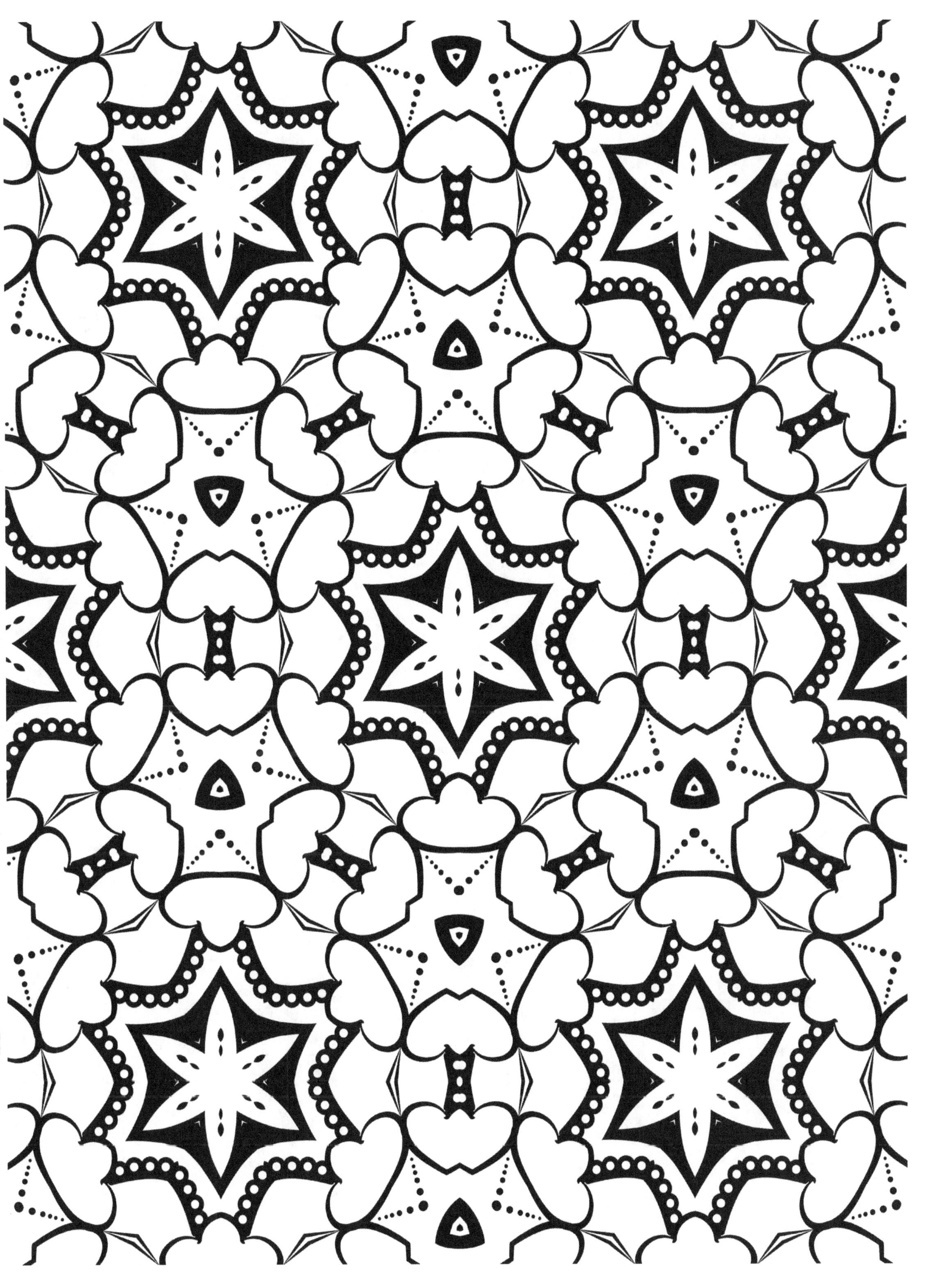